Book 2

PhonicsWorks™
Lesson Guide Advanced

k12

Book Staff and Contributors

Kristen Kinney   *Director, Primary Literacy*
Lenna King, Amy Rauen   *Instructional Designers*
Mary Beck Desmond   *Senior Text Editor*
Jill Tunick   *Text Editor*
Suzanne Montazer   *Creative Director, Print and ePublishing*
Sasha Blanton   *Senior Print Visual Designer*
David Batchelor, Carol Leigh   *Print Visual Designers*
Kim Barcas, Stephanie Williams   *Cover Designers*
Amy Eward   *Senior Manager, Writers*
Susan Raley   *Senior Manager, Editors*
Deanna Lacek   *Project Manager*

Maria Szalay   *Senior Vice President for Product Development*
John Holdren   *Senior Vice President for Content and Curriculum*
David Pelizzari   *Vice President, Content and Curriculum*
Kim Barcas   *Vice President, Creative*
Laura Seuschek   *Vice President, Instructional Design and Evaluation & Research*
Aaron Hall   *Vice President, Program Management*

Lisa Dimaio Iekel   *Production Manager*
John Agnone   *Director of Publications*

Credits

All illustrations © K12 Inc. unless otherwise noted
Cover: Turtle. © Photon75/Dreamstime.com

About K12 Inc.

K12 Inc., a technology-based education company, is the nation's leading provider of proprietary curriculum and online education programs to students in grades K–12. K12 provides its curriculum and academic services to online schools, traditional classrooms, blended school programs, and directly to families. K12 Inc. also operates the K12 International Academy, an accredited, diploma-granting online private school serving students worldwide. K12's mission is to provide any child the curriculum and tools to maximize success in life, regardless of geographic, financial, or demographic circumstances. K12 Inc. is accredited by CITA. More information can be found at www.K12.com.

978-1-60153-149-0

Printed by LSC Communications, Willard, OH, USA, April 2018   042018

Contents

Introduction . . . . PH viii

K¹² PhonicsWorks™ Program Overview . . . . PH ix

Contractions and Sound /z/ Spelled *s*

Contractions . . . . PH 483
Sound /z/ Spelled *s*. . . . . PH 488
Practice Contractions and Sound /z/ Spelled *s* (A) . . . . PH 493
Practice Contractions and Sound /z/ Spelled *s* (B) . . . . PH 497
Unit Checkpoint . . . . PH 501

Two-Syllable Words and Schwa Sound

Introduce Two-Syllable Words . . . . PH 505
Practice Two-Syllable Words . . . . PH 509
Introduce Schwa Sound . . . . PH 514
Practice Schwa Sound . . . . PH 519
Unit Checkpoint . . . . PH 524

Endings –*ing*, –*est*, and –*ed*

Introduce Endings –*ing* and –*est*. . . . . PH 527
Practice Endings –*ing* and –*est*. . . . . PH 532
Introduce Ending –*ed*. . . . . PH 536
Practice Endings –*ing*, –*est*, and –*ed* . . . . PH 541
Unit Checkpoint . . . . PH 546

Consonant Ending –*le* and Digraph *ph*

Introduce Consonant Ending –*le* . . . . PH 549
Practice Consonant Ending –*le*. . . . . PH 554
Introduce Digraph *ph*. . . . . PH 558
Practice Digraph *ph* . . . . PH 563
Unit Checkpoint . . . . PH 568

Spellings for Soft *c* and Soft *g* Sounds

Sound /s/ Spelled *c*. . . . . PH 571

Sound /j/ Spelled *g*. . . . . PH 576

Sound /j/ Spelled *dge* . . . . PH 581

Practice Spellings for Soft *c* and Soft *g* . . . . PH 585

Unit Checkpoint . . . . PH 589

Spellings for Sound /ā/

Introduce Spellings for Sound /ā/. PH 593

Practice Spellings for Sound /ā/ (A). . . . . PH 598

Practice Spellings for Sound /ā/ (B). . . . . PH 602

Practice Spellings for Sound /ā/ (C) . . . . PH 607

Unit Checkpoint . . . . PH 611

Spellings for Sound /ī/

Introduce Spellings for Sound /ī/ . . . . PH 615

Practice Spellings for Sound /ī/ (A) . . . . PH 620

Practice Spellings for Sound /ī/ (B) . . . . PH 624

Practice Spellings for Sound /ī/ (C) . . . . PH 628

Unit Checkpoint . . . . PH 632

Spellings for Sound /ō/

Introduce Spellings for Sound /ō/. PH 635

Practice Spellings for Sound /ō/ (A). . . . . PH 640

Practice Spellings for Sound /ō/ (B). . . . . PH 644

Practice Spellings for Sound /ō/ (C) . . . . PH 648

Unit Checkpoint . . . . PH 652

Spellings for Sound /ē/

Introduce Spellings for Sound /ē/ . . . . PH 655

Practice Spellings for Sound /ē/ (A) . . . . PH 660

Practice Spellings for Sound /ē/ (B) . . . . PH 664

Practice Spellings for Sound /ē/ (C) . . . . PH 668

Unit Checkpoint . . . . PH 672

Spellings for Sounds /ū/ and Long Double *o*

Introduce Spellings for Sound /ū/ . . . . PH 675

Introduce Spellings for Long Double *o* Sound . . . . PH 680

Practice Spellings for Sounds /ū/ and Long Double *o* (A) . . . . PH 684

Practice Spellings for Sounds /ū/ and Long Double *o* (B) . . . . PH 688

Unit Checkpoint . . . . PH 692

Spellings for Double *o* Sounds

Introduce Spellings for Short Double *o* Sound . . . . PH 695

Practice Spellings for Double *o* Sounds (A) . . . . PH 700

Practice Spellings for Double *o* Sounds (B) . . . . PH 704

Practice Spellings for Double *o* Sounds (C) . . . . PH 709

Unit Checkpoint . . . . PH 713

Review Long Vowels and Double *o* Sounds

Review Long Vowels and Double *o* Sounds (A) . . . . PH 717

Review Long Vowels and Double *o* Sounds (B) . . . . PH 723

Review Long Vowels and Double *o* Sounds (C) . . . . PH 727

Review Long Vowels and Double *o* Sounds (D) . . . . PH 731

Unit Checkpoint . . . . PH 735

Sound /er/ Spelled *–er*, *–ir*, *–ur*, and *–ear*

Introduce Sound /er/ Spelled *–er*, *–ir*, *–ur*, and *–ear* . . . . PH 739

Practice Sound /er/ Spelled *–er*, *–ir*, *–ur*, and *–ear* (A) . . . . PH 744

Practice Sound /er/ Spelled *–er*, *–ir*, *–ur*, and *–ear* (B) . . . . PH 748

Practice Sound /er/ Spelled *–er*, *–ir*, *–ur*, and *–ear* (C) . . . . PH 752

Unit Checkpoint . . . . PH 756

Sound /ĕ/ Spelled *ea*

Introduce Sound /ĕ/ Spelled *ea* . . . . PH 759

Practice Sound /ĕ/ Spelled *ea* (A) . . . . PH 764

Practice Sound /ĕ/ Spelled *ea* (B) . . . . PH 768

Practice Sound /ĕ/ Spelled *ea* (C) . . . . PH 773

Unit Checkpoint . . . . PH 776

Sound /oi/ Spelled *oi* and *oy*

Introduce Sound /oi/ Spelled *oi* and *oy* . . . . PH 779

Practice Sound /oi/ Spelled *oi* and *oy* (A) . . . . PH 784

Practice Sound /oi/ Spelled *oi* and *oy* (B) . . . . PH 788

Practice Sound /oi/ Spelled *oi* and *oy* (C) . . . . PH 792

Unit Checkpoint . . . . PH 796

Sound /aw/ Spelled *au* and *aw*

Introduce Sound /aw/ Spelled *au* and *aw*. . . . . PH 799

Practice Sound /aw/ Spelled *au* and *aw* (A). . . . . PH 804

Practice Sound /aw/ Spelled *au* and *aw* (B). . . . . PH 808

Practice Sound /aw/ Spelled *au* and *aw* (C). . . . . PH 812

Unit Checkpoint . . . . PH 816

Sound /ow/ Spelled *ou* and *ow*

Introduce Sound /ow/ Spelled *ou* and *ow* . . . . **PH 819**

Practice Sound /ow/ Spelled *ou* and *ow* (A) . . . . **PH 825**

Practice Sound /ow/ Spelled *ou* and *ow* (B). . . . . **PH 829**

Practice Sound /ow/ Spelled *ou* and *ow* (C). . . . . **PH 833**

Unit Checkpoint . . . . **PH 836**

Sound /ō/ Spelled *ow*

Introduce Sound /ō/ Spelled *ow* . . . . **PH 839**

Practice Sound /ō/ Spelled *ow* (A) . . . . **PH 844**

Practice Sound /ō/ Spelled *ow* (B) . . . . **PH 848**

Practice Sound /ō/ Spelled *ow* (C) . . . . **PH 852**

Unit Checkpoint . . . . **PH 856**

Introduction

This book provides the following information for K^{12} PhonicsWorks:

- ▸ About K^{12} PhonicsWorks
- ▸ Lesson Guide
- ▸ Activity Book
- ▸ Assessments Book
- ▸ PhonicsWorks Readers
- ▸ PhonicsWorks Online

The Lesson Guide contains detailed lesson plans for each day and is organized by unit. The lesson plans are placed in the order in which you will use them. Activity Book and Unit Checkpoint Answer Keys are included for you in the lesson plans.

The Activity Book supplements the Lesson Guide and provides an opportunity for students to do some work on their own. While many of the Activity Book pages can be completed independently, we recommend that you provide instruction and guidance (for instance, reviewing the instructions and sample task together) as necessary.

Note that the pages in the Lesson Guide and the Activity Book are also available online in the Materials list. The online version will match the book version unless it has an "update" label.

K¹² PhonicsWorks™ Program Overview

Reading is the most important skill for success in school and society.
— Susan L. Hall and Louisa C. Moats, *Straight Talk About Reading*

Introduction

You *can* teach your child to read!

The K¹² PhonicsWorks™ program is based on the best current research and years of firsthand experience. K¹²'s approach is—

- Explicit; lessons directly address relationships between sounds and letters.
- Systematic; lessons build logically, sequentially, and step by step.
- Multisensory; lessons engage students in a variety of visual, auditory, and tactile activities.

The PhonicsWorks program is organized into two parts—Basic and Advanced—typically completed over the course of two grades. When combined with instruction in literature (such as K¹² Language Arts Literature and Comprehension program for Kindergarten and K¹² Language Arts program for Grade 1), PhonicsWorks offers a comprehensive and balanced approach to help students acquire the critical skills and knowledge required for reading and literacy.

General Objectives

PhonicsWorks is designed to help students achieve these important goals:

- Recognize the relationship between sounds and letters.
- Blend sounds represented by letters into words.
- Read and spell longer, unfamiliar words by breaking them into syllables.
- Read grade-level text with fluency (appropriate speed and accuracy).
- Read "sight words" (high-frequency words such as *said* or *was*; many of these words do not follow the patterns that have been taught).

Before You Begin

Before you get started, familiarize yourself with the PhonicsWorks program.

Standard Curriculum Materials (K¹² Supplied)

PhonicsWorks Basic includes the following materials:

- *K¹² PhonicsWorks* training video
- K¹² PhonicsWorks Basic Kit
- *K¹² PhonicsWorks Readers Basic*
- *K¹² PhonicsWorks Basic Lesson Guide Book 1* and *Book 2*
- *K¹² PhonicsWorks Basic Activity Book*
- *K¹² PhonicsWorks Basic Assessments Book 1* and *Book 2*
- Online activities

PhonicsWorks Advanced includes all of the materials in the Basic course, as well as an Advanced Tile Kit.

Additional Materials (Learning Coach Supplied)

You will need to have the following materials on hand, which are labeled "Also Needed" in offline and online Materials lists:

- 3½ x 5-inch index cards
- Index card file box
- Black, nontoxic marker
- Dictation notebook (either loose-leaf paper in a binder or a spiral-bound notebook)
- Pencils
- Folder with loose-leaf paper (for portfolio materials and notes on student progress)

Prepare in Advance

When it's time to begin instruction, you will be well prepared if you take the time to *watch the video, read the lesson plans, and practice using the Tile Kit.* The *K¹² PhonicsWorks* video introduces the PhonicsWorks program, shows you how to use the Tile Kit, and explains teaching procedures.

Sounds and Letters: Basics of Phonics

Printed words are made up of letters that represent sounds. When we read words, we turn the letters into their corresponding speech sounds.

Consider the word *cat*, which has three letters:

c a t

The word *cat* also has three speech sounds, or phonemes (FO-neemz), which are written as follows:

/k/ /ă/ /t/

You will notice that sounds are written within slashes that we call *sound boxes*. The *K¹² PhonicsWorks* video provides a guide to pronouncing basic phonemes in the English language.

Let's look at one more word. Consider the word *boat*, which has four letters:

b o a t

Although the word *boat* has four letters, it has only three sounds:

/b/ /ō/ /t/

Over the course of the PhonicsWorks program, students will learn the following relationships between sounds and letters:

- Some sounds are represented by only one letter. For example, the sound /m/, as in <u>m</u>ouse, is almost always spelled with the letter *m*.
- Some sounds are represented by a combination of letters. For example, the sound /ch/, as in <u>ch</u>ip, is almost always spelled with the letters *ch*.
- Some sounds can be spelled more than one way. For example, the sound /k/ can be spelled *c*, as in <u>c</u>at; *k*, as in <u>k</u>ite; or *ck*, as in chi<u>ck</u>. The long o sound, /ō/, can be spelled *o*, as in n<u>o</u>; *oa*, as in b<u>oa</u>t; *oe*, as in t<u>oe</u>; *ow*, as in sn<u>ow</u>; and *o-e*, as in h<u>o</u>m<u>e</u>.

Course Instruction Guide

Number of Lessons

K[12] PhonicsWorks covers a total of 360 lessons: 180 in the Basic course and 180 in the Advanced course. Lessons are organized into groups of five lessons. Every fifth lesson presents online review activities and an assessment.

Lesson Time

These lesson times are estimates. You and students might take more or less time per lesson. Feel free to split the lessons into smaller segments and provide breaks for students as needed.

- ▸ **Basic:** 180 lessons; 30 minutes offline, 20 minutes online
- ▸ **Advanced:** 180 lessons; 30 minutes offline, 20 minutes online during the first semester and 15 minutes offline, 15 minutes online during the second semester.

Working Offline and Online

In the printed Lesson Guide, you will find step-by-step guidance for the offline portion of each lesson. These direct, explicit, and systematic lessons help students build a strong foundation of letter–sound knowledge. After the offline portion of the lesson is finished, students are ready to work independently online to reinforce, through engaging review and practice, the core lesson content. Some students may benefit from a short break between the offline and online portions of each lesson.

PhonicsWorks Basic Program: Lesson Guide Components

Unit Overview and Lesson Overview

Each new unit begins with a Unit Overview to help you understand the topics to be covered in the unit. A unit covers five days of instruction. Each day, the first page of the lesson plan indicates the materials; objectives; and any advance preparation, keywords, or Big Ideas you will need to be familiar with before you begin teaching.

Sight Words

Typically, students learn three new sight words every other week. Do not worry if students are unable to master all of the words for the week, because later lessons provide many opportunities to review them.

It is recommended that students work on no more than five sight words at a time. For example, if students master two of the three words for a given week, it is fine to add the third word to the following week's list, for a total of four words. However, if students are unable to master all three of the words, do not add all three to the following week's words.

Preparing sight word cards: You will need two sets of sight word cards to complete the Sight Words activities. One set of cards is supplied in your PhonicsWorks Kit. For the second set, you may either create your own using index cards or print a set from the online lesson and cut them into cards. If you create a set using index cards, you will need 3½ x 5-inch index cards and the list of words found in this section of the program overview. Use a bold black marker and print each word in neat, large, lowercase letters. Keep the two sets of cards somewhere convenient. As you work through the Phonics lessons, you will gradually add these cards to the file box (sight words box).

Here are the sight words in the Basic course:

- the, and, is
- on, to, in
- it, he, was
- says, have, with
- where, from, there
- that, of, put
- two, they, both
- you, went, we

- what, their, want
- said, your, so
- who, see, or
- for, she, her
- does, why, one
- were, my, are
- Mr., Mrs., Dr.

Get Ready

These activities help students review previously taught sounds and letters, and reinforce skills and concepts from earlier lessons.

Learn

In this section of the lesson, new concepts are introduced and practiced through a variety of multisensory activities, including the following:

- Listening to sounds in words
- Manipulating letter tiles
- Completing Activity Book pages with fun written activities
- Writing words and sentences that you dictate

In the first eight units, students practice phonological awareness. Phonological awareness is the ability to recognize and distinguish sounds of speech in language. We learn to speak before we learn to read; we learn to hear sounds before we learn which letters represent those sounds. Accordingly, in the first eight units of PhonicsWorks Basic, students focus on phonological awareness activities, distinguishing and manipulating sounds. Activities include Sound Chains; Finger Stretching; and Head, Waist, Toes.

Be patient. Do these activities thoroughly and well. Research has shown that explicit phonological awareness instruction leads to better reading.

Try It

This section of the lesson asks students to apply their new knowledge of a concept in a variety of ways. They may be asked to read from a PhonicsWorks Reader, write words or sentences in a Dictation activity, or complete an Activity Book page.

- **PhonicsWorks Readers:** The K[12] PhonicsWorks Readers are "decodable readers" with a carefully controlled vocabulary almost exclusively made up of letter–sound patterns and sight words students have already studied. Even though these stories are written in words students have studied, most beginning readers still need plenty of time to figure out the words. When students read the stories, you serve as a guide to help them when they have difficulty. The lessons offer detailed suggestions about how to help students read accurately and sound out challenging words.

Monitor progress: As students read, it is very important that you sit next to them and carefully observe their progress. Lesson plans provide instructions for taking notes while you listen to students read. These notes will help you decide which letters and sounds students still need to work on and which sight words are still difficult for them. You may want to keep a small notebook in which you can write the title of the reading assignment, the date, a list of skills students have mastered, and what they need to work on.

▸ **Dictation:** Early in the PhonicsWorks program, students will use letter tiles to create words dictated to them. As students' skills progress, students move to writing words and then sentences. It is important that you follow the instructions for Dictation as outlined in the Lesson Guide. Research indicates that these steps are the most effective for reinforcing students' letter–sound knowledge.

▸ **Activity Book Pages:** Students will complete two to four pages in each unit of PhonicsWorks. In most cases, after you have read the directions to students and observed them complete one or two examples, they may finish the page independently. Be sure to review students' completed work, making note of any letters and sounds they still need to work on and which sight words have yet to be mastered.

Online Overview

The last section of the Lesson Guide provides an overview of what students will accomplish during their online, independent review and practice of concepts taught to date. You may choose to sit with students during this time, but these activities were designed with plenty of audio and engaging animation to help them work independently.

Unit Checkpoint

Every fifth lesson in the PhonicsWorks program provides a Unit Checkpoint to help you determine how well students have learned the skills covered in the unit. On Unit Checkpoint days, students begin by spending time online completing review and practice activities. The activities provide a fun, interactive way to review concepts from the unit.

Unit Checkpoints and Answer Keys: You will find the Unit Checkpoint assessment pages in *K¹² PhonicsWorks Assessments*. You will find Answer Keys in the Lesson Guide. You can also print both the Unit Checkpoint pages and the Answer Key from the online lesson.

Please note: Throughout the PhonicsWorks program, the Lesson Guide for Unit Checkpoints contain test exercises that are not listed on students' Unit Checkpoint pages. This is not an error. The exercises printed only in the Lesson Guide are for you to assess students' listening skills. Please follow the directions and note students' verbal responses on the Unit Checkpoint page to use later when scoring the Checkpoint.

After you have scored the Unit Checkpoint, remember to ***return to the computer and enter the results***.

"Getting Stronger" Units

After the tenth unit of the Basic course, every other unit is called a "Getting Stronger" unit. These units are designed to strengthen students' skills through review and practice. If students are consistently scoring 100 percent on the Unit Checkpoints in prior units, you may choose to skip the Getting Stronger units. Before skipping the unit, have students take the Unit Checkpoint to make sure they have truly mastered the content. ***Please note: If you choose to skip these units, you will need to return to the computer and mark all the lessons in the unit as "completed."***

Should you skip ahead? Each student learns to read at his or her own pace. This variation is natural and is generally not a cause for concern. We have designed PhonicsWorks to meet the needs of a broad range of students, and we believe most students will benefit from working through all lessons in the program.

While some students might be able to skip some of the Getting Stronger lessons, most students will benefit from the review and practice. This practice helps ensure that they have thoroughly mastered early reading skills and that they are making progress toward achieving what cognitive psychologists call "automaticity." That is, they are on their way to becoming skilled readers who can automatically turn printed letters into their corresponding speech sounds without having to linger over individual letters and sounds. It's like reaching the point in math when students can quickly add and subtract mentally without having to count on their fingers, or in music when they can play "Twinkle, Twinkle, Little Star" on the piano without having to search for the notes.

Most students need repeated review and practice to achieve automaticity. When you come to the Getting Stronger lessons, however, you may feel that students have sufficiently mastered the skills taught in prior lessons. If they are consistently achieving perfect or near-perfect scores on the Unit Checkpoints and if you feel that they will not benefit from further review and practice, then you may skip the Getting Stronger lessons and move to the next unit.

Keep a Portfolio

To document students' progress, we recommend that you keep a portfolio of their work. You can compile a comprehensive portfolio by keeping all of the following items:

- ▶ The box of sight word cards
- ▶ Completed Activity Book pages and Dictation activities
- ▶ Your notes from Try It activities
- ▶ Completed Unit Checkpoint pages

PhonicsWorks Advanced Program: Lesson Components

In the Advanced course, lessons are presented much like the lessons in the Basic course (see above). The first four units of the Advanced course review the content of PhonicsWorks Basic, and the remaining units provide instruction in more advanced phonics concepts, such as blends, long vowels, and difficult spelling patterns.

Sight Words

The first four units of the Advanced course cover the 45 sight words from the Basic course. During this time, students will work on approximately 12 words per week. As in the Basic course, two sets of sight word cards are required. One set can be found in your PhonicsWorks Kit, and you may either make the second set yourself using index cards or print the second set from the online lesson. Here are the other sight words for the Advanced course:

- ▶ too, walk, talk
- ▶ again, out, pull
- ▶ next, my, friend
- ▶ goes, anything, begin
- ▶ down, know, after
- ▶ mother, father, only
- ▶ even, look, gone
- ▶ love, very, some
- ▶ none, more, held
- ▶ would, could, should
- ▶ brother, sister, baby

- ▶ many, animal, while
- ▶ together, people, other
- ▶ above, here, move
- ▶ these, against, now
- ▶ every, neighbor, behind
- ▶ once, come, about
- ▶ please, follow, saw
- ▶ everything, under, whether
- ▶ nothing, over, almost
- ▶ children, write, number
- ▶ because, its, first

The Tile Kit:
Multisensory Instruction

PhonicsWorks lessons incorporate *multisensory* instruction. Lesson activities ask students to look, listen, touch, move, and speak.

The Tile Kit is at the core of this multisensory instruction. The Tile Kit contains letters and letter combinations that represent sounds. Students use the magnetized tiles to manipulate sounds and letters in fun activities that combine visual, auditory, tactile, and oral learning.

How to Use the Tile Kit

The Tile Kit is used for a variety of gentle, interactive procedures, such as "build words," "touch and say," and "word chains." Detailed instructions for these procedures are provided in the lessons. (You can also see the Tile Kit used in the *K¹² PhonicsWorks* video.) The more you use the kit, the less you will need to consult the instructions, although the instructions are always available for you to use.

The Tile Kit helps students understand how speech is represented in print. For example, consider how we use the tiles to build the word *chin*. When students first build the word *chin*, they will be guided to select three tiles:

ch	i	n

The single sound /ch/ is represented by two letters, *c* and *h*. Because those two letters are printed on a single tile, students get both visual and tactile reinforcement of the simple but important concept that two letters can represent one sound.

Basic Letter Tiles

In the PhonicsWorks Basic course, you receive the Tile Kit, which consists of a binder with pages for the Basic letter tiles. These tiles include the following:

- ► Color tiles
- ► All uppercase (capital) letters
- ► All lowercase letters (multiple tiles provided for each letter)
- ► Digraphs *sh*, *ch*, *th*, *wh*, *ph*, and *ck* and trigraph *tch* (multiple tiles provided for each)
- ► Common word endings *–s*, *–es*, *–ed*, *–ing*, *–er*, and *–est*
- ► Double letter endings *–ff*, *–ll*, *–ss*, *–zz*, and *–all*
- ► Basic punctuation marks: period, question mark, exclamation point, comma, and apostrophe
- ► Vowels printed in red (to provide a visual cue for identifying those letters)

Advanced Letter Tiles

In PhonicsWorks Advanced, you receive the PhonicsWorks Basic course Tile Kit and the Advanced letter tile pages, which include letter tiles with common spellings for sounds that can be spelled in more than one way. The pages are organized to group together the various letters or combinations of letters that represent one sound.

For example, in one section of the binder you will find the following tiles for the long *o* vowel sound:

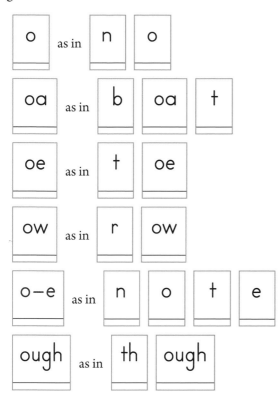

In another section you will find the following tiles to represent the consonant sound /j/:

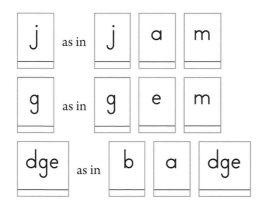

Here is the complete list of what you will receive (some tiles in multiples):

- ▶ All PhonicsWorks Basic tiles
- ▶ Word endings *ng, ang, ing, ong, ung*
- ▶ Word endings *nk, ank, ink, onk, unk*
- ▶ Long vowel sound /ā/: *a, e, ai, ay, eigh, a–e, ea*
- ▶ Long vowel sound /ē/: *e, e, ee, ea, ie, y, e–e*
- ▶ Long vowel sound /ī/: *i, e, ie, y, igh, i–e, y–e*
- ▶ Long vowel sound /ō/: *o, e, ow, oa, oe, o–e, ough*
- ▶ Long vowel sound /ū/: *u, e, u–e, ew, eu*
- ▶ Long double *o* sound (/o͞o/): *oo, e, u, ue, ew, u–e, ough*
- ▶ Short double *o* sound (/o͝o/): *oo, u, ou*
- ▶ Schwa sound: /ə/
- ▶ R-controlled vowels: *ar, or, er, ir, ur, ear, oar, ore*

My Accomplishments Chart

Research shows that rewarding students for quality work can increase their motivation. To aid you in rewarding students, you will receive a My Accomplishments chart and sticker sheet for use throughout the course. This chart gives students a tangible and concrete representation of their progress and accomplishments throughout the PhonicsWorks course (and other courses in which they may be enrolled), which they can proudly display and share with others. When students score 80% or above on a Unit Checkpoint, have them add a sticker for that unit to the My Accomplishments chart. Encourage students to set goals and watch their stickers accumulate. Verbally reinforce their progress to help them understand the connection between their own growing skill set and the My Accomplishments chart.

How to Correct Errors: "Accentuate the Positive"

All students will make mistakes as they learn to read. They may have to try repeatedly to grasp concepts that strike experienced readers as painfully obvious. When correcting mistakes, we need to remain patient and encouraging.

PhonicsWorks lessons suggest specific phrases for you to use when students make an error. These suggestions are meant to help make the experience of learning to read a positive one that focuses on success.

For example, imagine that you ask students to touch the letter *b* and they touch the letter *d*. You want to avoid a negative (and potentially discouraging) response such as, "No, that's not right. Try again." Instead, say, "You touched the letter *d*. This is the letter *b*. Touch this letter and say *b*." These words inform students that they did indeed touch a letter, and they serve as a reminder of the name of the letter touched. They also provide immediate and gentle guidance about how to give the right answer.

PhonicsWorks Keywords

accent – the emphasis, by stress or pitch, on a word or syllable. For example, in the word *garden*, the accent falls on the first syllable, *gar*.

base word – the part of a word that contains a prefix, suffix, or both. A base word can stand on its own.

blend – a combination of two or three consonants in which you hear the sound of each consonant; for example, the two letters *st* can each be heard in the word *stop*, and the three letters *str* can each be heard in the word *string*.

compound word – a word made from two smaller words (for example, baseball)

decode – the ability to translate written forms into their corresponding speech sounds. For example, students decode when they recognize that *d* represents /d/, *o* represents /ŏ/, *g* represents /g/, and therefore that combination of letters (*d-o-g*) is the word *dog*.

digraph – two letters together that make one sound. For example, the two letters *sh* in the word *fish* make one sound.

onset – the part of a word preceding the first vowel. For example, in the word *smart*, *sm* is the onset.

phonemes – the smallest units of sound. Phonemes are combined to make words.

phonological awareness – the ability to identify and manipulate sound parts in words. The ability to identify similar sounds in words, create rhyming words, and count syllables are all signs of phonological awareness.

rime – the part of a word that includes the first vowel and what follows it. For example, in the word *smart*, *art* is the rime.

schwa – an unstressed vowel indistinct in pronunciation, often similar to short *u*. In the word *garden*, the unstressed syllable *den* contains the schwa sound. In the word *alone*, the unstressed syllable *a* is the schwa sound. The schwa sound is represented by the symbol ə.

trigraph – three letters together that make one sound. For example, the three letters *tch* in the word *match* make one sound.

Contractions

Unit Overview

In this unit, students will
- ▶ Review sight words.
- ▶ Learn to make and write contractions.
- ▶ Practice identifying individual sounds in words.
- ▶ Build words.

Materials

Supplied
- *K¹² PhonicsWorks Advanced Activity Book,* p. PH 37
- small whiteboards (3)
- whiteboard, student
- Tile Kit

Also Needed
- sight words box

Lesson Overview

Offline FOCUS: Contractions		**15** minutes
Sight Words	Review Sight Words	
Learn	Introduce Contractions	
	Make Contractions	
	Make Contractions with Two *n*'s	
	Write Contractions	
Try It	Alphabet Subtraction	

Online REVIEW: Contractions	**15** minutes

Advance Preparation

If you have not already done so, create a second set of the sight words cards either by writing words on 3½ x 5-inch index cards (the list of words can be found in the Sight Words section of the Lesson Guide introduction) or printing a set from the online lesson. In addition, you will be instructed throughout the semester to make a series of word cards for individual activities. Save these cards for further use.

Note that the amount of time for offline and online phonics instruction changes in Semester 2, from 30 minutes offline to 15 minutes offline and from 20 minutes online to 15 minutes online. As students spend less time on PhonicsWorks, they should spend more time working Spelling or Writing Skills.

⟨ Offline ⟩ ⏱ 15 minutes

FOCUS: Contractions

Work **together** with students to complete offline Sight Words, Learn, and Try It activities.

Sight Words ●

Review Sight Words

Help students learn to recognize sight words.

1. Gather all the sight word cards students have yet to master from their sight words box. Stack the cards on the table face down.

2. Have students pick a word and read it to you.

3. If they read it quickly and correctly, put the card in one stack. If they hesitate or do not read the word correctly, put it in another stack. The second stack should have words that they will review again.

4. Take the stack of words that students read correctly and dictate each word to them. They may choose to either write the word or spell it aloud.

5. If students spell the word correctly, they have mastered the word. If they misspell the word, add it to the stack of cards to review again.

6. Chart students' progress on the back of each card.

   ▸ Divide the back of the card into two columns.
   ▸ Label the first column "Read" and the second column "Spell."
   ▸ Record the dates that students read or spell the word correctly. When students can read and spell the word correctly three times in a row, they have mastered the word. You may want to put a star or sticker on their card when they have mastered that word.

   TIP Even if students can read and spell all the words correctly, it is still beneficial for them to review sight words. Choose as many additional words as you would like for each subsequent activity.

Objectives
- Read sight words.
- Spell sight words.
- Write sight words.

Learn ●

Introduce Contractions

Introduce the concept of contractions to students using the examples *did not* and *didn't*.

1. Write the following sentences on students' whiteboard:

   ▸ *She did not go.*
   ▸ *She didn't go.*

Objectives
- Identify, create, and read contractions.
- Write words by applying grade-level phonics knowledge.
- Identify and use contractions.

2. **Say:** We're going to learn about a special group of words. You've already seen some of these words in the stories you have read. We call these words **contractions**. If something contracts, it shrinks and gets smaller. Contractions are words we make by taking two words and shrinking them into one word.

3. Have students read both sentences.

   Say: In the first sentence, you read the words *did not*, and in the second sentence, you read those two words as *didn't*. *Didn't* is the contraction for *did not*. Contractions are a faster way to say two words.

4. Have students touch and say the words *did not* and *didn't*.

5. Point to the apostrophe.

   Say: This is called an **apostrophe**. Touch it and say *apostrophe*.

6. **Say:** When we combine two words into a contraction, we take out one letter and put an apostrophe in its place. I'll show you how this happens.

7. Point to the words *did not*.

   Say: When I say *did not*, I clearly say the /ŏ/ sound in the word *not*.

8. Point to the word *didn't*.

   Say: When I say *didn't*, I don't say the sound /ŏ/. To spell *didn't*, I push the two words together and take out the letter *o* because the sound /ŏ/ is gone.

9. Point to the apostrophe in *didn't*.

   Say: I replaced the sound /ŏ/ with an apostrophe, but the apostrophe doesn't stand for a sound.

Make Contractions

Have students practice making contractions.

1. Place the apostrophe tile and the following letter tiles at the top of students' whiteboard: *a, e, h, i, n, o, r, s, t,* and *w*.

2. **Say:** We can say this sentence, "She is not having any fun today," or we can say this sentence, "She isn't having any fun today." Both sentences mean the same thing. We just changed the words *is not* to the contraction *isn't*. I will say two words to you and you will use those words to make a contraction. I'll do the first one for you. The words are *is* and *not*.

   ▸ Make the words *is* and *not*.
   ▸ Push the letter tiles for *is* and *not* together.
   ▸ Take out the letter *o* for the sound /ŏ/, and replace it with an apostrophe to make the contraction *isn't*.

3. Say the following word pairs to students, and have them follow the procedure to make the contractions:

   ▸ *has* and *not hasn't*
   ▸ *are* and *not aren't*
   ▸ *was* and *not wasn't*

Make Contractions with Two *n*'s

Have students practice making contractions that have two *n*'s together.

1. Place the apostrophe tile and the following letter tiles at the top of students' whiteboard: *a, c, n, n, o,* and *t.*

2. **Say:** We can say this sentence, "I can not go today," or we can say this sentence, "I can't go today." Both sentences mean the same thing. We just changed the words *can not* to the contraction *can't.*

3. Have students make the contraction *can't.* Guide them with the following directions:

   Say: Make the words *can* and *not.* Push the two words *can* and *not* together. Notice that you have two *n*'s together. When we make the contraction, we are going to take out the letter *o,* as usual, but this time we will also take out one letter *n.*

4. Have students remove one of the *n*'s, take out the letter *o* for the sound /ŏ/, and replace it with an apostrophe.

   ▸ What contraction did you spell? *can't*
   ▸ How is the contraction *can't* different from the other contractions we learned today? One of the letter *n*'s was removed.

Write Contractions

Have students practice making and writing contractions. Grab three small whiteboards.

1. **Say:** You are going to write contractions. I will say a pair of words to you. Your job is to spell and write each of the words I say. I'll do the first one for you.

2. Write the words *was* and *not* on a small whiteboard, using one board per word.

3. Push the two boards together and make the contraction.

   Say: To make the contraction, you will erase the letter or letters that need to be taken out and write an apostrophe in place of that letter or letters. You will write the contraction on another small whiteboard.

4. Write the contraction *wasn't* on a third small whiteboard.

5. Dictate the following pairs of words. Have students write each word pair and the contraction.

   ▸ *can* and *not can't*
   ▸ *did* and *not didn't*
   ▸ *is* and *not isn't*
   ▸ *has* and *not hasn't*

Try It

Alphabet Subtraction

Have students complete page PH 37 in *K[12] PhonicsWorks Advanced Activity Book* for more practice with making contractions. First have students read the two words aloud. Then have them write the contraction by putting the two words together and replacing the letter *o* (or letters *no* in *can not*) with an apostrophe.

Try It
Contractions
Alphabet Subtraction

Read the two words aloud, and then write them as one contraction.
(Where the *o* should be, write an apostrophe.)

1. is not   −   o   =   __isn't__

2. did not   −   o   =   __didn't__

3. are not   −   o   =   __aren't__

4. has not   −   o   =   __hasn't__

5. was not   −   o   =   __wasn't__

6. can not   −   no   =   __can't__

LANGUAGE ARTS GREEN   PH 37

[Online] 15 minutes

REVIEW: Contractions

Students will work online independently to

▸ Practice making contractions.
▸ Practice decoding text by reading a story.

Help students locate the online activities and provide support as needed.

Offline Alternative

No computer access? Have students say or write the two words that are used in the contractions *aren't*, *can't*, *didn't*, *hasn't*, *isn't*, *it's*, and *let's*. Vice versa, have students say or write the contractions made by the words *are not*, *can not*, *did not*, *has not*, *is not*, *it is*, and *let us*. You might also ask students to make up sentences using contractions.

Sound /z/ Spelled *s*

Lesson Overview

📃 **[Offline]** FOCUS: Sound /z/ Spelled *s*		🕘 **15** minutes
Sight Words	Use Words in Sentences	
Get Ready	Build Contractions	
Learn	Introduce Sound /z/ Spelled *s*	
	Build Words	
Try It	"Eve Loves Rules"	

🖥️ **[Online]** REVIEW: Sound /z/ Spelled *s*　🕘 **15** minutes

[Materials]

Supplied

- *K¹² PhonicsWorks Readers Advanced 6,* pp. 19–24
- whiteboard, Learning Coach
- whiteboard, student
- Tile Kit

Also Needed

- sight words box

〖 Offline 〗 ⑮ minutes

FOCUS: Sound /z/ Spelled *s*

Work **together** with students to complete offline Sight Words, Get Ready, Learn, and Try It activities.

Sight Words

Use Words in Sentences

Help students use sight words in sentences.

1. Gather all the sight word cards students have yet to master from their sight words box. Spread the sight word cards on the table.

2. **Say:** Let's use sight words in sentences.

3. Have students

   ▸ Touch each card and read the word on it.
   ▸ Make up a sentence using the word.
   ▸ Put the card in a pile after using the word in a sentence.
   ▸ Go through the pile of cards and read each sight word again.
   ▸ Spell each word.

TIP If students have difficulty with any of the sight words, place those cards in a pile to review again.

> **Objectives**
> • Read sight words.
> • Spell sight words.

Get Ready

Build Contractions

Help students build contractions.

1. Place the apostrophe tile and the following letter tiles at the top of students' whiteboard: *a, c, d, d, e, h, i, n, n, o, r, s, t,* and *w*.

2. **Say:** Let's use letters and the apostrophe to build the contraction *isn't*.

3. Have students

   ▸ Say the two words the contraction stands for. *is* and *not*
   ▸ Identify the sounds in *isn't*.
   ▸ Choose the corresponding letter for each of the sounds.
   ▸ Move the apostrophe to the correct location in the word.
   ▸ Say and write the contraction on the whiteboard.

> **Objectives**
> • Identify, create, and read contractions.
> • Identify and use contractions.

4. Repeat the activity to build the following contractions:

- ▸ *did* and *not didn't*
- ▸ *are* and *not aren't*
- ▸ *can* and *not can't*
- ▸ *has* and *not hasn't*
- ▸ *was* and *not wasn't*

TIP If students have difficulty remembering what a contraction is, remind them that it is two words pushed together to make one word with an apostrophe in the place of the missing letter or letters. Tell them that the word **contract** means to make shorter.

Learn

Introduce Sound /z/ spelled s

Help students learn the sound /z/ spelled with the letter *s*. Grab your whiteboard and dry-erase marker.

1. **Say:** In some words that end with the letter *s*, like *cats*, the *s* makes the sound /s/. In other words that end in *s*, like *bugs*, *has*, and *was*, the *s* makes the sound /z/.

2. Write the letter *s* on your whiteboard and point to it. State the following:

- ▸ What are the sounds for this letter? /s/ or /z/
- ▸ Touch and say the sounds for the letter *s*.

3. **Say:** I will write some words that have the sound /z/ for the letter *s*. The first word is *is*.

- ▸ Touch and say the word.
- ▸ What sound does the letter *s* make in the word *is*? /z/

4. Repeat this procedure for the following words:

- ▸ *use* /z/
- ▸ *dose* /s/
- ▸ *rose* /z/

Objectives

- Identify the letter, given the sounds /s/ and /z/.
- Identify the sounds, given the letter *s*.
- Identify ending sounds in words.
- Identify, create, and read contractions.
- Identify and use contractions.

Build Words

Help students use letters and sounds to build words.

1. Place the following letter tiles at the top of students' whiteboard: *a, ch, e, e, h, i, o, s,* and *th*.

2. Draw two horizontal lines across the middle of students' whiteboard to represent the sounds in a word.

3. **Say:** Let's use letters and sounds to build the word *as*.

4. Have students finger stretch the sounds in *as*.

5. Have students

  ▸ Identify the first and last sounds in *as*.
  ▸ Choose the corresponding letter for each sound.
  ▸ Move the letters to the correct lines on their whiteboard.

6. Guide students with these questions:

  ▸ What is the first sound in *as*? /ă/
    Which line does the letter for that sound go on? the first one
  ▸ What's the last sound in *as*? /z/
    Which line does the letter for that sound go on? the last one

7. Redirect students if they select the incorrect letter.

  Say: That sound is in the word [word], and it is the [first, second] sound. We want the sound [target sound].

  Continue until students select the correct letter.

8. Have students touch and say the word.

9. Have them say the word as they use a dry-erase marker to write the word on the whiteboard.

10. Draw three horizontal lines across the middle of students' whiteboard that represent the number of sounds in each word. Repeat the activity to build the following words:

  ▸ *has* /h/ /ă/ /z/
  ▸ *his* /h/ /ĭ/ /z/
  ▸ *these* /th/ /ĕ/ /z/
  ▸ *those* /th/ /ō/ /z/
  ▸ *chose* /ch/ /ō/ /z/

TIP Remind students that when building words with the silent *e* on the end, there is no line on which to place the *e*. This reinforces the fact that the vowel and the *e* work together to make the long vowel sound, and the silent *e* does not make a sound on its own. Have students put the silent *e* on the end of the word.

Try It

"Eve Loves Rules"

Have students read "Eve Loves Rules" on page 19 of *K¹² PhonicsWorks Readers Advanced 6*.

Students should read the story silently once or twice before reading the story aloud. When students miss a word that can be sounded out, point to it and give them three to six seconds to try the word again. If students still miss the word, tell them the word so the flow of the story isn't interrupted.

After reading the story, make a list of all the words students missed, and go over those words with them. You may use letter tiles to show students how to read the words.

Objectives
- Read aloud grade-level text with appropriate automaticity, prosody, accuracy, and rate.
- Decode words by applying grade-level word analysis skills.

 **15 minutes**

REVIEW: Sound /z/ Spelled *s*

Students will work online independently to

▶ Practice the sound /z/ spelled *s*.

Help students locate the online activities and provide support as needed.

Offline Alternative

No computer access? Have students spell words that end with the sound /z/ spelled with the letter *s*, such as *is*, *as*, *was*, *has*, and *dogs*.

Objectives
- Identify the letter, given the sounds /s/ and /z/.
- Identify the sounds, given the letter *s*.
- Identify ending sounds in words.
- Identify, create, and read contractions.
- Identify and use contractions.

Practice Contractions and Sound /z/ Spelled *s* (A)

Lesson Overview

[Offline]	**FOCUS:** Practice Contractions and Sound /z/ Spelled *s*	**15** minutes

Sight Words	Sight Word Concentration
Get Ready	Checkup: Two Sounds for *s*
Learn	Introduce Contractions *Let's* and *It's*
Try It	Best Pick

[Online]	**REVIEW:** Contractions and Sound /z/ Spelled *s*	**15** minutes

[Materials]

Supplied
- *K¹² PhonicsWorks Advanced Activity Book*, p. PH 38
- whiteboard, student
- Tile Kit

Also Needed
- sight words box
- index cards (14)

Advance Preparation

Gather two sets of the sight word cards that students have yet to master.

For Checkup: Two Sounds for *s*, print each of the following words on index cards, using one card per word: *is, was, these, those, rise, rose, hose, pose, chose, use, gas, dose, mass,* and *kiss.*

〔 Offline 〕 🕖 minutes

FOCUS: Practice Contractions and Sound /z/ Spelled *s*

Work **together** with students to complete offline Sight Words, Get Ready, Learn, and Try It activities.

Sight Words ....

Sight Word Concentration

Help students review sight words.

1. Gather the two sets of sight word cards.

2. Scramble both sets of sight word cards and place them face down on the table or floor.

3. Turn over two cards at a time; take turns with students. If the cards match, the person turning over the matching cards reads the word and uses it in a sentence. If the cards don't match, the person turns them back over.

4. Remove and save the matching cards.

5. Continue the activity until all the cards are paired.

6. Have students read all the words.

7. Take the stack of words that students read correctly and dictate each word to them.

8. Have students write each word or spell it aloud.

TIP If students have difficulty with any sight words, let them work at their own pace to really master these words.

Objectives
- Read sight words.
- Spell sight words.
- Write sight words.

Get Ready ....

Checkup: Two Sounds for *s*

Have students practice identifying the ending sound in words that end with the sound /z/ spelled *s*.

1. Gather the index cards you prepared.

2. Have students

   ▸ Choose a card.
   ▸ Read the word.
   ▸ Say if the word ends with the sound /z/ for the letter *s*.
   Sound /z/ Words: *is, was, these, those, rise, rose, hose, pose, chose, use*
   Sound /s/ Words: *gas, dose, mass, kiss*

Objectives
- Identify the letter, given the sounds /s/ and /z/.
- Identify the sounds, given the letter *s*.
- Identify ending sounds in words.

Learn •••

Introduce Contractions *Let's* and *It's*

Help students learn the contractions *let's* and *it's*.

1. Place the apostrophe tile and the following letter tiles at the top of students' whiteboard: *e, i, i, l, s, t,* and *u.*

2. **Say:** We will make the contraction *let's.* This contraction is made from the words *let* and *us.* When you speak or read, you don't usually use *let* and *us.* It is easier to spell *let's* if you know that it comes from the words *let* and *us.* I will use *let's* in the sentence *Let's go to the store.* Without the contraction, the sentence would be *Let us go to the store.*

3. Have students

   ▸ Spell the words *let* and *us* with the letter tiles on their whiteboard.
   ▸ Push the letter tiles for *let* and *us* together.
   ▸ Take out the vowel *u* and replace it with an apostrophe to make the contraction *let's.*

4. Ask students the following questions:

   ▸ What contraction did you spell? *let's*
   ▸ What are the two words the contraction stands for? *let* and *us*

5. **Say:** Now we will make the contraction *it's.* This contraction is made from the words *it* and *is.* I will use *it's* in the sentence *It's hot outside.* Without the contraction, the sentence would be *It is hot outside.*

6. Have students

   ▸ Spell the words *it* and *is* with the letter tiles on their whiteboard.
   ▸ Push the letter tiles for *it* and *is* together.
   ▸ Take out the vowel *i* from *is* and replace it with an apostrophe to make the contraction *it's.*

7. Ask students the following questions:

   ▸ What contraction did you spell? *it's*
   ▸ What are the two words the contraction stands for? *it* and *is*

TIP If students have difficulty remembering what a contraction is, remind them that it is two words pushed together to make one word with an apostrophe in the place of the missing letter or letters. Tell them that the word **contract** means to make shorter.

Objectives

- Identify, create, and read contractions.
- Identify and use contractions.

Try It

Best Pick

Have students complete page PH 38 in *K¹² PhonicsWorks Advanced Activity Book* for practice with making sentences. Have them choose the word that best completes the sentence and write the word. Have them read the sentence aloud.

Try It

Practice Contractions and Sound /z/ Spelled *s* (A)

Best Pick

Read the sentence aloud and circle the word that best completes it. Then write the word.

1. The mule **didn't** want to go. wasn't (didn't)
2. The cats **aren't** together. (aren't) can't
3. Let's **chase** the kite. (chase) cute
4. She **hasn't** gone home yet. isn't (hasn't)
5. They didn't **want** to go there. (want) went
6. He didn't **use** his chopsticks. (use) us

PH 38   LANGUAGE ARTS GREEN

⟦ Online ⟧ 🕐 minutes

REVIEW: Contractions and Sound /z/ Spelled *s*

Students will work online independently to

▸ Practice contractions and the sound /z/ spelled *s*.
▸ Practice decoding text by reading a story.

Help students locate the online activities and provide support as needed.

Offline Alternative

No computer access? Have students practice making contractions such as *let's*, *it's*, *can't*, and *aren't*. Have them tell you the two words that each contraction represents. Vice versa, have students say or write the contractions made by the words *let us*, *it is*, *can not*, *are not*, and so on. In addition, have students spell words that end with the sound /z/ spelled with the letter *s*, such as *is*, *was*, *beds*, *pans*, *lids*, *rubs*, *hugs*, *pins*, *gabs*, *buns*, and *fins*.

Practice Contractions and Sound /z/ Spelled s (B)

Lesson Overview

Offline — **FOCUS:** Practice Contractions and Sound /z/ Spelled s — **15** minutes

Sight Words	Pick a Pair
Practice	Practice Contractions
	Practice Sound /z/ Spelled s
Try It	"Where Is Dane?"
	Dictation: Write Sentences

Online — **REVIEW:** Contractions and Sound /z/ Spelled s — **15** minutes

Materials

Supplied
- *K¹² PhonicsWorks Readers Advanced 6*, pp. 25–30
- whiteboard, Learning Coach

Also Needed
- sight words box
- dictation notebook

[Offline] 🕐 15 minutes

FOCUS: Practice Contractions and Sound /z/ Spelled *s*

Work **together** with students to complete offline Sight Words, Practice, and Try It activities.

Sight Words ···

Pick a Pair

Play a card game with students for more practice with sight words.

1. Gather the sight word cards that students are reviewing. Choose two words and place the cards on the table.

2. Ask questions to help students identify each word. For example, if the words are *or* and *one*, you could ask, "Which word names a number?" If the words are *on* and *but*, you could ask, "Which word is the opposite of *off*?"

3. Continue the activity until students identify all the words.

4. Take the stack of words that students read correctly and dictate each word to them.

5. Have students write each word or spell it aloud.

> **Objectives**
> - Read sight words.
> - Write sight words.
> - Spell sight words.

Practice ···

Practice Contractions

Have students practice making contractions and using them in sentences.

1. **Say:** I will say a contraction. You will repeat the contraction and use it in a sentence. You will say the same sentence using the two words that make the contraction. I will do the first one. The word is *isn't*. I will say the contraction in a sentence, *That dog isn't very cute*. I'll repeat the sentence using the two words that *isn't* is made from, *That dog **is not** very cute*. Now it's your turn. The contraction is *aren't*.

2. Have students
   - ► Say the contraction *aren't*.
   - ► Make up a sentence using the contraction *aren't*.
   - ► Repeat the sentence using the two words the contraction is made from, *are* and *not*.

3. Continue the same procedure for the contractions *let's, hasn't, wasn't, it's, can't,* and *didn't*.

> **Objectives**
> - Identify, create, and read contractions.
> - Identify and use contractions.
> - Identify the letter, given the sounds /s/ and /z/.
> - Identify the sounds, given the letter *s*.
> - Identify ending sounds in words.

Practice Sound /z/ Spelled *s*

Have students practice identifying the ending sound in words that end with the sound /s/ or /z/ for the letter *s*.

1. **Say:** I will say two words. Your job is to listen for the ending sound in each word. After I say the words, you repeat them. Tell me which word ends in the sound /s/ and which word ends in the sound /z/.

2. Say the following pairs of words. Have students say which word has the sound /s/ and which word has the sound /z/.

   ▸ *hats, bugs /s/ hats; /z/ bugs*
   ▸ *pins, walks /s/ walks; /z/ pins*
   ▸ *sings, hops /s/ hops; /z/ sings*
   ▸ *mitts, swims /s/ mitts; /z/ swims*
   ▸ *books, plays /s/ books; /z/ plays*

Try It

"Where Is Dane?"

Have students read "Where Is Dane?" on page 25 of *K¹² PhonicsWorks Readers Advanced 6*.

Students should read the story silently once or twice before reading the story aloud. When students miss a word that can be sounded out, point to it and give them three to six seconds to try the word again. If students still miss the word, tell them the word so the flow of the story isn't interrupted.

After reading the story, make a list of all the words students missed, and go over those words with them. You may use letter tiles to show students how to read the words.

Dictation: Write Sentences

Use sentences to help students identify individual sounds in words.

1. Gather a pencil and the dictation notebook. Say the sentence, *Let's take this gift to Rose.* Then give these directions to students:

   ▸ Repeat the sentence.
   ▸ Write the sentence in your notebook.
   ▸ Read the sentence aloud.

2. When students have finished, write the following sentence on your whiteboard: *Let's take this gift to Rose.*

3. Have them compare their answer to your correct version.

4. Repeat this procedure with the following sentences: *The hose isn't in the box. Steve wasn't at the shop.*

   ▸ If students make an error and don't see it, help them correct their mistake by having them finger stretch the sounds in the word they missed.
   ▸ If students are having difficulty selecting the correct letters or sounds, review those letters or sounds that are confusing them.
   ▸ If students have difficulty with first, middle, and last sounds, have them finger stretch the sounds in words.

Objectives
- Read aloud grade-level text with appropriate automaticity, prosody, accuracy, and rate.
- Decode words by applying grade-level word analysis skills.
- Write words by applying grade-level phonics knowledge.
- Write sight words.
- Follow three-step directions.
- Identify, create, and read contractions.

 **minutes**

REVIEW: Contractions and Sound /z/ Spelled *s*

Students will work online independently to

▶ Practice contractions and the sound /z/ spelled *s*.

Help students locate the online activities and provide support as needed.

Offline Alternative

No computer access? Have students practice making contractions such as *let's*, *it's*, *didn't*, and *wasn't*. Have them tell you the two words that each contraction represents. Vice versa, have students say or write the contractions made by the words *let us*, *it is*, *did not*, *was not*, and so on. In addition, have students spell words that end with the sound /z/ spelled with the letter *s*, such as *his*, *hers*, *bins*, *pens*, *lads*, *ribs*, *mugs*, *kids*, *grabs*, *fans*, and *wins*.

Objectives

- Identify, create, and read contractions.
- Identify and use contractions.
- Identify the letter, given the sounds /s/ and /z/.
- Identify the sounds, given the letter *s*.
- Identify ending sounds in words.

Unit Checkpoint

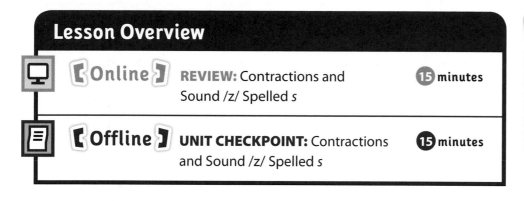

Lesson Overview

🖥 **[Online]** **REVIEW:** Contractions and Sound /z/ Spelled *s* — 🕙 **15** minutes

📄 **[Offline]** **UNIT CHECKPOINT:** Contractions and Sound /z/ Spelled *s* — 🕙 **15** minutes

【 Materials 】

Supplied
- *K¹² PhonicsWorks Advanced Assessments*, pp. PH 109–114

⭐ Objectives

- Identify, create, and read contractions.
- Identify and use contractions.
- Identify the letter, given the sounds /s/ and /z/.
- Identify the sounds, given the letter *s*.
- Identify individual sounds in words.
- Identify ending sounds in words.
- Given the letter, identify the most common sound.
- Given the sound, identify the most common letter or letters.

- Read instructional-level text with 90% accuracy.
- Read aloud grade-level text with appropriate automaticity, prosody, accuracy, and rate.
- Write words by applying grade-level phonics knowledge.
- Write sight words.
- Read sight words.

【 Online 】 🕙 **15** minutes

REVIEW: **Contractions and Sound /z/ Spelled *s***

Students will review contractions and the sound /z/ spelled *s* to prepare for the Unit Checkpoint. Help students locate the online activities and provide support as needed.

〖 Offline 〗 ⑮ minutes

UNIT CHECKPOINT: Contractions and Sound /z/ Spelled *s*

Explain that students are going to show what they have learned about sounds, letters, and words.

1. Give students the Unit Checkpoint pages for the Contractions and Sound /z/ Spelled *s* unit and print the Unit Checkpoint Answer Key, if you'd like.

2. Use the instructions below to help administer the Checkpoint to students. On the Answer Key or another sheet of paper, note student answers to oral response questions to help with scoring the Checkpoint later.

3. Use the Answer Key to score the Checkpoint, and then enter the results online.

Part 1. Count Sounds Have students read each word aloud, count the number of sounds, and write that number.

Part 2. Matching Have students read the words aloud and draw a line to match the words to their contraction.

Part 3. Sound /z/ or /s/ Spelled *s* Have students read each word aloud and identify the ending sound. Have them write *s* for words that end with the sound /s/ and *z* for words that end with the sound /z/.

Part 4. Writing Read each sentence to students. Have them repeat and write the sentence.

19. *Pete can't use these.*

20. *Let's run those hills.*

21. *It's time for lunch, isn't it?*

Part 5. Read Aloud Listen to students read the sentences aloud. Count and note the number of words they read correctly.

Part 6. Read Words Have students read each word aloud. Note any words they read incorrectly.

Part 7. Read Nonsense Words Have students read each nonsense word aloud. Note any words they read incorrectly.

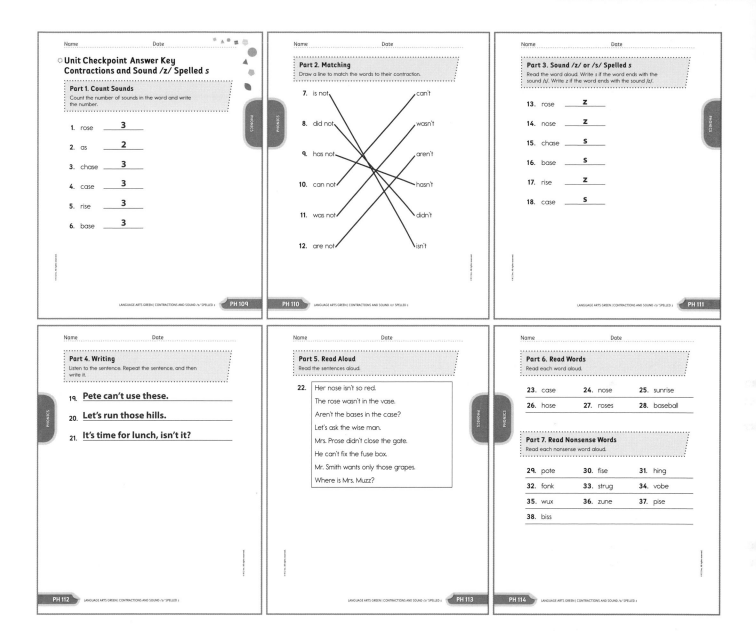

Unit Checkpoint Answer Key
Contractions and Sound /z/ Spelled s

Part 1. Count Sounds
Count the number of sounds in the word and write the number.

1. rose _____3_____
2. as _____2_____
3. chase _____3_____
4. case _____3_____
5. rise _____3_____
6. base _____3_____

Part 2. Matching
Draw a line to match the words to their contraction.

7. is not — can't
8. did not — wasn't
9. has not — aren't
10. can not — hasn't
11. was not — didn't
12. are not — isn't

Part 3. Sound /z/ or /s/ Spelled s
Read the word aloud. Write s if the word ends with the sound /s/. Write z if the word ends with the sound /z/.

13. rose _____z_____
14. nose _____z_____
15. chase _____s_____
16. base _____s_____
17. rise _____z_____
18. case _____s_____

Part 4. Writing
Listen to the sentence. Repeat the sentence, and then write it.

19. **Pete can't use these.**
20. **Let's run those hills.**
21. **It's time for lunch, isn't it?**

Part 5. Read Aloud
Read the sentences aloud.

22.
Her nose isn't so red.
The rose wasn't in the vase.
Aren't the bases in the case?
Let's ask the wise man.
Mrs. Prose didn't close the gate.
He can't fix the fuse box.
Mr. Smith wants only those grapes.
Where is Mrs. Muzz?

Part 6. Read Words
Read each word aloud.

23. case   24. nose   25. sunrise
26. hose   27. roses   28. baseball

Part 7. Read Nonsense Words
Read each nonsense word aloud.

29. pote   30. fise   31. hing
32. fonk   33. strug   34. vobe
35. wux   36. zune   37. pise
38. biss

Introduce Two-Syllable Words

Unit Overview

In this unit, students will
- ▸ Learn the sight words *brother*, *sister*, and *baby*.
- ▸ Learn two-syllable words.
- ▸ Learn the schwa sound.
- ▸ Practice making contractions.
- ▸ Read a story silently and aloud.

[Materials]

Supplied
- *K¹² PhonicsWorks Advanced Activity Book*, p. PH 39
- whiteboard, student
- Tile Kit

Also Needed
- sight words box

Lesson Overview

[Offline] FOCUS: Introduce Two-Syllable Words	**15** minutes

Sight Words	Introduce Sight Words
Get Ready	Recognize Words and Syllables
Learn	Introduce Two-Syllable Words
Try It	Careful Counting

[Online] REVIEW: Two-Syllable Words	**15** minutes

Offline   🕐 minutes

FOCUS: Introduce Two-Syllable Words

Work **together** with students to complete offline Sight Words, Get Ready, Learn, and Try It activities.

Sight Words

Introduce Sight Words

Help students learn the sight words *brother, sister,* and *baby.*

1. Gather the sight word cards *brother, sister,* and *baby.*

2. Show students the *brother* card.

3. **Say:** This is the word *brother.* We see this word so often that we want to be able to read and spell it quickly without thinking about it. Look closely at the word *brother.* Spell the word *brother.* Take a picture of the word *brother* in your mind. When you think you can spell *brother* yourself, turn the card over and use your letter tiles to spell the word *brother.* Check the card to see if you spelled the word *brother* correctly. Read aloud the word you spelled with the letter tiles.

4. Repeat the activity with the remaining sight words.

5. Chart students' progress on the back of each card.
   - ▸ Divide the back of the card into two columns.
   - ▸ Label the first column "Read" and the second column "Spell."
   - ▸ Record the dates that students read or spell the word correctly. When students can read and spell the word correctly three times in a row, they have mastered the word. You may want to put a star or sticker on their card when they have mastered that word.

6. Add the cards to students' sight words box.

TIP Sight words can be very difficult for some students. Let students work at their own pace and really master these words, as they occur frequently in reading and writing.

> **Objectives**
> - Read sight words.
> - Spell sight words.

Get Ready

Recognize Words and Syllables

Practice the concept of syllables with students.

1. **Say:** When we talk, we make words by pushing air out of our mouths. Each push of air in a word is called a **syllable**. Each word has one or more syllables. You can think of syllables as chunks of words.

> **Objectives**
> - Identify syllables in words.
> - Identify individual sounds in words.
> - Identify the number of sounds within words.

2. **Say:** Let's break some words into syllables.

> ▸ I'll say a word. I'll repeat the word.
> ▸ You'll say the word after me, and you'll break it into syllables by saying the separate chunks of the word and tapping your fist on the table as you say each chunk.
> ▸ For example, I'll say *inside,* and then I'll say it again.
> ▸ You'll say *in / side* and tap your fist on the table as you say each syllable.

3. Say each word and repeat it. Have students fist tap on the table as they say the syllables in each word.

> ▸ *basket bas / ket*
> ▸ *muffin muf / fin*
> ▸ *rabbit rab / bit*
> ▸ *until un / til*
> ▸ *helpful help / ful*

TIP Have students name items in a category, such as foods, furniture, or animals, and fist tap the syllables with you. For example, have them name and fist tap words such as *ta / ble* and *win / dow.* Challenge students to name and fist tap something with several syllables (for example, *tel / e / vi / sion*).

Learn

Introduce Two-Syllable Words

Help students build words with two syllables.

1. Place the following letter tiles on students' whiteboard: *a, c, c, e, f, h, i, i, k, l, l, n, n, p, s, t,* and *u.*

2. **Say:** Syllables are chunks of words. Each word has one or more syllables. We are going to make words with two syllables. We will take two syllables and push them together to make a word. I will do the first one.

3. Use the letter tiles to build the syllables *nap* and *kin* on students' whiteboard and read each syllable aloud.

4. Push the syllables together to make the word *napkin.*

5. Write the word *napkin,* saying each syllable as you write it on the whiteboard.

6. **Say:** Now it's your turn. The two syllables are *pic* and *nic.*

> ▸ Use the letter tiles to build each syllable.
> ▸ Push the syllables together to make a word. What is the word? *picnic*
> ▸ Say and write the word.

7. Continue the procedure with the following words:

> ▸ *un / til until*
> ▸ *help / ful helpful*
> ▸ *up / set upset*

> **Objectives**
> - Identify syllables in words.
> - Identify individual sounds in words.
> - Identify the number of sounds within words.
> - Write words by applying grade-level phonics knowledge.

Try It

Careful Counting

Have students complete page PH 39 in *K¹² PhonicsWorks Advanced Activity Book* for more practice with syllables. Have students count the number of syllables they hear in the word and write the number. They should make sure they have only one vowel sound in each syllable.

Try It

Introduce Two-Syllable Words
Careful Counting

Count how many syllables you hear in the word and write the number.

1.	hope	1	9.	velvet	2
2.	picnic	2	10.	kittens	2
3.	basketball	3	11.	tent	1
4.	pumpkin	2	12.	lemonade	3
5.	rabbit	2	13.	muffins	2
6.	insect	2	14.	admit	2
7.	rake	1	15.	fantastic	3
8.	stack	1	16.	napkin	2

LANGUAGE ARTS GREEN   **PH 39**

⟦Online⟧ 🕐 minutes

REVIEW: Two-Syllable Words

Students will work online independently to

▶ Practice two-syllable words.
▶ Practice decoding text by reading a story.

Help students locate the online activities and provide support as needed.

Offline Alternative

No computer access? Have students fist tap and count the number of syllables in the words *basket, muffin, rabbit, until, helpful,* and *upset.* You might also tell students two syllables and have them say the word made by the two syllables (for example, *ta / ble, win / dow, mit / ten, car / toon, fin / ish, mis / take, pre / tend, ap / ple, flow / er,* and *gar / den*).

Practice Two-Syllable Words

Lesson Overview

Offline — FOCUS: Practice Two-Syllable Words — 15 minutes

Sight Words	Sight Word Fun
Get Ready	Write Contractions
Practice	Build Words
Try It	"Quinn and Kent's Lunch"
	Dictation: Write Words

Online — REVIEW: Two-Syllable Words — 15 minutes

Materials

Supplied

- *K¹² PhonicsWorks Readers Advanced 7*, pp. 1–9
- small whiteboards (3)
- whiteboard, Learning Coach
- whiteboard, student
- Tile Kit

Also Needed

- sight words box
- dictation notebook

[Offline] ⓯ minutes

FOCUS: Practice Two-Syllable Words

Work **together** with students to complete offline Sight Words, Get Ready, Practice, and Try It activities.

Sight Words ···

Sight Word Fun

Help students learn the sight words *brother*, *sister*, and *baby*, and up to two additional sight words they have yet to master.

1. Gather the sight word cards *brother*, *sister*, and *baby*, and up to two additional sight word cards.

2. Choose one sight word card to begin.

   Say: Look at this word and take a picture of it in your mind. When you think you can spell the word yourself, turn the card over and use your letter tiles to spell the word.

3. After students spell the word, have them check the card to see if they spelled the word correctly.

   Say: Read aloud the word you spelled with the letter tiles.

4. Repeat the activity with the remaining sight words.

   TIP Sight words can be very difficult for some students. Let students work at their own pace and really master these words.

> **Objectives**
> - Read sight words.
> - Spell sight words.

Get Ready ···

Write Contractions

Have students practice making and writing contractions. Grab the three small whiteboards.

1. **Say:** You are going to write contractions. I will say a pair of words to you. Your job is to spell and write each of the words I say. I'll do the first one for you.

2. Write the words *is* and *not* on a small whiteboard, using one board per word.

3. Push the two boards together and make the contraction.

   Say: To make the contraction, you will erase the letter or letters that need to be taken out and make an apostrophe in place of that letter or letters. You will write the contraction on another small whiteboard.

> **Objectives**
> - Identify, create, and read contractions.
> - Write words by applying grade-level phonics knowledge.
> - Identify and use contractions.

4. Write the contraction *isn't* on a third board.

5. Dictate the following pairs of words. Have students write each word pair and the contraction.

   ▸ *did* and *not didn't*
   ▸ *are* and *not aren't*
   ▸ *has* and *not hasn't*
   ▸ *was* and *not wasn't*
   ▸ *can* and *not can't*
   ▸ *let* and *us let's*

Practice

Build Words

Help students use letters and sounds to build two syllable words.

1. Place the following letter tiles at the top of your whiteboard: *a, a, b, b, c, c, d, e, f, f, g, i, k, k, l, m, n, o, p, p, r, s, t, t,* and *u.*

2. Draw six horizontal lines across the middle of students' whiteboard to represent the sounds in a word.

3. **Say:** Let's use letters and sounds to build the word *magnet.*

4. Have students finger stretch the sounds in *magnet.*

5. Have students

   ▸ Identify the first, next, and last sounds in *magnet.*
   ▸ Choose the corresponding letter for each sound.
   ▸ Move the letters to the correct lines on their whiteboard.

6. Guide students with these questions:

   ▸ What is the first sound in *magnet*? /m/
     Which line does the letter for that sound go on? the first one
   ▸ What is the second sound in *magnet*? /ă/
     Which line does the letter for that sound go on? the second one
   ▸ What's the third sound in *magnet*? /g/
     Which line does the letter for that sound go on? the third one
   ▸ What's the next sound in *magnet*? /n/
     Which line does the letter for that sound go on? the fourth one
   ▸ What's the next sound in *magnet*? /ĕ/
     Which line does the letter for that sound go on? the fifth one
   ▸ What's the last sound in *magnet*? /t/
     Which line does the letter for that sound go on? the last one

7. Have them say the word as they use a dry-erase marker to write the word on the whiteboard.

8. Have students touch and say the word.

9. Have them say the syllables in the word.

Objectives

- Blend sounds to create words.
- Identify individual sounds in words.
- Identify syllables in words.
- Write words by applying grade-level phonics knowledge.

10. Redirect students if they select the incorrect letter.

    Say: That sound is in the word [word], and it is the [first, second, third, fourth, fifth, sixth] sound. We want the sound [target sound].

    Continue until students select the correct letter.

11. Draw horizontal lines across the middle of students' whiteboard that represent the number of sounds in each word. Repeat the activity to build the following words:

    ▸ *muffin* /m/ /ŭ/ /f/ /f/ /ĭ/ /n/
    ▸ *rabbit* /r/ /ă/ /b/ /b/ /ĭ/ /t/
    ▸ *laptop* /l/ /ă/ /p/ /t/ /ŏ/ /p/
    ▸ *backpack* /b/ /ă/ /k/ /p/ /ă/ /k/
    ▸ *dentist* /d/ /ĕ/ /n/ /t/ /ĭ/ /s/ /t/
    ▸ *basket* /b/ /ă/ /s/ /k/ /ĕ/ /t/

Try It

"Quinn and Kent's Lunch"

Have students read "Quinn and Kent's Lunch" on page 1 of *K¹² PhonicsWorks Readers Advanced 7*.

Students should read the story silently once or twice before reading the story aloud. When students miss a word that can be sounded out, point to it and give them three to six seconds to try the word again. If students still miss the word, tell them the word so the flow of the story isn't interrupted.

After reading the story, make a list of all the words students missed, and go over those words with them. You may use letter tiles to show students how to read the words.

Objectives

- Read aloud grade-level text with appropriate automaticity, prosody, accuracy, and rate.
- Decode words by applying grade-level word analysis skills.
- Write words by applying grade-level phonics knowledge.
- Follow three-step directions.

Dictation: Write Words

Have students practice identifying sounds and writing words.

1. Gather a pencil and the dictation notebook. Say the word *upset*. Then give these directions to students:

    ▸ Repeat the word.
    ▸ Write the word in your notebook.
    ▸ Read the word aloud.

2. When students have finished, write the following word on your whiteboard: *upset*.

3. Have them compare their answer to your correct version.

4. Repeat this procedure with the following words: *mistake, unzip, helpful,* and *hopeful*.

    ▸ If students make an error and don't see it, help them correct their mistake by having them finger stretch the sounds in the word they missed.
    ▸ If students are having difficulty selecting the correct letters or sounds, review those letters or sounds that are confusing them.
    ▸ If students have difficulty with first, middle, and last sounds, have them finger stretch the sounds in words.

[Online] ⏱ minutes

REVIEW: Two-Syllable Words

Students will work online independently to

► Practice two-syllable words.

Help students locate the online activities and provide support as needed.

Objectives
- Identify syllables in words.
- Identify individual sounds in words.
- Identify the number of sounds within words.

Offline Alternative

No computer access? Have students fist tap and count the number of syllables in the words *jacket*, *bunny*, *zebra*, *later*, *bashful*, and *wooden*. You might also tell students two syllables and have them say the word made by the two syllables (for example, *hap / py*, *el / bow*, *writ / ten*, *chim / ney*, *dol / phin*, *din / ner*, *o / ver*, *so / fa*, *pen / cil*, and *cray / on*).

Introduce Schwa Sound

Lesson Overview

〔Offline〕 **FOCUS:** Introduce Schwa Sound — **15** minutes

Sight Words	Sight Word Fun
Learn	Introduce Accent
	Introduce the Schwa Symbol and Sound
Try It	Match It

〔Online〕 **REVIEW:** Schwa Sound — **15** minutes

Materials

Supplied
- *K¹² PhonicsWorks Advanced Activity Book,* p. PH 40
- whiteboard, Learning Coach
- whiteboard, student
- Tile Kit

Also Needed
- sight words box

[Offline] 🕒 minutes

FOCUS: Introduce Schwa Sound

Work **together** with students to complete offline Sight Words, Learn, and Try It activities.

Sight Words ....

Sight Word Fun

Help students learn the sight words *brother*, *sister*, and *baby*, and up to two additional sight words they have yet to master.

1. Gather the sight word cards *brother*, *sister*, and *baby*, and up to two additional sight word cards.

2. Choose one sight word card to begin.

   Say: Look at this word and take a picture of it in your mind. When you think you can spell the word yourself, turn the card over and use your letter tiles to spell the word.

3. After students spell the word, have them check the card to see if they spelled the word correctly.

   Say: Read aloud the word you spelled with the letter tiles.

4. Repeat the activity with the remaining sight words.

TIP Sight words can be very difficult for some students. Let students work at their own pace and really master these words.

> **Objectives**
> - Read sight words.
> - Spell sight words.

Learn ....

Introduce Accent

Introduce the concept of **accent** to students.

1. **Say:** We usually say one syllable in a word a little bit louder than the other one. The syllable that we say louder is the accented syllable. For example, in the word *wagon*, the accent is placed on the first syllable, *wag*. Let's do a test to show where the accent naturally falls in the word *wagon*.

2. Repeat the word *wagon*, saying the first syllable loudly with emphasis. Say the second syllable softly.

3. Repeat the word *wagon* again, this time saying the first syllable softly and the second syllable loudly.

   Say: Notice that when I say *wagon* this way [word emphasizing the second syllable], the word doesn't sound correct because we usually say *wag* a little bit louder than *on*. Let's test some more words to learn where the accent falls.

> **Objectives**
> - Identify the accented syllable, given the word.
> - Identify syllables in words.
> - Identify individual sounds in words.
> - Identify and use the schwa sound.

4. Have students test the following words using the procedure to decide which syllable sounds more natural when it is said aloud:

  ▶ *rabbit* accent falls on *rab*
  ▶ *insect* accent falls on *in*
  ▶ *invite* accent falls on *vite*
  ▶ *confuse* accent falls on *fuse*
  ▶ *grapevine* accent falls on *grape*
  ▶ *athlete* accent falls on *ath*

TIP Hearing the accented syllable is an important task that can be difficult for students. You may need to demonstrate which syllable is the accented one several times before students can recognize it on their own.

___

Introduce the Schwa Symbol and Sound
Introduce the schwa sound to students.

1. Place the schwa letter tile ə and the following letter tiles on your whiteboard: *a, a, b, b, d, d, e, e, g, h, i, k, l, n, n, o, r, s, t, t, u, v,* and *w.*

2. Take the letter tiles from your whiteboard to make the word *wagon* on students' whiteboard.

3. **Say:** In some words, the vowel sound in the unaccented syllable gets lost and turns into the sound /ŭ/. When this happens, we say the vowel has a **schwa** sound. The symbol for the schwa sound is an upside down *e.*

4. Point to the schwa letter tile and say /ŭ/.

5. **Say:** The schwa sound is /ŭ/. This is the same sound we make for the short vowel *u.* Let's look at a word with the schwa sound. Here we have the word *wagon* again. The word *wagon* has two syllables and the loud, accented syllable is *wag.* The unaccented syllable *on* becomes /ŭn/ instead of /ŏn/ because we say it softly. I am going to put the schwa letter tile on top of the vowel in the second syllable.

6. Build the word *garden* on students' whiteboard.

7. **Say:** Listen for the schwa sound in the words that I spell on your whiteboard. I will do the first word, *garden.* I will separate the word into the syllables *gar* and *den,* and touch and say each syllable. One syllable has a schwa sound. The syllable with the schwa sound is *den* because we say it more softly than the syllable *gar. Den* is pronounced /dŭn/ instead of /dĕn/. Now it's your turn. The word is *hidden.*

8. Have students

  ▶ Separate the word into syllables.
  ▶ Touch and say each syllable.
  ▶ Listen for the schwa sound.
  ▶ Say which syllable has the schwa sound.

9. Continue the activity with the following words:

- ▸ *seven* second syllable
- ▸ *button* second syllable
- ▸ *basket* second syllable
- ▸ *ribbon* second syllable
- ▸ *instant* second syllable

10. **Say:** In all of the words you just spelled, the schwa sound is in the second syllable. I will spell some more words. This time, listen for the schwa sound in the first syllable. All of the first syllables start with the letter *a*. The *a* will be pronounced as the schwa sound /ŭ/. The first word is *alone*.

11. Have students

- ▸ Separate the word into syllables.
- ▸ Touch and say each syllable.
- ▸ Listen for the schwa sound.
- ▸ Say which syllable has the schwa sound.

12. Continue the activity with the following words:

- ▸ *alive* first syllable
- ▸ *awake* first syllable
- ▸ *along* first syllable

TIP When separating the words into syllables, students may have to divide a word with double consonants between the two consonants. Although the consonants are only said once, this procedure is correct.

Try It

Match It

Have students complete page PH 40 in *K¹² PhonicsWorks Advanced Activity Book* for more practice reading words with the schwa sound. Have students draw a line to the picture that matches the sentence. Have them read the sentence aloud.

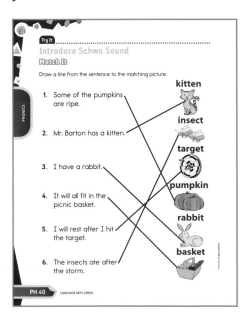

Objectives
- Read aloud grade-level text with appropriate automaticity, prosody, accuracy, and rate.
- Identify and use the schwa sound.

 **15** minutes

REVIEW: Schwa Sound

Students will work online independently to

▶ Practice the schwa sound.
▶ Practice decoding text by reading a story.

Help students locate the online activities and provide support as needed.

Offline Alternative

No computer access? Have students practice breaking words into syllables and identifying the syllable with the schwa sound. Use the following words: *a / dult* (first syllable), *a / jar* (first syllable), *a / larm* (first syllable), *a / part* (first syllable), *a / shore* (first syllable), *a / side* (first syllable), *a / ware* (first syllable), *a / while* (first syllable), *a / woke* (first syllable); *bas / ket* (second syllable), *but / ton* (second syllable), *in / stant* (second syllable), *rib / bon* (second syllable), *sev / en* (second syllable), and *wag / on* (second syllable).

Objectives

- Identify and use the schwa sound.
- Identify individual sounds in words.
- Identify syllables in words.
- Read aloud grade-level text with appropriate automaticity, prosody, accuracy, and rate.
- Decode words by applying grade-level word analysis skills.

Practice Schwa Sound

Lesson Overview

[Offline] FOCUS: Practice Schwa Sound — **15** minutes

Sight Words	Sight Word Fun
Practice	Accented Syllables
	Find Schwa in Words
	Words with Three Syllables
Try It	"The Wagon Ride"
	Dictation: Write Sentences

[Online] REVIEW: Schwa Sound — **15** minutes

[Materials]

Supplied
- *K¹² PhonicsWorks Readers Advanced 7*, pp. 10–15
- whiteboard, Learning Coach
- whiteboard, student
- Tile Kit

Also Needed
- sight words box
- dictation notebook
- index cards (47)

Advance Preparation

For Accented Syllables, print the following syllables on index cards, using one card per syllable: *un, til, mor, ning, un, zip, in, hale, in, tend, in, sist, con,* and *test.* Keep the cards in order.

For Find Schwa in Words, print the following syllables on index cards, using one card per syllable: *car, ton, tar, get, dark, ness, horn, et, lem, on, pock,* and *et.* Keep the cards in order.

For Words with Three Syllables, print the following syllables on index cards, using one card per syllable: capital *At, lan, tic, bas, ket, ball, es, tab, lish, snap, drag, on, con, sis, tent, won, der, ful, fan, tas,* and *tic.* Keep the cards in order.

⟦ Offline ⟧ 🕒 15 minutes

FOCUS: Practice Schwa Sound

Work **together** with students to complete offline Sight Words, Practice, and Try It activities.

Sight Words ••

Sight Word Fun

Help students learn the sight words *brother, sister,* and *baby,* and up to two additional sight words they have yet to master.

1. Gather the sight word cards *brother, sister,* and *baby,* and up to two additional sight word cards.

2. Choose one sight word card to begin.

   Say: Look at this word and take a picture of it in your mind. When you think you can spell the word yourself, turn the card over and use your letter tiles to spell the word.

3. After students spell the word, have them check the card to see if they spelled the word correctly.

   Say: Read aloud the word you spelled with the letter tiles.

4. Repeat the activity with the remaining sight words.

TIP Sight words can be very difficult for some students. Let students work at their own pace and really master these words.

> **Objectives**
> - Read sight words.
> - Spell sight words.

Practice ••

Accented Syllables

Have students practice identifying the accent on syllables.

1. Gather the index cards you prepared.

2. Place the syllable cards (in the correct order) on the table for the first word: *un, til.*

3. **Say:** Let's put syllables together to make words. You will tell me the syllable the accent occurs on. The first syllables are *un / til.*

4. Have students

   ▸ Read the word. *until*
   ▸ Identify the accented syllable. *til*

> **Objectives**
> - Identify individual sounds in words.
> - Identify the accented syllable, given the word.
> - Identify syllables in words.
> - Identify and use the schwa sound.

5. Repeat the activity with the syllable cards for the following words:

- *mor, ning morning, mor*
- *un, zip unzip, zip*
- *in, hale inhale, hale*
- *in, tend intend, tend*
- *in, sist insist, sist*
- *con, test contest, con*

Find Schwa in Words

Have students make words from syllables, identify the accented syllable, and name the vowel that makes the schwa sound.

1. Gather the index cards you prepared.

2. Place the syllable cards (in the correct order) on the table for the first word: *car, ton*.

3. **Say:** Let's put syllables together to make words. You will tell me the syllable the accent occurs on and name the vowel that makes the schwa sound. The first syllables are *car / ton*.

4. Have students

- Read the word. *carton*
- Identify the accented syllable. *car*
- Identify the vowel that makes the schwa sound in the unaccented syllable. *o*

5. Repeat the activity with the syllable cards for the following words:

- *tar, get target, tar, o*
- *dark, ness darkness, dark, e*
- *horn, et hornet, hor, e*
- *lem, on lemon, lem, o*
- *pock, et pocket, pock, e*

Words with Three Syllables

Have students make three-syllable words.

1. Gather the index cards you prepared, students' whiteboard, and the dry-erase marker.

2. Place the syllable cards on the table (in the correct order) for the first word: *At, lan, tic*.

3. **Say:** Let's put syllables together to make words that have three syllables. The first syllables are *At / lan / tic*.

4. Have students

- Put the syllables together.
- Read the word. *Atlantic*
- Say the word as they use the dry-erase marker to write the word on their whiteboard.

5. Repeat the activity with the syllable cards for the following words:

- *bas, ket, ball basketball*
- *es, tab, lish establish*
- *snap, drag, on snapdragon*
- *con, sis, tent consistent*
- *won, der, ful wonderful*
- *fan, tas, tic fantastic*

Try It

"The Wagon Ride"
Have students read "The Wagon Ride" on page 10 of *K¹² PhonicsWorks Readers Advanced 7*.

Students should read the story silently once or twice before reading the story aloud. When students miss a word that can be sounded out, point to it and give them three to six seconds to try the word again. If students still miss the word, tell them the word so the flow of the story isn't interrupted.

After reading the story, make a list of all the words students missed, and go over those words with them. You may use letter tiles to show students how to read the words.

Objectives

- Read aloud grade-level text with appropriate automaticity, prosody, accuracy, and rate.
- Decode words by applying grade-level word analysis skills.
- Write words by applying grade-level phonics knowledge.
- Write sight words.
- Follow three-step directions.

Dictation: Write Sentences
Use sentences to help students identify individual sounds in words.

1. Gather a pencil and the dictation notebook. Say the sentence, *The ship will cross the Atlantic.* Then give these directions to students:

   - Repeat the sentence.
   - Write the sentence in your notebook.
   - Read the sentence aloud.

2. When students have finished, write the following sentence on your whiteboard: *The ship will cross the Atlantic.*

3. Have them compare their answer to your correct version.

4. Repeat this procedure with the sentence, *Jane likes basketball.*

   - If students make an error and don't see it, help them correct their mistake by having them finger stretch the sounds in the word they missed.
   - If students are having difficulty selecting the correct letters or sounds, review those letters or sounds that are confusing them.
   - If students have difficulty with first, middle, and last sounds, have them finger stretch the sounds in words.

[Online] ⑮ minutes

REVIEW: Schwa Sound

Students will work online independently to

► Practice the schwa sound.

Help students locate the online activities and provide support as needed.

Offline Alternative

No computer access? Have students practice breaking words into syllables and identifying the syllable with the schwa sound. Use the following words: *a / bout* (first syllable), *a / fraid* (first syllable), *a / rrive* (first syllable), *a / ttempt* (first syllable), *a / way* (first syllable), *ad / just* (first syllable), *a / ware* (first syllable), *sev / en* (first syllable), *sel / dom* (second syllable), *gol / den* (second syllable), *doc / tor* (second syllable), *vi / sor* (second syllable), *sail / or* (second syllable), and *ad / just* (second syllable).

Objectives

- Identify individual sounds in words.
- Identify the accented syllable, given the word.
- Identify syllables in words.
- Identify and use the schwa sound.

Unit Checkpoint

Lesson Overview

🖥	**[Online]**	**REVIEW:** Two-Syllable Words and Schwa Sound	**15** minutes
📄	**[Offline]**	**UNIT CHECKPOINT:** Two-Syllable Words and Schwa Sound	**15** minutes

⭐ Objectives

- Identify individual sounds in words.
- Identify and use the schwa sound.
- Identify syllables in words.
- Given the letter, identify the most common sound.
- Given the sound, identify the most common letter or letters.
- Read instructional-level text with 90% accuracy.
- Read aloud grade-level text with appropriate automaticity, prosody, accuracy, and rate.
- Write words by applying grade-level phonics knowledge.
- Write sight words.
- Read sight words.

[Materials]

Supplied
- *K¹² PhonicsWorks Advanced Assessments,* pp. PH 115–120

[Online] 15 minutes

REVIEW: Two-Syllable Words and Schwa Sound

Students will review two-syllable words and the schwa sound to prepare for the Unit Checkpoint. Help students locate the online activities and provide support as needed.

[Offline] 🖫 minutes

UNIT CHECKPOINT: Two-Syllable Words and Schwa Sound

Explain that students are going to show what they have learned about sounds, letters, syllables, and words.

1. Give students the Unit Checkpoint pages for the Two-Syllable Words and Schwa Sound unit and print the Unit Checkpoint Answer Key, if you'd like.

2. Use the instructions below to help administer the Checkpoint to students. On the Answer Key or another sheet of paper, note student answers to oral response questions to help with scoring the Checkpoint later.

3. Use the Answer Key to score the Checkpoint, and then enter the results online.

Part 1. Count Syllables Have students read each word aloud, count the number of syllables, and write that number.

Part 2. Vowel or Consonant Say each letter to students. Have them decide if the letter is a vowel or consonant and write that letter in the correct column.

7. *a*

8. *k*

9. *o*

10. *e*

Part 3. True or False Read each statement to students and have them write *T* if the statement is true and *F* if the statement is false.

11. *Every word has at least one syllable.*

12. *Every syllable has one vowel sound.*

Part 4. Writing Read each sentence to students. Have them repeat and write the sentence.

13. *This cake is fantastic.*

14. *Pete lost his backpack.*

15. *Let's invite Morgan to go with us.*

Part 5. Read Aloud Listen to students read the sentences aloud. Count and note the number of words they read correctly.

Part 6. Say Sounds Say each word to students. Have them say if the schwa sound is in the first or second syllable.

17. *wagon*

18. *above*

19. *organ*

20. *doctor*

21. *awhile*

22. *about*

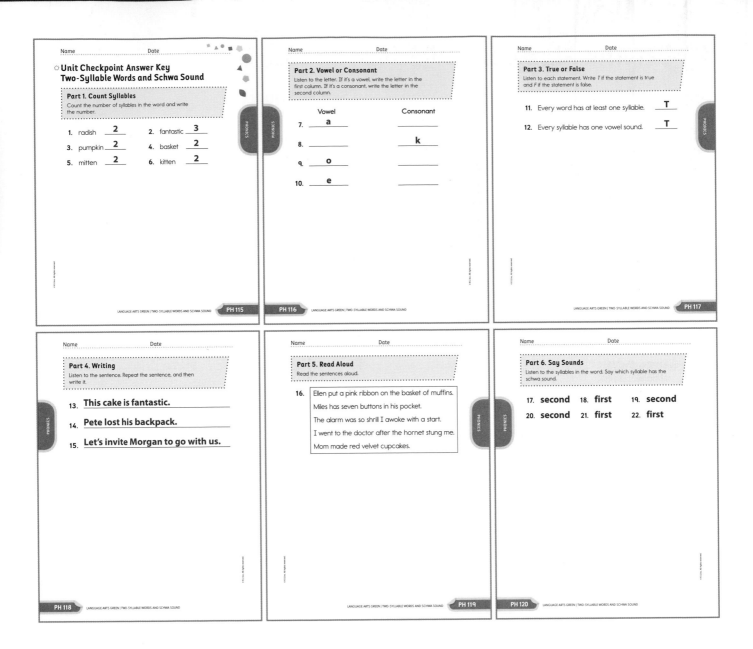

Name _____ Date _____

Unit Checkpoint Answer Key
Two-Syllable Words and Schwa Sound

Part 1. Count Syllables
Count the number of syllables in the word and write the number.

1. radish __2__   2. fantastic __3__

3. pumpkin __2__   4. basket __2__

5. mitten __2__   6. kitten __2__

Name _____ Date _____

Part 2. Vowel or Consonant
Listen to the letter. If it's a vowel, write the letter in the first column. If it's a consonant, write the letter in the second column.

Vowel	Consonant
7. **a**	
8.	**k**
9. **o**	
10. **e**	

Name _____ Date _____

Part 3. True or False
Listen to each statement. Write T if the statement is true and F if the statement is false.

11. Every word has at least one syllable. __T__

12. Every syllable has one vowel sound. __T__

Name _____ Date _____

Part 4. Writing
Listen to the sentence. Repeat the sentence, and then write it.

13. **This cake is fantastic.**

14. **Pete lost his backpack.**

15. **Let's invite Morgan to go with us.**

Name _____ Date _____

Part 5. Read Aloud
Read the sentences aloud.

16.
Ellen put a pink ribbon on the basket of muffins.

Miles has seven buttons in his pocket.

The alarm was so shrill I awoke with a start.

I went to the doctor after the hornet stung me.

Mom made red velvet cupcakes.

Name _____ Date _____

Part 6. Say Sounds
Listen to the syllables in the word. Say which syllable has the schwa sound.

17. **second** 18. **first** 19. **second**

20. **second** 21. **first** 22. **first**

Introduce Endings –*ing* and –*est*

Unit Overview

In this unit, students will
- Learn the sight words *many*, *animals*, and *while*.
- Practice multisyllable words.
- Learn the endings –*ing*, –*est*, and –*ed*.
- Read a story silently and aloud.

Materials

Supplied
- *K¹² PhonicsWorks Advanced Activity Book*, p. PH 41
- whiteboard, student
- Tile Kit

Also Needed
- sight words box
- index cards (31)

Lesson Overview

[Offline] FOCUS: Introduce Endings –*ing* and –*est* **15** minutes

Sight Words	Introduce Sight Words
Get Ready	Read Multisyllable Words
Learn	Introduce Endings –*ing* and –*est*
	Add Endings –*ing* and –*est* to Base Words
Try It	Alphabet Addition

[Online] REVIEW: Endings –*ing* and –*est* **15** minutes

Advance Preparation

For Read Multisyllable Words, print the following syllables on index cards, using one card per syllable: *pub, lish, base, ment, dic, tate, ad, ver, tise, pan, cake, a, long, wed, ding, pun, ish, ment, a, lone, in, com, plete, in, di, cate, ex, plode,* capital *A, las,* and *ka.*

[Offline] ⏱ 15 minutes

FOCUS: Introduce Endings –ing and –est

Work **together** with students to complete offline Sight Words, Get Ready, Learn, and Try It activities.

Sight Words ....

Introduce Sight Words

Help students learn the sight words *many*, *animal*, and *while*.

1. Gather the sight word cards *many*, *animal*, and *while*.

2. Show students the *many* card.

3. **Say:** This is the word *many*. We see this word so often that we want to be able to read and spell it quickly without thinking about it. Look closely at the word *many*. Spell the word *many* aloud. Take a picture of the word *many* in your mind. When you think you can spell *many* yourself, turn the card over and use your letter tiles to spell the word *many*. Check the card to see if you spelled the word *many* correctly. Read aloud the word you spelled with the letter tiles.

4. Repeat the activity with the remaining sight words.

5. Chart students' progress on the back of each card.

   ▸ Divide the back of the card into two columns.
   ▸ Label the first column "Read" and the second column "Spell."
   ▸ Record the dates that students read or spell the word correctly. When students can read and spell the word correctly three times in a row, they have mastered the word. You may want to put a star or sticker on the card when they have mastered that word.

6. Add the cards to students' sight words box.

TIP Sight words can be very difficult for some students. Let students work at their own pace and really master these words, as they occur frequently in reading and writing.

> **Objectives**
> - Read sight words.
> - Spell sight words.

Get Ready •••

Read Multisyllable Words

Have students practice making words that have two or more syllables.

1. Gather the index cards you prepared. Scatter the following syllable cards face up on the table: *pub / lish, base / ment,* and *ad / ver / tise.*

2. **Say:** Let's put syllables together to make words.

   ▸ I'll say a word. You'll say the word after me.
   ▸ You'll break the word into syllables by saying the separate chunks in the word while tapping your fist on the table as you say each chunk.
   ▸ You'll find the cards on the table with the syllables in the word and put the cards together to make the word.

3. **Say:** I'll do the first one for you. The word is *publish.*

4. Perform the following steps for students:

   ▸ Repeat the word *publish.*
   ▸ Fist tap *pub* and *lish.*
   ▸ Find the syllable *pub* and pull that card down.
   ▸ Find the syllable *ish* and put that card to the right of *pub.*
   ▸ Read the word.
   ▸ Pick up the cards and put them in a pile.

5. **Say:** Now it's your turn. The word is *basement.*

6. Have students

   ▸ Repeat the word.
   ▸ Fist tap the syllables.
   ▸ Find the cards with the syllables for the word.
   ▸ Put the cards together and read the word.
   ▸ Pick up the cards and put them in a pile.

7. Continue this procedure until all of the cards on the table are used. Then place new syllable cards on the table so that there are always enough syllables to make three words.

TIP If students have difficulty with this activity, you may want to start with only four syllable cards that have obvious matches, such as *pub / lish* and *base / ment.*

Objectives
• Identify syllables in words.
• Identify individual sounds in words.

Learn

Introduce Endings –*ing* and –*est*

Help students learn the endings –*ing* and –*est*.

1. Place the following letter tiles on students' whiteboard: *ing* and *est*.

2. **Say:** We're going to learn two common endings for longer words. We add endings to a **base word** to change the meaning of the word. The first ending is spelled *ing*.

   Point to the *ing* tile and say /ing/.

3. **Say:** Touch the tile and say /ing/.

4. **Say:** The second ending is spelled *est*.

   Point to the *est* tile and say /est/.

5. **Say:** Touch the tile and say /est/.

> ### Objectives
> - Identify syllables in words.
> - Identify individual sounds in words.
> - Identify ending sounds in words.
> - Identify, read, and write words ending with –*ing*.
> - Identify, read, and write words ending with –*est*.

Add Endings –*ing* and –*est* to Base Words

Help students learn words that end in –*ing* and –*est* by having them add the endings to base words.

1. Place the following letter tiles at the top of students' whiteboard: *a, c, d, f, g, h, i, k, l, m, n, o, p, r, s,* and *t*.

2. Place the following letter tiles at the bottom of students' whiteboard: *ing* and *est*.

3. **Say:** We are going to add the endings –*ing* and –*est* to base words. I'll do the first one for you. The base word is *fast*.

   - ▸ Make the word *fast*.
   - ▸ Put the tile with the ending –*est* at the end of the base word *fast*.
   - ▸ Read the new word *fastest*.

4. Say the following words and endings to students, and have them spell the word with the tiles and read the new word aloud:

   - ▸ *hard* and –*est hardest*
   - ▸ *long* and –*est longest*
   - ▸ *short* and –*est shortest*
   - ▸ *ask* and –*ing asking*
   - ▸ *fish* and –*ing fishing*
   - ▸ *camp* and –*ing camping*
   - ▸ *pick* and –*ing picking*

Try It

Alphabet Addition

Have students complete page PH 41 in *K¹² PhonicsWorks Advanced Activity Book* for more practice with the endings *–ing* and *–est*. Have them add the letters together to make a new word and write the word. Have students read the words and the silly sentences aloud.

> **Objectives**
> - Identify ending sounds in words.
> - Identify, read, and write words ending with *–ing*.
> - Identify, read, and write words ending with *–est*.
> - Identify individual sounds in words.

Online 15 minutes

REVIEW: Endings *–ing* and *–est*

Students will work online independently to

► Practice the endings *–ing* and *–est*.
► Practice decoding text by reading a story.

Help students locate the online activities and provide support as needed.

Offline Alternative

No computer access? Have students name words ending in the letters *ing* and *est*, such as *barking* and *hardest*. You might also ask them to spell the words and state the base word, the ending, and the consonant letter that is doubled if it is needed.

> **Objectives**
> - Identify, read, and write words ending with *–ing*.
> - Identify, read, and write words ending with *–est*.
> - Identify ending sounds in words.
> - Identify individual sounds in words.
> - Read aloud grade-level text with appropriate automaticity, prosody, accuracy, and rate.
> - Decode words by applying grade-level phonics knowledge.

Practice Endings –*ing* and –*est*

Lesson Overview

Offline FOCUS: Practice Endings –*ing* and –*est*		**15** minutes
Sight Words	Sight Word Fun	
Practice	Practice Words with Endings –*ing* and –*est*	
	Work with –*ing* and –*est*	
Try It	"Mitch"	
Online REVIEW: Endings –*ing* and –*est*		**15** minutes

Materials

Supplied
- *K¹² PhonicsWorks Readers Advanced 7*, pp. 16–20
- whiteboard, student
- Tile Kit

Also Needed
- sight words box
- index cards (8)

Advance Preparation

For Work with –*ing* and –*est*, print the following words on index cards, using one card per word: *biggest, thinnest, hottest, fattest, stopping, skipping, tagging,* and *running.* Keep the cards in order.

[Offline] ⑮ minutes

FOCUS: Practice Endings –*ing* and –*est*

Work **together** with students to complete offline Sight Words, Practice, and Try It activities.

Sight Words ....

Sight Word Fun

Help students learn the sight words *many*, *animal*, and *while*, and up to two additional sight words they have yet to master.

1. Gather the sight word cards *many*, *animal*, and *while*, and up to two additional sight word cards.

2. Choose one sight word card to begin.

   Say: Look at this word and take a picture of it in your mind. When you think you can spell the word yourself, turn the card over and use your letter tiles to spell the word.

3. After students spell the word, have them check the card to see if they spelled the word correctly.

   Say: Read aloud the word you spelled with the letter tiles.

4. Repeat the activity with the remaining sight words.

TIP Sight words can be very difficult for some students. Let students work at their own pace and really master these words.

> **Objectives**
> - Read sight words.
> - Spell sight words.

Practice ....

Practice Words with Endings –*ing* and –*est*

Help students practice spelling words that end in –*ing* and –*est* by having them identify the base word, the ending, and the consonant letter that is doubled to spell the word correctly.

1. **Say:** We are going to review words that end in –*ing* and –*est*. When we have a base word that ends with a vowel followed by a consonant, we have to double the consonant before we add the ending. I'm going to say a base word, and you will write the word on your whiteboard. Then I'll say an ending. Your job is to decide whether to double the last letter before adding the ending. I'll do the first one. The word is *fast*.

   ▸ Write the word *fast* on your whiteboard.
   ▸ Say the word *fastest*.
   ▸ Write the ending –*est* at the end of the word *fast*.

> **Objectives**
> - Identify, read, and write words ending with –*ing*.
> - Identify, read, and write words ending with –*est*.
> - Identify individual sounds in words.
> - Identify ending sounds in words.
> - Write words by applying grade-level phonics knowledge.

2. **Say:** I do not have to double the last letter because the word *fast* does not end with a vowel followed by a consonant. Now you try one.

3. **Say:** The word is *sit*.

   ▸ Write the word *sit* on your whiteboard.
   ▸ The ending word is *sitting*. Write the word *sitting* correctly.
   ▸ Do you have to double the last letter before adding the ending? Yes

4. Continue this procedure with the following words:

   ▸ *sing*   *singing* No
   ▸ *quick*   *quickest* No
   ▸ *flash*   *flashing* No
   ▸ *big*   *biggest* Yes
   ▸ *tap*   *tapping* Yes
   ▸ *short*   *shortest* No
   ▸ *ask*   *asking* No
   ▸ *shop*   *shopping* Yes
   ▸ *fat*   *fattest* Yes
   ▸ *dim*   *dimmest* Yes

Work with *–ing* and *–est*

Help students learn the spellings of words that end in *–ing* and *–est* by having them identify the base word, the ending, and the consonant letter that is doubled to spell the word correctly.

1. Gather the index cards you prepared, turn the word *biggest* face up, and then stack the rest of the cards face down in a pile on the table.

2. **Say:** When we have a base word that ends with a vowel followed by a consonant, we have to double the consonant before we add the ending *–ing* or *–est*. I'm going to show you some words on cards. You are going to identify the base word, the ending, and the consonant letter that is doubled to spell the word. I'll do the first one for you. The word is *biggest*.

3. Repeat the word *biggest*. Have students

   ▸ Name the base word. *big*
   ▸ Name the ending and underline it. *–est*
   ▸ Name and circle the double letters. *gg*

4. Continue this procedure with the remaining words in the stack.

   ▸ *thinnest thin, –est, nn*
   ▸ *hottest hot, –est, tt*
   ▸ *fattest fat, –est, tt*
   ▸ *stopping stop, –ing, pp*
   ▸ *skipping skip, –ing, pp*
   ▸ *tagging tag, –ing, gg*
   ▸ *running run, –ing, nn*

Try It

"Mitch"

Have students read "Mitch" on page 16 of *K¹² PhonicsWorks Readers Advanced 7*.

Students should read the story silently once or twice before reading the story aloud. When students miss a word that can be sounded out, point to it and give them three to six seconds to try the word again. If students still miss the word, tell them the word so the flow of the story isn't interrupted.

After reading the story, make a list of all the words students missed, and go over those words with them. You may use letter tiles to show students how to read the words.

Objectives
- Read aloud grade-level text with appropriate automaticity, prosody, accuracy, and rate.
- Decode words by applying grade-level word analysis skills.

 **15 minutes**

REVIEW: Endings *–ing* and *–est*

Students will work online independently to

▶ Practice the endings *–ing* and *–est*.

Help students locate the online activities and provide support as needed.

Objectives
- Identify, read, and write words ending with *–ing*.
- Identify, read, and write words ending with *–est*.
- Identify ending sounds in words.
- Identify individual sounds in words.

Offline Alternative

No computer access? Have students name words ending in the letters *ing* and *est*, such as *farming* and *darkest*. You might also ask them to spell the words and state the base word, the ending, and the consonant letter that is doubled if it is needed.

Introduce Ending –ed

Lesson Overview

Offline FOCUS: Introduce Ending –ed · **15** minutes

Sight Words	Sight Word Fun
Learn	Introduce Sounds for the Ending –ed
	Spelling Rules for Adding the Ending –ed
	Ending –ed Pronounced /ed/
	Ending –ed Pronounced /d/
	Ending –ed Pronounced /t/
Try It	Practice What You Know

Online REVIEW: Ending –ed · **15** minutes

Materials

Supplied

- *K¹² PhonicsWorks Advanced Activity Book,* p. PH 42
- whiteboard, student
- Tile Kit

Also Needed

- sight words box
- index cards (45)

Advance Preparation

For Spelling Rules for Adding the Ending –ed, print the following words on index cards, using one card per word: *batted, locked, hugged, hopped,* and *blended.*

For Ending –ed Pronounced activities, print the following words on index cards, using one card per word: *bat, batted, dot, dotted, pat, patted, rot, rotted, hand, handed, nod,* and *nodded; call, called, hug, hugged, spill, spilled, smell, smelled, rob, robbed, slam, slammed, fan, fanned, quiz, quizzed, plug,* and *plugged;* and *clap, clapped, pick, picked, match, matched, ask, asked, kick,* and *kicked.*

【 Offline 】 ⑮ minutes

FOCUS: Introduce Ending –ed
Work **together** with students to complete offline Sight Words, Learn, and Try It activities.

Sight Words

Sight Word Fun
Help students learn the sight words *many*, *animal*, and *while*, and up to two additional sight words they have yet to master.

1. Gather the sight word cards *many*, *animal*, and *while*, and up to two additional sight word cards.

2. Choose one sight word card to begin.

   Say: Look at this word and take a picture of it in your mind. When you think you can spell the word yourself, turn the card over and use your letter tiles to spell the word.

3. After students spell the word, have them check the card to see if they spelled the word correctly.

   Say: Read aloud the word you spelled with the letter tiles.

4. Repeat the activity with the remaining sight words.

TIP Sight words can be very difficult for some students. Let students work at their own pace and really master these words.

> **Objectives**
> - Read sight words.
> - Spell sight words.

Learn

Introduce Sounds for the Ending –ed
Introduce the sounds and letters for the ending –ed.

1. Place the following letter tile at the top of students' whiteboard: *ed*.

2. Place the following sound tiles across the middle of students' whiteboard: /ed/, /d/, and /t/.

3. **Say:** You can pronounce the ending –ed three ways: /ed/, /d/, and /t/. Touch each of these sound tiles and say the sound.

> **Objectives**
> - Identify individual sounds in words.
> - Identify ending sounds in words.
> - Identify and use ending –ed for /ed/, /d/, and /t/.

Spelling Rules for Adding the Ending –ed

Help students learn the rules for adding the ending –ed to words by having them practice identifying the correct spelling.

1. Gather the index cards you prepared, turn the word *batted* face up, and then stack the rest of the cards face down in a pile on the table.

2. **Say:** Let's learn about the ending spelled with the letters *ed*. When we add the ending –ed to a base word, the last letter is doubled if the base word ends in a vowel and a consonant. Let's look at words with the ending –ed. The first word is *batted*.

   ▸ What is the base word? *bat*
   ▸ What is the ending? *–ed*
   ▸ Was the last letter of the base word doubled? Yes, the last letter was doubled because the end of the base word ends with a vowel and a consonant.
   ▸ Read the word again. *batted*

3. Continue the procedure with the remaining words.

   ▸ *locked lock, –ed*, No
   ▸ *hugged hug, –ed*, Yes
   ▸ *hopped hop, –ed*, Yes
   ▸ *blended blend, –ed*, No

Ending –ed Pronounced /ed/

Help students practice reading words with the sound /ed/ for the ending –ed.

1. Place the following sound tiles across the middle of students' whiteboard: /ed/, /d/, and /t/.

2. Gather the index cards you prepared: *bat, batted, dot, dotted, pat, patted, rot, rotted, hand, handed, nod,* and *nodded.*

3. Place the words *bat* and *batted* on the table.

4. **Say:** We are going to read words that have the ending –ed pronounced /ed/.

5. Point to the /ed/ sound tile and say the sound.

6. **Say:** The word *bat* becomes *batted* when I add the ending –ed. You'll say each word as I lay it on the table. Listen for the sound /ed/ at the end of the word.

7. Continue the procedure with the remaining words.

Ending –ed Pronounced /d/

Help students practice reading words with the sound /d/ for the ending –ed.

1. Place the following sound tiles across the middle of students' whiteboard: /ed/, /d/, and /t/.

2. Gather the index cards you prepared: *call, called, hug, hugged, spill, spilled, smell, smelled, rob, robbed, slam, slammed, fan, fanned, quiz, quizzed, plug,* and *plugged.*

3. **Say:** Sometimes when we add the ending –ed to a base word, it sounds just like the sound /d/. The sound /d/ is a noisy sound, so you can feel your voice box when you hear the sound /d/ at the end of a word.

4. Point to the /d/ sound tile and say the sound.

5. Place the words *call* and *called* on the table.

6. **Say:** The word *call* becomes *called* when I add the ending –ed. You'll say each word as I lay it on the table. Listen for the sound /d/ at the end of the word.

7. Continue the procedure with the remaining words.

Ending –ed Pronounced /t/

Help students practice reading words with the sound /t/ for the ending –ed.

1. Place the following sound tiles across the middle of students' whiteboard: /ed/, /d/, and /t/.

2. Gather the index cards you prepared: *clap, clapped, pick, picked, match, matched, ask, asked, kick,* and *kicked.*

3. **Say:** We are going to read words that have the ending –ed pronounced /t/. The sound /t/ is a whispered sound. When you say words ending in –ed pronounced /t/, you won't feel your voice box.

4. Point to the /t/ sound tile and say the sound.

5. Place the words *clap* and *clapped* on the table.

6. **Say:** The word *clap* becomes *clapped* when I add the ending –ed. You'll say each word as I lay it on the table. Listen for the sound /t/ at the end of the word.

7. Continue the procedure with the remaining words.

Practice What You Know

Have students complete page PH 42 in *K¹² PhonicsWorks Advanced Activity Book* for more practice with identifying words ending in *–ed* and *–ing*. Have students read each word aloud. Then have them rewrite the base word, adding the endings *–ed* and *–ing* in the correct columns. Have students read aloud the new words they wrote.

Objectives

- Write words by applying grade-level phonics knowledge.
- Identify individual sounds in words.
- Identify ending sounds in words.
- Identify and use ending *–ed* for /ed/, /d/, and /t/.

[Online] ⏱ minutes

REVIEW: Ending *–ed*

Students will work online independently to

▶ Practice the ending *–ed*.
▶ Practice decoding text by reading a story.

Help students locate the online activities and provide support as needed.

Offline Alternative

No computer access? Have students practice identifying the sounds /d/, /t/, and /ed/ for words ending in *–ed*. Refer to the list of words provided in the Advance Preparation of this lesson. You might also have students spell the words.

Objectives

- Identify individual sounds in words.
- Identify ending sounds in words.
- Identify and use ending *–ed* for /ed/, /d/, and /t/.
- Read aloud grade-level text with appropriate automaticity, prosody, accuracy, and rate.
- Decode words by applying grade-level word analysis skills.

Practice Endings –*ing*, –*est*, and –*ed*

[Materials]

Supplied
- *K¹² PhonicsWorks Readers Advanced 7*, pp. 22–30
- whiteboard, Learning Coach
- whiteboard, student
- Tile Kit

Also Needed
- sight words box
- dictation notebook
- index cards (9)

Lesson Overview

[Offline] FOCUS: Practice Endings –*ing*, –*est*, and –*ed*		**15** minutes

Sight Words	Sight Word Fun
Practice	Build Words
	Sort Words with the Ending –*ed*
Try It	"Nell and Jack Have Fun"
	Dictation: Write Sentences

[Online] REVIEW: Endings –*ing*, –*est*, and –*ed*		**15** minutes

Advance Preparation

For Sort Words with the Ending –*ed*, print the following words on index cards, using one card per word: *hunted, published, rejected, sniffed, dumped, called, ended, rubbed,* and *jumped.*

[Offline] 🕐 minutes

FOCUS: Practice Endings *–ing*, *–est,* and *–ed*

Work **together** with students to complete offline Sight Words, Practice, and Try It activities.

Sight Words ••

Sight Word Fun

Help students learn the sight words *many*, *animal*, and *while*, and up to two additional sight words they have yet to master.

1. Gather the sight word cards *many*, *animal*, and *while*, and up to two additional sight word cards.

2. Choose one sight word card to begin.

   Say: Look at this word and take a picture of it in your mind. When you think you can spell the word yourself, turn the card over and use your letter tiles to spell the word.

3. After students spell the word, have them check the card to see if they spelled the word correctly.

   Say: Read aloud the word you spelled with the letter tiles.

4. Repeat the activity with the remaining sight words.

   TIP Sight words can be very difficult for some students. Let students work at their own pace and really master these words.

> **Objectives**
> - Read sight words.
> - Spell sight words.

Practice ••

Build Words

Help students use letters and sounds to build words.

1. Place the following letter tiles at the top of students' whiteboard: *a, b, c, ck, d, d, est, i, ing, j, m, p, qu, t, t,* and *u.*

2. Draw five horizontal lines across the middle of students' whiteboard to represent the sounds in a word.

3. **Say:** Let's use letters and sounds to build the word *jumping.*

4. Have students finger stretch the sounds in *jumping.*

5. Have students
   - ► Identify the first, next, and last sounds in *jumping.*
   - ► Choose the corresponding letter for each of the sounds.
   - ► Move the letters to the correct lines on their whiteboard.

> **Objectives**
> - Identify individual sounds in words.
> - Identify ending sounds in words.
> - Blend sounds to create words.
> - Identify and use ending *–ed* for /ed/, /d/, and /t/.
> - Write words by applying grade-level phonics knowledge.
> - Identify, read, and write words ending with *–ing.*
> - Identify, read, and write words ending with *–est.*

6. Guide students with these questions:

   ▸ What is the first sound in *jumping*? /j/
     Which line does the letter for that sound go on? the first one
   ▸ What is the second sound in *jumping*? /ŭ/
     Which line does the letter for that sound go on? the second one
   ▸ What's the third sound in *jump*? /m/
     Which line does the letter for that sound go on? the third one
   ▸ What's the next sound in *jumping*? /p/
     Which line does the letter for that sound go on? the fourth one
   ▸ What's the last sound in *jumping*? /ing/
     Which line do the letters for that sound go on? the last one

7. Redirect students if they select the incorrect letter or letters.

   Say: That sound is in the word [word], and it is the [first, second, third, fourth, fifth] sound. We want the sound [target sound].

   Continue until students select the correct letter or letters.

8. Have students touch and say the word.

9. Have them say the word as they use a dry-erase marker to write the word on the whiteboard.

10. Draw four horizontal lines across the middle of students' whiteboard to represent the sounds in a word. Repeat the activity to build the following words:

    ▸ *batting* /b/ /ă/ /t/ /ing/
    ▸ *baddest* /b/ /ă/ /d/ /est/
    ▸ *acting* /ă/ /k/ /t/ /ing/
    ▸ *quickest* /kw/ /ĭ/ /k/ /est/

Sort Words with the Ending –*ed*

Help students practice words with the ending –*ed* by having them sort words ending with the sounds /ed/, /d/, and /t/.

1. Gather the index cards you prepared.

2. Place the following sound tiles across the middle of students' whiteboard: /ed/, /d/, and /t/.

3. **Say:** You are going to sort words by their ending sounds. Let's do the first one together. The word is *hunted*. Which sound should this word go under? /ed/

4. Show the word to students and have them

   ▸ Read the word.
   ▸ Say the ending sound.
   ▸ Place the card under the tile with the correct sound.

5. Continue the procedure with the remaining words:

- ► *published* /t/
- ► *rejected* /ed/
- ► *sniffed* /t/
- ► *dumped* /t/
- ► *called* /d/
- ► *ended* /ed/
- ► *rubbed* /d/
- ► *jumped* /t/

(TIP) If students have difficulty distinguishing between the ending sounds /d/ and /t/, have them place a hand on their throat as they say the words. If they can feel their voice box (if the word ending is "noisy"), then the ending is the sound /ed/ or the sound /d/. If they cannot feel their voice box (if the word ending is "quiet"), then the ending is the sound /t/.

Try It

"Nell and Jack Have Fun"
Have students read "Nell and Jack Have Fun" on page 21 of *K¹² PhonicsWorks Readers Advanced 7.*

Students should read the story silently once or twice before reading the story aloud. When students miss a word that can be sounded out, point to it and give them three to six seconds to try the word again. If students still miss the word, tell them the word so the flow of the story isn't interrupted.

After reading the story, make a list of all the words students missed, and go over those words with them. You may use letter tiles to show students how to read the words.

Objectives

- Read aloud grade-level text with appropriate automaticity, prosody, accuracy, and rate.
- Decode words by applying grade-level word analysis skills.
- Write words by applying grade-level phonics knowledge.
- Write sight words.
- Follow three-step directions.

Dictation: Write Sentences
Use sentences to help students identify individual sounds in words.

1. Gather a pencil and the dictation notebook. Say the sentence, *I am camping with Dad.* Then give these directions to students:

- ► Repeat the sentence.
- ► Write the sentence in your notebook.
- ► Read the sentence aloud.

2. When students have finished, write the following sentence on your whiteboard: *I am camping with Dad.*

3. Have them compare their answer to your correct version.

4. Repeat this procedure with the following sentences: *This pen has the darkest ink. The ball landed in the backyard.*

   ▸ If students make an error and don't see it, help them correct their mistake by having them finger stretch the sounds in the word they missed.
   ▸ If students are having difficulty selecting the correct letters or sounds, review those letters or sounds that are confusing them.
   ▸ If students have difficulty with first, middle, and last sounds, have them finger stretch the sounds in words.

[Online] ⒖ minutes

REVIEW: Endings *–ing*, *–est,* and *–ed*

Students will work online independently to

   ▸ Practice the endings *–ing*, *–est,* and *–ed.*

Help students locate the online activities and provide support as needed.

Offline Alternative

No computer access? Have students practice words ending in *–ed* for the sounds /ed/, /d/, and /t/. Say words that end in the letters *–ed* and have students tell you the ending sound in the word (for example *batted,* /ed/; *called,* /d/; and *clapped,* /t/). Have students add the endings *–ing* and *–est* to base words and spell the words aloud.

> ### Objectives
> - Identify individual sounds in words.
> - Identify ending sounds in words.
> - Identify and use ending *–ed* for /ed/, /d/, and /t/.
> - Identify, read, and write words ending with *–ing*.
> - Identify, read, and write words ending with *–est*.

Unit Checkpoint

Lesson Overview

[Online] REVIEW: Endings *–ing, –est,* and *–ed*   **15** minutes

[Offline] UNIT CHECKPOINT: Endings *–ing, –est,* and *–ed*   **15** minutes

[Materials]

Supplied

- *K¹² PhonicsWorks Advanced Assessments,* pp. PH 121–126

Objectives

- Identify ending sounds in words.
- Identify and use ending *–ed* for /ed/, /d/, and /t/.
- Identify, read, and write words ending with *–ing.*
- Identify, read, and write words ending with *–est.*
- Identify syllables in words.
- Given the letter, identify the most common sound.
- Given the sound, identify the most common letter or letters.

- Read instructional-level text with 90% accuracy.
- Read aloud grade-level text with appropriate automaticity, prosody, accuracy, and rate.
- Write words by applying grade-level phonics knowledge.
- Write sight words.
- Read sight words.

 **15** minutes

REVIEW: Endings *–ing, –est,* and *–ed*

Students will review the endings *–ing, –est,* and *–ed* to prepare for the
Unit Checkpoint. Help students locate the online activities and provide
support as needed.

[Offline] ⓯ minutes

UNIT CHECKPOINT: Endings *–ing*, *–est,* and *–ed*

Explain that students are going to show what they have learned about sounds, letters, and words.

1. Give students the Unit Checkpoint pages for the Endings *–ing, –est,* and *–ed* unit and print the Unit Checkpoint Answer Key, if you'd like.

2. Use the instructions below to help administer the Checkpoint to students. On the Answer Key or another sheet of paper, note student answers to oral response questions to help with scoring the Checkpoint later.

3. Use the Answer Key to score the Checkpoint, and then enter the results online.

Part 1. Count Syllables Have students read each word aloud, count the number of syllables, and write that number.

Part 2. Identify Ending Sounds Say each word to students and have them decide whether the word ends with the sound /ed/, /d/, or /t/. Then have them write *ed, d,* or *t* and read the word aloud.

7. *hopped*	10. *stalled*
8. *jumped*	11. *slammed*
9. *trusted*	12. *acted*

Part 3. Read Sight Words Have students read each sight word aloud. Note any words they read incorrectly.

Part 4. Writing Read each sentence to students. Have them repeat and write the sentence.

21. *I am packing for a trip.*

22. *Jane switched the boxes.*

23. *Ted is the fastest and Jeb is the shortest.*

Part 5. Read Aloud Listen to students read the sentences aloud. Count and note the number of words they read correctly.

Part 6. Read Words Have students read each word aloud. Note any words they read incorrectly.

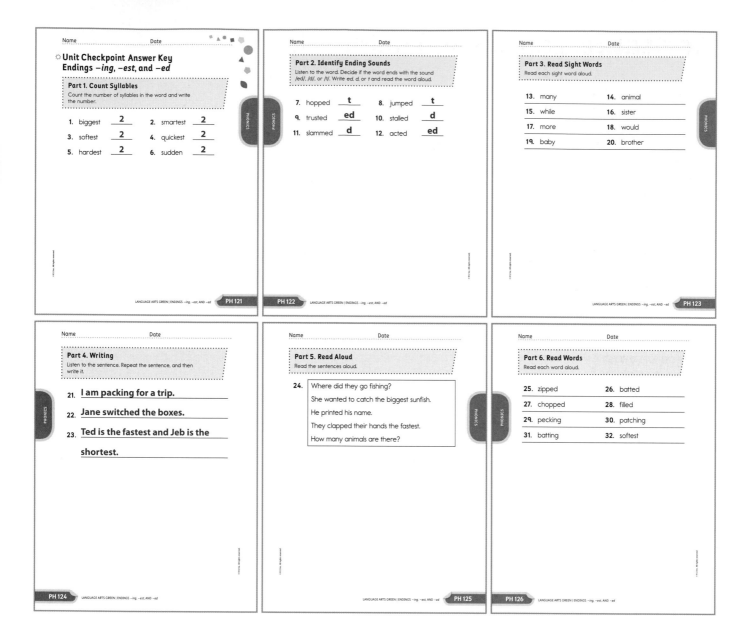

Unit Checkpoint Answer Key
Endings –ing, –est, and –ed

Part 1. Count Syllables

Count the number of syllables in the word and write the number.

1. biggest __2__
2. smartest __2__
3. softest __2__
4. quickest __2__
5. hardest __2__
6. sudden __2__

Part 2. Identify Ending Sounds

Listen to the word. Decide if the word ends with the sound /ed/, /d/, or /t/. Write ed, d, or t and read the word aloud.

7. hopped __t__
8. jumped __t__
9. trusted __ed__
10. stalled __d__
11. slammed __d__
12. acted __ed__

Part 3. Read Sight Words

Read each sight word aloud.

13. many
14. animal
15. while
16. sister
17. more
18. would
19. baby
20. brother

Part 4. Writing

Listen to the sentence. Repeat the sentence, and then write it.

21. **I am packing for a trip.**
22. **Jane switched the boxes.**
23. **Ted is the fastest and Jeb is the shortest.**

Part 5. Read Aloud

Read the sentences aloud.

24. Where did they go fishing?
    She wanted to catch the biggest sunfish.
    He printed his name.
    They clapped their hands the fastest.
    How many animals are there?

Part 6. Read Words

Read each word aloud.

25. zipped
26. batted
27. chopped
28. filled
29. pecking
30. patching
31. batting
32. softest

Introduce Consonant Ending –*le*

Unit Overview

In this unit, students will

- ▶ Review sight words.
- ▶ Learn the consonant ending –*le* and the digraph *ph*.
- ▶ Build words.
- ▶ Read stories silently and aloud.

Materials

Supplied

- *K¹² PhonicsWorks Advanced Activity Book*, p. PH 43
- whiteboard, student
- Tile Kit

Also Needed

- sight words box
- index cards (6)

Lesson Overview

🗎	**Offline** FOCUS: Introduce Consonant Ending –*le*	**15** minutes

Sight Words	Review Sight Words
Learn	Introduce the Consonant Ending –*le*
	Consonant Ending –*le*
Try It	Alphabet Addition

🖥	**Online** REVIEW: Consonant Ending –*le*	**15** minutes

Advance Preparation

For Consonant Ending –*le*, print the following words on index cards, using one card per word: *candle*, *jumble*, *giggle*, *purple*, *bottle*, and *puzzle*.

[Offline] ⏱ 15 minutes

FOCUS: Introduce Consonant Ending –*le*

Work **together** with students to complete offline Sight Words, Learn, and Try It activities.

Sight Words

Review Sight Words

Help students learn to recognize sight words.

1. Gather all the sight word cards students have yet to master from their sight words box. Stack the cards on the table face down.

2. Have students pick a word and read it to you.

3. If they read it quickly and correctly, put the card in one stack. If they hesitate or do not read the word correctly, put it in another stack. The second stack should have words that they will review again.

4. Take the stack of words that students read correctly and dictate each word to them. They may choose to either write the word or spell it aloud.

5. If students spell the word correctly, they have mastered the word. If they misspell the word, add it to the stack of cards to review again.

6. Chart students' progress on the back of each card.

   ▶ Divide the back of the card into two columns.
   ▶ Label the first column "Read" and the second column "Spell."
   ▶ Record the dates that students read or spell the word correctly. When students can read and spell the word correctly three times in a row, they have mastered the word. You may want to put a star or sticker on their card when they have mastered that word.

TIP Even if students can read and spell all the words correctly, it is still beneficial for them to review sight words. Choose as many additional words as you would like for each subsequent activity.

Objectives
- Read sight words.
- Spell sight words.
- Write sight words.

Learn

Introduce the Consonant Ending –*le*

Help students learn the consonant ending –*le*, which is used in a special three-letter syllable called the consonant –*le* syllable.

1. Place the following letter tiles at the top of students' whiteboard: *a*, *b*, *le*, and *t*.

2. **Say:** The consonant –*le* syllable has only three letters, and two of the letters are always the letters *l* and *e* together. We have a special *le* letter tile that we will use to help us when we are spelling words that end with the letters *le*.

3. Pull down the *le* letter tile to the middle of the whiteboard and point to it.

4. **Say:** These two letters spell the sound /ul/ when they are in a consonant –*le* syllable. Touch the letter tile and say /ul/.

5. Put the letter *b* in front of the *le* letter tile.

6. **Say:** If we put a *b* in front of the letters *le*, we say /bul/. Run your finger under the tiles and say /bul/.

7. **Say:** Let's look at the word *table*. Add the letters *t* and *a* in front of the letters *ble* to make the word *table*. Touch and say the word *table*.

8. Break *table* into the syllables *ta / ble*.

9. **Say:** When we break the word *table* into syllables, it has two syllables. The consonant –*le* syllable always has three letters.

10. Have students touch and say the syllables *ta / ble*.

Consonant Ending –*le*

Have students practice identifying the consonant ending –*le* in words and syllables.

1. Gather the index cards you prepared.

2. Place the following letter tiles at the top of students' whiteboard: *b*, *d*, *g*, *le*, *p*, *t*, and *z*.

3. Pull down the *le* letter tile to the middle of the whiteboard and point to it.

4. **Say:** These two letters spell the sound /ul/ when they are in a consonant –*le* syllable. Touch the letter tile and say /ul/.

5. Put the letter *d* in front of the *le* letter tile.

6. **Say:** If we put a *d* in front of *le*, we say /dul/. Run your finger under the tiles and say /dul/.

7. Place the index card with the word *candle* on the table.

8. **Say:** I will underline the consonant –*le* syllable, and then read the word and say the syllables. *can<u>dle</u>, can / dle*

> ### Objectives
> - Identify and use –*le* spelling pattern.
> - Identify syllables in words.
> - Identify ending sounds in words.
> - Write words by applying grade-level phonics knowledge.

9. **Say:** Now it's your turn.

10. Have students put the *b* letter tile in front of the *le* letter tile, and show them the index card with the word *jumble*.

11. Have students

- ▸ Run their finger under the tiles and say /bul/.
- ▸ Underline the consonant –*le* syllable on the card and read the word aloud. jum<u>ble</u>
- ▸ Say the syllables. *jum / ble*

12. Repeat the activity with the remaining words.

- ▸ *giggle* gig<u>gle</u>, *gig / gle*
- ▸ *purple* pur<u>ple</u>, *pur / ple*
- ▸ *bottle* bot<u>tle</u>, *bot / tle*
- ▸ *puzzle* puz<u>zle</u>, *puz / zle*

Try It

Alphabet Addition

Have students complete page PH 43 in *K¹² PhonicsWorks Advanced Activity Book* for more practice with the consonant ending –*le*. First have students read the two word parts aloud. Then have them add the letters together to make a new word and write the word. Have them read the new word aloud.

Objectives

- Identify and use –*le* spelling pattern.
- Write words by applying grade-level phonics knowledge.

Try It

Introduce Consonant Ending –*le*
Alphabet Addition

Add the letters to make a word. Write the word, and then read it aloud.

1. ap + ple = **apple**
2. can + dle = **candle**
3. pud + dle = **puddle**
4. bun + dle = **bundle**
5. bub + ble = **bubble**
6. puz + zle = **puzzle**
7. lit + tle = **little**

PHONICS

LANGUAGE ARTS GREEN   **PH 43**

〔Online〕 ⑮ minutes

REVIEW: Consonant Ending –*le*

Students will work online independently to

▶ Practice the consonant ending –*le*.

▶ Practice decoding text by reading a story.

Help students locate the online activities and provide support as needed.

Offline Alternative

No computer access? Have students point out and name things or words that contain the consonant ending –*le* (for example, *candle* or *puzzle*). You might also ask students to spell words that contain the consonant ending –*le*.

Objectives

- Identify and use –*le* spelling pattern.
- Identify syllables in words.
- Read aloud grade-level text with appropriate automaticity, prosody, accuracy, and rate.
- Decode words by applying grade-level word analysis skills.

Practice Consonant Ending –le

Lesson Overview

Offline **FOCUS:** Practice Consonant Ending –le — **30** minutes

Sight Words	Use Words in Sentences
Practice	Build Words from Syllables
	Introduce –stle
Try It	"Russ and His Baby Brother"

Online **REVIEW:** Consonant Ending –le — **15** minutes

Materials

Supplied
- *K¹² PhonicsWorks Readers Advanced 8,* pp. 1–7
- whiteboard, student
- Tile Kit

Also Needed
- sight words box

[Offline] (15) minutes

FOCUS: Practice Consonant Ending –*le*

Work **together** with students to complete offline Sight Words, Practice, and Try It activities.

Sight Words ....

Use Words in Sentences

Help students use sight words in sentences.

> **Objectives**
> • Read sight words.
> • Spell sight words.

1. Gather all the sight word cards students have yet to master from their sight words box. Spread the sight word cards on the table.

2. **Say:** Let's use sight words in sentences.

3. Have students

   ‣ Touch each card and read the word on it.
   ‣ Make up a sentence using the word.
   ‣ Put the card in a pile after using the word in a sentence.
   ‣ Go through the pile of cards and read each sight word again.
   ‣ Spell each word.

TIP If students have difficulty with any of the sight words, place those cards in a pile to review again.

Practice ....

Build Words from Syllables

Help students build words and identify syllables that have the ending consonant –*le* syllable.

> **Objectives**
> • Identify and use –*le* spelling pattern.
> • Identify ending sounds in words.
> • Identify syllables in words.

1. Place the following letter tiles at the top of students' whiteboard: *a, b, c, d, i, le, m, n, p, s, t, th,* and *u*.

2. **Say:** A consonant –*le* syllable has only three letters, and two of the letters are always the letters *l* and *e* together. We have a special *le* letter tile that we will use to help us when we are spelling words that have consonant –*le*.

3. **Say:** You are going to spell words that have the consonant –*le* syllable. How many letters are in a consonant –*le* syllable? three

4. **Say:** Let's begin. The first word is *candle*.

5. Have students

- ▸ Repeat the word.
- ▸ Fist tap the syllables in the word on the table. *can / dle*
- ▸ Build the word with the letter tiles.
- ▸ Touch and say the word.
- ▸ Say and write the word.
- ▸ Underline the *–le* syllable. *can / dle*

6. Repeat the activity to build the following words and syllables:

- ▸ *bundle bun / dle, bun<u>dle</u>*
- ▸ *dimple dim / ple, dim<u>ple</u>*
- ▸ *simple sim / ple, sim<u>ple</u>*
- ▸ *stumble stum / ble, stum<u>ble</u>*
- ▸ *thimble thim / ble, thim<u>ble</u>*

Introduce *–stle*

Help students build words that have the special consonant *–le* syllable with *–stle*.

1. Place the following letter tiles at the top of students' whiteboard: *a, c, e, h, i, le, n, s, t, u,* and *wh*.

2. Build the following word on your whiteboard: *castle*.

3. **Say:** Let's learn about a special consonant *–le* syllable in the word *castle*.

4. Fist tap the word *castle* and break it into syllables. *ca / stle*

5. **Say:** In the word *castle*, we don't pronounce the sound /t/ in the second syllable. That is because the *t* is not pronounced when the letters *stle* are in a word. There are only a few of these words in the English language, but you may see them in the stories you read. We are going to read some more words with the letters *stle*.

6. Build the word *whistle* on your whiteboard.

7. Have students

- ▸ Point to the *–stle* in the word.
- ▸ Break the word into syllables. *whi / stle*
- ▸ Identify the letter that is not pronounced. *t*
- ▸ Read the word.
- ▸ Point to the first syllable in the word. *whi*
- ▸ Identify the last letter in the first syllable. *i*
- ▸ Say whether the last letter in the first syllable is a vowel or consonant. vowel

8. Repeat the activity with the following words:

- ▸ *nestle ne / stle*
- ▸ *hustle hu / stle*

 Try It •

"Russ and His Baby Brother"

Have students read "Russ and His Baby Brother" on page 1 of *K¹² PhonicsWorks Readers Advanced 8.*

Students should read the story silently once or twice before reading the story aloud. When students miss a word that can be sounded out, point to it and give them three to six seconds to try the word again. If students still miss the word, tell them the word so the flow of the story isn't interrupted.

After reading the story, make a list of all the words students missed, and go over those words with them. You may use letter tiles to show students how to read the words.

 **15** minutes

REVIEW: Consonant Ending –*le*

Students will work online independently to

▶ Practice the consonant ending –*le*.

Help students locate the online activities and provide support as needed.

Offline Alternative

No computer access? Have students point out and name things or words that contain the consonant ending –*le* (for example, *stumble* or *thimble*). You might also ask students to spell words that contain the consonant ending –*le*.

Objectives
- Read aloud grade-level text with appropriate automaticity, prosody, accuracy, and rate.
- Decode words by applying grade-level word analysis skills.

Objectives
- Identify and use –*le* spelling pattern.
- Identify ending sounds in words.
- Identify syllables in words.

Introduce Digraph *ph*

Lesson Overview

Offline FOCUS: Introduce Digraph *ph* **15** minutes

Sight Words	Sight Word Concentration
Get Ready	Read Words with the Consonant Ending –*le*
Learn	Introduce the Sound for *ph*
	Read One-Syllable Words with *ph*
	Read Multisyllable Words with *ph*
Try It	Match It

Online REVIEW: Digraph *ph* **15** minutes

Materials

Supplied

- *K¹² PhonicsWorks Advanced Activity Book,* p. PH 44
- whiteboard, Learning Coach
- whiteboard, student
- Tile Kit

Also Needed

- sight words box
- index cards (7)

Advance Preparation

Gather two sets of the sight word cards that students have yet to master.

For Read Words with the Consonant Ending –*le*, print each of the following words on index cards, using one card per word: *table, cable, fable, sable, staple, maple,* and *rifle.*

[Offline] ⏱ 15 minutes

FOCUS: Introduce Digraph *ph*

Work **together** with students to complete offline Sight Words, Get Ready, Learn, and Try It activities.

Sight Words ···

Sight Word Concentration

Help students review sight words.

1. Gather the two sets of sight word cards.

2. Scramble both sets of sight word cards and place them face down on the table or floor.

3. Turn over two cards at a time; take turns with students. If the cards match, the person turning over the matching cards reads the word and uses it in a sentence. If the cards don't match, the person turns them back over.

4. Remove and save the matching cards.

5. Continue the activity until all the cards are paired.

6. Have students read all the words.

7. Take the stack of words that students read correctly and dictate each word to them.

8. Have students write each word or spell it aloud.

TIP If students have difficulty with any sight words, let them work at their own pace to really master these words.

> **Objectives**
> - Read sight words.
> - Spell sight words.
> - Write sight words.

Get Ready ···

Read Words with the Consonant Ending –*le*

Have students practice reading words that have the consonant ending –*le*.

1. Gather the index cards you prepared and place them in a stack face down on the table.

2. **Say:** You are going to read words that have a long vowel sound in the first syllable and the consonant ending –*le* in the second syllable.

3. Have students

> ► Choose a card.
> ► Read the word silently.
> ► Underline each syllable.
> ► Read the word aloud.

> **Objectives**
> - Identify and use –*le* spelling pattern.
> - Identify syllables in words.
> - Identify ending sounds in words.

4. Continue the activity with all of the words in the pile.

- ▸ *table ta / ble*
- ▸ *cable ca / ble*
- ▸ *fable fa / ble*
- ▸ *sable sa / ble*
- ▸ *staple sta / ple*
- ▸ *maple ma / ple*
- ▸ *rifle ri / fle*

Learn

Introduce the Sound for *ph*

Introduce the sound /f/ for the digraph *ph* to students.

1. Place the letter tile for the digraph *ph* at the top of students' whiteboard.

2. **Say:** We're going to learn a sound spelled with two letters. It's a sound you know already. It's the sound /f/. What is one way that you know how to spell the sound /f/? *f*

3. Point to the *ph* tile.

   Say: In some words, /f/ is spelled with the digraph *ph*, like in the word *telephone*.

4. Have students touch the *ph* letter tile and say the sound /f/.

Objectives

- Identify and use *ph* for the sound /f/.
- Identify the sound /f/, given the digraph *ph*.
- Identify the digraph *ph*, given the sound /f/.
- Identify and use the digraph *ph*.
- Identify syllables in words.

Read One-Syllable Words with *ph*

Have students practice reading one-syllable words that have the digraph *ph* for the sound /f/. Grab your whiteboard and dry-erase marker.

1. Place the following letter tiles at the top of students' whiteboard: *a, e, g, i, l, n, o, ph*, and *r*.

2. Build the word *phone* on students' whiteboard.

   - ▸ Touch and say the word *phone*.
   - ▸ Write the word *phone* on your whiteboard.
   - ▸ Have students say the sounds in the word *phone*. /f/ /ō/ /n/

3. Repeat the activity with the following words:

   - ▸ *Ralph* /r/ /ă/ /l/ /f/
   - ▸ *Phil* /f/ /ĭ/ /l/
   - ▸ *graph* /g/ /r/ /ă/ /f/

TIP Reinforce with students the use of the capital letter when you write the proper nouns *Ralph* and *Phil* on the whiteboard.

Read Multisyllable Words with *ph*

Have students practice reading multisyllable words that have the digraph *ph* for the sound /f/. Grab your whiteboard and dry-erase marker.

1. Write the word *elephant* on your whiteboard.

   ▸ Read the word *elephant*.
   ▸ Underline each syllable in the word. *el / e / phant*
   ▸ Circle the digraph that spells the sound /f/. *ph*

2. Have students touch and say the word.

3. Repeat the activity with the following words:

   ▸ *alphabet al / pha / bet*
   ▸ *digraph di / graph*

Try It

Match It

Have students complete page PH 44 in *K¹² PhonicsWorks Advanced Activity Book* for more practice with the digraph *ph*. Have students read each sentence aloud and draw a line to the picture that matches the sentence.

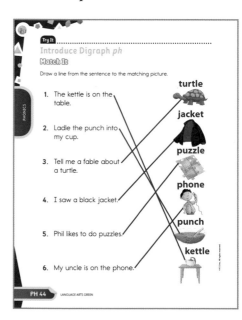

 **15 minutes**

REVIEW: Digraph *ph*

Students will work online independently to

► Practice the digraph *ph* for the sound /f/.
► Practice decoding text by reading a story.

Help students locate the online activities and provide support as needed.

Offline Alternative

No computer access? Have students practice identifying words that have the digraph *ph* for the sound /f/, such as *alphabet* and *telephone*. You might also ask them to spell words that have the digraph *ph* for the sound /f/.

Objectives

- Identify and use *ph* for the sound /f/.
- Identify the sound /f/, given the digraph *ph*.
- Identify the digraph *ph*, given the sound /f/.
- Identify and use the digraph *ph*.
- Read aloud grade-level text with appropriate automaticity, prosody, accuracy, and rate.
- Decode words by applying grade-level word analysis skills.

Practice Digraph *ph*

Lesson Overview

[Offline] FOCUS: Practice Digraph *ph* **15** minutes

Sight Words	Pick a Pair
Practice	Sort Words Ending in *–stle*
	Word Chains
	Build Words
Try It	"Phil's Lost Phone"

[Online] REVIEW: Digraph *ph* **15** minutes

[Materials]

Supplied
- *K¹² PhonicsWorks Readers Advanced 8*, pp. 8–14
- whiteboard, Learning Coach
- whiteboard, student
- Tile Kit

Also Needed
- sight words box
- index cards (8)

Advance Preparation

For Sort Words Ending in *–stle,* print each of the following words on index cards, using one card per word: *castle, cable, whistle, fable, thistle, bundle, bumble,* and *cuddle.*

[Offline] 30 minutes

FOCUS: Practice Digraph *ph*

Work **together** with students to complete offline Sight Words, Practice, and Try It activities.

Sight Words ....

Pick a Pair

Play a card game with students for more practice with sight words.

1. Gather the sight word cards that students are reviewing. Choose two words and place the cards on the table.

2. Ask questions to help students identify each word. For example, if the words are *or* and *one*, you could ask, "Which word names a number?" If the words are *on* and *but*, you could ask, "Which word is the opposite of *off*?"

3. Continue the activity until students identify all the words.

4. Take the stack of words that students read correctly and dictate each word to them.

5. Have students write each word or spell it aloud.

> **Objectives**
> - Read sight words.
> - Spell sight words.
> - Write sight words.

Practice ....

Sort Words Ending in *–stle*

Help students practice identifying words ending in *–le* and *–stle*.

1. Gather the index cards you prepared.

2. Place the word *castle* face up in front of students.

   Say: You are going to sort words by their ending letters. You will read each word that I show you and place the word in two different piles: one pile for words ending in *–le* and the other pile for words ending in *–stle*. I'll do the first one for you. This is the word *castle*. I will put the card in the *–stle* pile because it ends with the letters *–stle*. Now it's your turn.

3. Place the next card face up in front of students. Have them

   ▸ Read the word.
   ▸ Say the ending letters.
   ▸ Sort the card into one of two piles.

4. Continue the procedure with the remaining words:

   ▸ **Ending *–le* Words:** *cable, fable, bundle, bumble, cuddle*
   ▸ **Ending *–stle* Words:** *whistle, thistle*

> **Objectives**
> - Identify and use *–le* spelling pattern.
> - Identify the new word when one sound is changed in a word.
> - Identify individual sounds in words.
> - Identify and use *ph* for the sound /f/.
> - Identify the sound /f/, given the digraph *ph*.
> - Identify the digraph *ph*, given the sound /f/.
> - Identify and use the digraph *ph*.

Word Chains

Have students build words by adding and changing letters to help them recognize and use the individual sounds in words.

1. Place the following letter tiles at the top of students' whiteboard: *a, b, c, e, n, o, ph, r, s,* and *t.*

2. **Say:** I am going to build the first word in a chain. The word is *bone.*

   ▸ I will pull down the letters for the sounds /b/, /ō/, and /n/ to spell the word *bone.*
   ▸ I will touch and say *bone.* To change *bone* to *tone,* I will think about which sound is changed from the word *bone* to *tone.* I will replace the letter *b* with the letter *t.*
   ▸ Touch and say the word *tone.* Now it's your turn to change *tone* to *phone.* You can spell *phone* by making only one change. Touch and say the new word.

3. Redirect students if they select the incorrect letter for any sound.

   Say: That letter is for the sound [incorrect sound]. We want the letter for the sound [target sound]. What letter makes that sound? Answers will vary.

4. Redirect students if they name the sound incorrectly.

   Say: To change the word [first word] to [target word], we need the letter for the sound [target sound].

   Show students how to make the change. Have them touch and say the new word after they move the letters.

5. Follow this procedure to make the following words: *cone, cane, case, phase, phrase.*

6. For every new word, have students add, replace, or remove only one letter tile.

   TIP If students struggle, review the sounds and letters that are confusing them.

Build Words

Help students use letters and sounds to build words.

1. Place the following letter tiles at the top of students' whiteboard: *a, e, g, l, m, n, o, ph, r, s,* and *x.*

2. Draw three horizontal lines across the middle of students' whiteboard to represent the sounds in a word.

3. **Say:** Let's use letters and sounds to build the word *phone.* Remember, the silent *e* works with the letter *o* to make the sound /ō/.

4. Have students finger stretch the sounds in *phone.*

5. Have students

- Identify the first, next, and last sounds in *phone*.
- Choose the corresponding letter for each of the sounds.
- Move the letters to the correct lines on their whiteboard.

6. Guide students with these questions:

- What is the first sound in *phone*? /ph/
  Which line do the letters for that sound go on? the first one
- What is the second sound in *phone*? /ō/
  Which line does the letter for that sound go on? the second one
- What is the third sound in *phone*? /n/
  Which line does the letter for that sound go on? the last one

7. Redirect students if they select the incorrect letter.

Say: That sound is in the word [word], and it is the [first, second, third] sound. We want the sound [target sound].

Continue until students select the correct letter.

8. Have students touch and say the word. Be sure to check that students are using their index and middle fingers to touch the *o* and *e* at the same time before they touch and say the last letter and sound.

9. Have them say the word as they use a dry-erase marker to write the word on the whiteboard.

10. Draw horizontal lines across the middle of students' whiteboard to represent the sounds in each word. Repeat the activity to build the following words:

- *phlox* /f/ /l/ /ŏ/ /ks/
- *phase* /f/ /ā/ /z/
- *morph* /m/ /or/ /f/
- *graph* /g/ /r/ /a/ /f/

TIP Remind students that when building words with the silent *e* on the end, there is no line on which to place the *e*. This reinforces the fact that the vowel and the *e* work together to make the long vowel sound, and the silent *e* does not make a sound on its own. Have students put the silent *e* on the end of the word.

Try It

"Phil's Lost Phone"
Have students read "Phil's Lost Phone" on page 8 of *K¹² PhonicsWorks Readers Advanced 8.*

Students should read the story silently once or twice before reading the story aloud. When students miss a word that can be sounded out, point to it and give them three to six seconds to try the word again. If students still miss the word, tell them the word so the flow of the story isn't interrupted.

After reading the story, make a list of all the words students missed, and go over those words with them. You may use letter tiles to show students how to read the words.

Objectives
- Read aloud grade-level text with appropriate automaticity, prosody, accuracy, and rate.
- Decode words by applying grade-level word analysis skills.

[Online] 15 minutes

REVIEW: Digraph *ph*

Students will work online independently to

▶ Practice the digraph *ph* for the sound /f/.

Help students locate the online activities and provide support as needed.

Offline Alternative

No computer access? Have students practice identifying words that have the digraph *ph* for the sound /f/, such as *graph* and *Ralph*. You might also ask them to spell words that have the digraph *ph* for the sound /f/.

Objectives

- Identify and use *ph* for the sound /f/.
- Identify the sound /f/, given the digraph *ph*.
- Identify the digraph *ph*, given the sound /f/.
- Identify and use the digraph *ph*.

Unit Checkpoint

Lesson Overview

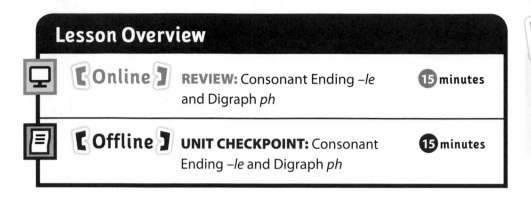

	[Online]	**REVIEW:** Consonant Ending –*le* and Digraph *ph*	**15** minutes
	[Offline]	**UNIT CHECKPOINT:** Consonant Ending –*le* and Digraph *ph*	**15** minutes

Materials

Supplied

- *K¹² PhonicsWorks Advanced Assessments,* pp. PH 127–132

Objectives

- Identify and use *ph* for the sound /f/.
- Identify the sound /f/, given the digraph *ph*.
- Identify the digraph *ph*, given the sound /f/.
- Identify and use the digraph *ph*.
- Identify syllables in words.
- Identify and use –*le* spelling pattern.
- Identify individual sounds in words.
- Identify ending sounds in words.
- Given the letter, identify the most common sound.
- Given the sound, identify the most common letter or letters.
- Read instructional-level text with 90% accuracy.
- Read aloud grade-level text with appropriate automaticity, prosody, accuracy, and rate.
- Write words by applying grade-level phonics knowledge.
- Write sight words.
- Read sight words.

[Online] **15** minutes

REVIEW: Consonant Ending –*le* and Digraph *ph*

Students will review the consonant ending –*le* and digraph *ph* to prepare for the Unit Checkpoint. Help students locate the online activities and provide support as needed.

UNIT CHECKPOINT: Consonant Ending *–le* and Digraph *ph*

Explain that students are going to show what they have learned about sounds, letters, and words.

1. Give students the Unit Checkpoint pages for the Consonant Ending *–le* and Digraph *ph* unit and print the Unit Checkpoint Answer Key, if you'd like.

2. Use the instructions below to help administer the Checkpoint to students. On the Answer Key or another sheet of paper, note student answers to oral response questions to help with scoring the Checkpoint later.

3. Use the Answer Key to score the Checkpoint, and then enter the results online.

Part 1. Count Syllables Have students read each word aloud, count the number of syllables, and write that number.

Part 2. Vowel or Consonant Say each letter to students. Have them decide if the letter is a vowel or consonant and write that letter in the correct column.

7. *o*

8. *s*

9. *u*

10. *r*

Part 3. True or False Read each statement to students and have them write *T* if the statement is true and *F* if the statement is false.

11. *Every syllable has one vowel sound.*

12. *The letters* ph *spell the sound /f/.*

Part 4. Writing Read each sentence to students. Have them repeat and write the sentence.

13. *The phone rang six times.*

14. *Ralph made a sand castle.*

15. *I lost the smallest marble.*

Part 5. Read Aloud Listen to students read the sentences aloud. Count and note the number of words they read correctly.

Part 6. Read Sight Words Have students read each sight word aloud. Note any words they read incorrectly.

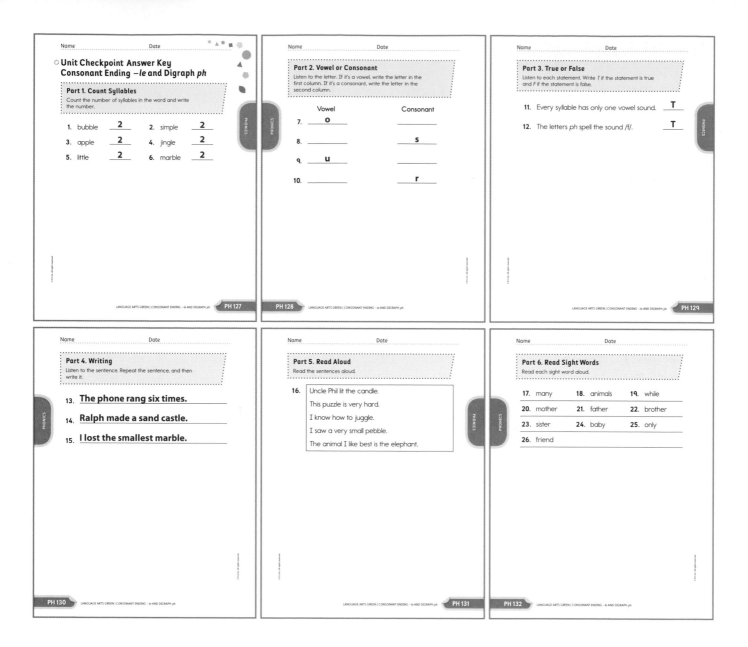

Unit Checkpoint Answer Key
Consonant Ending –le and Digraph ph

Part 1. Count Syllables
Count the number of syllables in the word and write the number.

1. bubble __2__   2. simple __2__

3. apple __2__   4. jingle __2__

5. little __2__   6. marble __2__

Part 2. Vowel or Consonant
Listen to the letter. If it's a vowel, write the letter in the first column. If it's a consonant, write the letter in the second column.

	Vowel	Consonant
7.	o	_____
8.	_____	s
9.	u	_____
10.	_____	r

Part 3. True or False
Listen to each statement. Write T if the statement is true and F if the statement is false.

11. Every syllable has only one vowel sound. __T__

12. The letters ph spell the sound /f/. __T__

Part 4. Writing
Listen to the sentence. Repeat the sentence, and then write it.

13. **The phone rang six times.**

14. **Ralph made a sand castle.**

15. **I lost the smallest marble.**

Part 5. Read Aloud
Read the sentences aloud.

16. Uncle Phil lit the candle.

This puzzle is very hard.

I know how to juggle.

I saw a very small pebble.

The animal I like best is the elephant.

Part 6. Read Sight Words
Read each sight word aloud.

17. many   18. animals   19. while

20. mother   21. father   22. brother

23. sister   24. baby   25. only

26. friend

Sound /s/ Spelled c

Unit Overview

In this unit, students will
- ▶ Learn the sight words *other*, *together*, and *people*.
- ▶ Learn the sound /s/ spelled with the letter *c*.
- ▶ Learn the sound /j/ spelled with the letter *g*.
- ▶ Learn the sound /j/ spelled with the letters *dge*.
- ▶ Read a story silently and aloud.

Lesson Overview

	[Offline] FOCUS: Sound /s/ Spelled *c*	**15** minutes
Sight Words	Introduce Sight Words	
Learn	Sound /s/ Spelled *c*	
	Sound /s/ Spelled *c* with Silent *e*	
	More Words with Sound /s/ Spelled *c*	
Try It	Careful Counting	

	[Online] REVIEW: Sound /s/ Spelled *c*	**15** minutes

Advance Preparation

For Sound /s/ Spelled *c*, print each of the following words on index cards, using one card per word: *cot, cat, cup, cost, cape,* and *cute*.

For Sound /s/ Spelled *c* with Silent *e*, print each of the following words on index cards, using one card per word: *face, ace, lace, place, ice, nice, twice, spice,* and *advice*.

For More Words with Sound /s/ Spelled *c*, print each of the following words on index cards, using one card per word: *fence, glance, prince, since, chance, France, sentence,* and *convince*.

〔 Offline 〕 ⏱ 15 minutes

FOCUS: Sound /s/ Spelled *c*

Work **together** with students to complete offline Sight Words, Learn, and Try It activities.

Sight Words ●●

Introduce Sight Words

Help students learn the sight words *other*, *together*, and *people*.

1. Gather the sight word cards *other*, *together*, and *people*.

2. Show students the *other* card.

3. **Say:** This is the word *other*. We see this word so often that we want to be able to read and spell it quickly without thinking about it. Look closely at the word *other*. Spell the word *other* aloud. Take a picture of the word *other* in your mind. When you think you can spell *other* yourself, turn the card over and use your letter tiles to spell the word *other*. Check the card to see if you spelled the word *other* correctly. Read aloud the word you spelled with the letter tiles.

4. Repeat the activity with the remaining sight words.

5. Chart students' progress on the back of each card.

   ▸ Divide the back of the card into two columns.
   ▸ Label the first column "Read" and the second column "Spell."
   ▸ Record the dates that students read or spell the word correctly. When students can read and spell the word correctly three times in a row, they have mastered the word. You may want to put a star or sticker on their card when they have mastered that word.

6. Add the cards to students' sight words box.

TIP Sight words can be very difficult for some students. Let students work at their own pace and really master these words, as they occur frequently in reading and writing.

> **Objectives**
> - Read sight words.
> - Spell sight words.

Sound /s/ Spelled c

When the letter *c* is followed by a consonant or the vowels *a*, *o*, and *u*, it usually makes the sound /k/, as in the words *cringe*, *cape*, *cop*, and *cut*. However, when the letter *c* is followed by the letters *e*, *i*, or *y*, the letter *c* often makes the sound /s/. Help students learn the sound /s/ spelled with the letter *c*.

1. Gather the index cards you prepared.

2. Place the following letter tiles on students' whiteboard: *c*, *ch*, *e*, *i*, *n*, *s*, *t*, and *y*.

3. Put the letter *s* in the middle of students' whiteboard and point to it.

   Say: The letter *s* can have two different sounds. The letter *s* can have the sound /s/, as in the word *sit*, or the sound /z/, as in the word *has*.

4. Put the letter *c* in the middle of students' whiteboard and point to it.

   Say: Today we will learn about another letter that can have two different sounds. That letter is *c*.

5. Place the following index cards in front of students and have them read the words: *cot*, *cat*, *cup*, *cost*, *cape*, and *cute*.

   Say: What sound do you hear the letter *c* make? /k/

6. Make the word *cinch* and point to it.

   Say: The letter *c* can have the sound /s/ when it is followed by the letters *e*, *i*, or *y*. This is the word *cinch*. The word *cinch* has the letter *c* followed by the letter *i*. The letter *i* means the letter *c* says /s/.

7. Have students

   ▸ Touch and say *cinch*.
   ▸ Say and write the word *cinch*.
   ▸ Say the sound for the letter *c*. /s/
   ▸ Explain why the letter *c* will make the sound /s/. The letter *c* makes the sound /s/ because it is followed by the letter *i*.

8. Repeat this procedure for the words *cent* and *cyst*.

Sound /s/ Spelled c Spelled with Silent e

Help students learn the sound /s/ spelled with the letter *c* when followed by a letter *e* that is silent at the end of the word.

1. Gather the index cards you prepared.

2. Place the following letter tiles on students' whiteboard: *a*, *c*, *e*, and *r*.

3. Make the word *race* and point to it.

   Say: This is the word *race*. We learned that when the letter *c* is followed by *i*, *y*, or *e*, sometimes it says the sound /s/. Let's touch and say the sounds in the word *race*.

Objectives

- Identify and use *c* for the sound /s/
- Identify and use silent *e*.
- Read aloud grade-level text with appropriate automaticity, prosody, accuracy, and rate.
- Write words by applying grade-level phonics knowledge.

4. Have students

- ► Touch and say *race*.
- ► Say and write the word *race*.
- ► Say the sound for the letter *c*. /s/
- ► Explain why the letter *c* will make the sound /s/. The letter *c* makes the sound /s/ because it is followed by the letter *e*, which is silent at the end of the word.

5. Repeat this procedure using the index cards with the following words: *face, ace, lace, place, ice, nice, twice, spice,* and *advice*.

More Words with Sound /s/ Spelled *c*

Have students practice reading words that have the sound /s/ spelled with the letter *c* when the word has vowels separated between two sounds and the letter *c* is followed by a letter *e*.

1. Gather the index cards you prepared.

2. Place the following letter tiles on students' whiteboard: *a, c, e, d,* and *n*.

3. Make the word *dance* and point to it.

   Say: This is the word *dance*. Let's finger stretch the sounds in the word *dance*: /d/, /ă/, /n/, /s/. There are two sounds between the first vowel *a* and the silent *e* at the end of the word—the sound /n/ and the sound /s/. The first vowel *a* has the short sound /ă/. The letter *c* is followed by the letter *e*, which tells us that the letter *c* makes the sound /s/.

4. **Say:** Before, when we had a silent *e*, we would read the long vowel sound. But in the word *dance*, the *a* is short. There are two sounds between the vowel and the *e*, so the *e* does the job of telling us that the *c* says /s/.

5. Have students

- ► Touch and say *dance*. (Make sure that students touch both the *c* and *e* letter tiles at the same time when they say the /s/ sound.)
- ► Say and write the word *dance*.
- ► Say the sound for the letter *c*. /s/
- ► Explain why the letter *c* will make the sound /s/. The letter *c* is followed by the letter *e*.

6. Redirect students if they misread the letter *c* as the sound /k/. Have them state what letter follows the *c*. Then explain to them that the letter *c* makes the sound /s/ if the next letter after the letter *c* is *e, i,* or *y*.

7. Repeat this procedure using the index cards with the following words: *fence, glance, prince, since, chance, France, sentence,* and *convince*.

Try It

Careful Counting

Have students complete page PH 45 in *K¹² PhonicsWorks Advanced Activity Book* for more practice with words that have the sound /s/ spelled *c*. Have them count the number of syllables they hear in the word and write that number.

Try It

Sound /s/ Spelled *c*

Careful Counting

Count how many syllables you hear in the word and write the number.

1.	race	1	8.	convince	2
2.	bracelet	2	9.	spice	1
3.	pencil	2	10.	racetrack	2
4.	icebox	2	11.	since	1
5.	trace	1	12.	placement	2
6.	Bruce	1	13.	rice	1
7.	playmate	2	14.	sentence	2

LANGUAGE ARTS GREEN   PH 45

Online 15 minutes

REVIEW: Sound /s/ Spelled *c*

Students will work online independently to

► Practice the sound /s/ spelled *c*.
► Practice decoding text by reading a story.

Help students locate the online activities and provide support as needed.

Offline Alternative

No computer access? Have students spell words that have the sound /s/ spelled *c*, such as *face*, *cite*, *lacy*, and *fence*.

Sound /j/ Spelled *g*

Lesson Overview

[Offline] FOCUS: Sound /j/ Spelled *g* **15** minutes

Sight Words	Sight Word Fun
Get Ready	Practice Sound /s/ Spelled *c*
Learn	Sound /j/ Spelled *g*
	Sound /j/ Spelled *g* with Silent *e*
	More Words with Sound /j/ Spelled *g*
Try It	"Lance"

[Online] REVIEW: Sound /j/ Spelled *g* **15** minutes

Materials

Supplied
- *K¹² PhonicsWorks Readers Advanced 8,* pp. 15–21
- whiteboard, student
- Tile Kit

Also Needed
- sight words box
- index cards (44)

Advance Preparation

For Practice Sound /s/ Spelled *c*, print each of the following words on index cards, using one card per word: *face, trace, place, race, pace, spice, ice, nice, twice, slice, mice, dice, space, grace, force, brace, dance, fence, since, wince, Bruce, spruce, lace, rice, trance, embrace, misplace, disgrace, sentence,* and *convince.*

For Sound /j/ Spelled *g*, print each of the following words on index cards, using one card per word: *game, gum,* and *got.*

For Sound /j/ Spelled *g* with Silent *e*, print each of the following words on index cards, using one card per word: *age, rage, stage, wage,* and *cage.*

For More Words with Sound /j/ Spelled *g*, print each of the following words on index cards, using one card per word: *change, large, fringe, hinge, Marge,* and *orange.*

〔Offline〕 ⏱ 15 minutes

FOCUS: Sound /j/ Spelled *g*

Work **together** with students to complete offline Sight Words, Get Ready, Learn, and Try It activities.

Sight Words ·····································

Sight Word Fun

Help students learn the sight words *other*, *together*, and *people*, and up to two additional sight words they have yet to master.

1. Gather the sight word cards *other*, *together*, and *people*, and up to two additional sight word cards.

2. Choose one sight word card to begin.

   Say: Look at this word and take a picture of it in your mind. When you think you can spell the word yourself, turn the card over and use your letter tiles to spell the word.

3. After students spell the word, have them check the card to see if they spelled the word correctly.

   Say: Read aloud the word you spelled with the letter tiles.

4. Repeat the activity with the remaining sight words.

TIP Sight words can be very difficult for some students. Let students work at their own pace and really master these words.

Objectives
- Read sight words.
- Spell sight words.

Get Ready ·····································

Practice Sound /s/ Spelled *c*

Have students practice reading words that have the sound /s/ spelled with the letter *c*.

1. Gather the index cards you prepared.

2. Give students the stack of cards and have them read as many words as possible in one minute.

3. If students finish the stack in less than one minute, have them start over.

4. Have students read the stack of words three times.

Objectives
- Identify and use *c* for the sound /s/.
- Identify and use silent *e*.
- Read aloud grade-level text with appropriate automaticity, prosody, accuracy, and rate.

Learn

Sound /j/ Spelled *g*

When the letter *g* is followed by a consonant or the vowels *a*, *o*, and *u*, it usually makes the sound /g/, as in the words *grape*, *glance*, *gap*, and *gum*. However, when the letter *g* is followed by the letters *e*, *i*, or *y*, the letter *g* often makes the sound /j/. Help students learn the sound /j/ spelled with the letter *j*.

1. Gather the index cards you prepared.

2. Place the following letter tiles on students' whiteboard: *e*, *g*, *m*, *r*, and *y*.

3. Put the letter *g* in the middle of students' whiteboard and point to it.

   Say: Today we will learn about another letter that can have two different sounds. That letter is *g*.

4. Place the following index cards in front of students and have them read the words: *game*, *gum*, and *got*.

   Say: What sound do you hear the letter *g* make? /g/

5. Make the word *gym* and point to it.

   Say: The letter *g* can have the sound /j/ when it is followed by the letters *e*, *i*, or *y*. This is the word *gym*. The word *gym* has the letter *g* followed by the letter *y*. The letter *y* means the letter *g* says the sound /j/.

6. Have students

   ▸ Touch and say *gym*.
   ▸ Say and write the word *gym*.
   ▸ Say the sound for the letter *g*. /j/
   ▸ Explain why the letter *g* will make the sound /j/. The letter *g* makes the sound /j/ because it is followed by the letter *y*.

7. Repeat this procedure for the words *gem* and *germ*.

Sound /j/ Spelled *g* with Silent *e*

Help students learn the sound /j/ spelled with the letter *g* when followed by a letter *e* that is silent at the end of the word.

1. Gather the index cards you prepared.

2. Place the following letter tiles on students' whiteboard: *a*, *e*, *g*, and *p*.

3. Make the word *page* and point to it.

   Say: The letter *g* can have the sound /j/ when it is followed by the letters *e*, *i*, or *y*. This is the word *page*. The word *page* has a letter *e* after the letter *g*. The letter *e* is silent at the end of the word.

Objectives

- Identify and use *g* for the sound /j/.
- Identify and use silent *e*.
- Write words by applying grade-level phonics knowledge.
- Read aloud grade-level text with appropriate automaticity, prosody, accuracy, and rate.

4. Have students

   ▸ Touch and say *page*.
   ▸ Say and write the word *page*.
   ▸ Say the sound for the letter *g*. /j/
   ▸ Explain why the letter *g* will make the sound /j. The letter *g* makes the sound /j/ because it is followed by the letter *e*, which is silent at the end of the word.

5. Repeat this procedure using the index cards with the following words: *age*, *rage*, *stage*, *wage*, and *cage*.

More Words with Sound /j/ Spelled *g*

Have students practice reading words that have sound /j/ spelled with the letter *g* when the word has vowels separated between two sounds and the letter *g* is followed by a letter *e*.

1. Gather the index cards you prepared.

2. Place the following letter tiles on students' whiteboard: *a, e, g, h, i, n, r, s,* and *t*.

3. Make the word *strange* and point to it.

   Say: This is the word *strange*. Let's finger stretch the sounds in the word *strange*: /s/, /t/, /r/, /ā/, /n/, /j/. When a silent *e* is at the end of the word, it often makes the first vowel sound long, and the vowel says its name. But we know when the letter *e* follows the letter *g*, it does the job of telling us to say /j/ when we read the letter *g*.

4. Have students

   ▸ Touch and say *strange*. (Make sure that students touch both the *g* and *e* letter tiles at the same time when they say the sound /j/.)
   ▸ Say and write the word *strange*.
   ▸ Say the sound for the letter *g*. /j/
   ▸ Explain why the letter *g* will make the sound /j/. The letter *g* is followed by the letter *e*.

5. Make the word *hinge* and point to it.

   Say: This is the word *hinge*. Let's finger stretch the sounds in the word *hinge*: /h/, /ĭ/, /n/, /j/. When a silent *e* is at the end of the word, it often makes the first vowel sound long, and the vowel says its name. In this word, though, the *i* is short, and the *e* at the end of the word tells us the *g* says the sound /j/.

6. Redirect students if they misread the letter *g* as the sound /g/. Have them state what letter follows the *g*. Then explain to them that the letter *g* makes the sound /j/ if the next letter after the letter *g* is *e*.

7. Have students
   ▸ Touch and say *hinge*. (Make sure that students touch both the *g* and *e* letter tiles at the same time when they say the sound /j/.)
   ▸ Say and write the word *hinge*.
   ▸ Say the sound for the letter *g*. /j/
   ▸ Explain why the letter *g* will make the sound /j/. The letter *g* is followed by the letter *e*.

8. Repeat this procedure using the index cards with the following words: *change, large, fringe, hinge, Marge,* and *orange*.

Try It •••

"Lance"

Have students read "Lance" on page 15 of *K¹² PhonicsWorks Readers Advanced 8*.

Students should read the story silently once or twice before reading the story aloud. When students miss a word that can be sounded out, point to it and give them three to six seconds to try the word again. If students still miss the word, tell them the word so the flow of the story isn't interrupted.

After reading the story, make a list of all the words students missed, and go over those words with them. You may use letter tiles to show students how to read the words.

Objectives
- Read aloud grade-level text with appropriate automaticity, prosody, accuracy, and rate.
- Decode words by applying grade-level word analysis skills.

〔Online〕 15 minutes

REVIEW: Sound /j/ Spelled *g*

Students will work online independently to

▸ Practice /j/ spelled *g*.

Help students locate the online activities and provide support as needed.

Objectives
- Identify individual sounds in words.
- Identify and use *g* for the sound /j/.
- Identify and use silent *e*.

Offline Alternative

No computer access? Have students spell words that have the sound /j/ spelled *g*, such as *age, magic, gym,* and *hinge*. You might also ask students to name words that have a long vowel sound and the letters *ange*, such as *change* or *strange*.

Sound /j/ Spelled –dge

Sound /j/ Spelled –dge

Lesson Overview

📄 **[Offline]** FOCUS: Sound /j/ Spelled –dge		**15** minutes
Sight Words	Sight Word Fun	
Learn	Sound /j/ Spelled –dge in One-Syllable Words	
	Sound /j/ Spelled –dge in Two-Syllable Words	
Try It	Finish the Job	
🖥 **[Online]** REVIEW: Sound /j/ Spelled –dge		**15** minutes

Materials

Supplied
- *K¹² PhonicsWorks Advanced Activity Book*, p. PH 46
- whiteboard, student
- Tile Kit

Also Needed
- sight words box
- index cards (13)

Advance Preparation

For Sound /j/ Spelled –dge in One-Syllable Words, print each of the following words on index cards, using one card per word: *edge, ledge, wedge, badge, dodge, bridge, ridge,* and *smudge.*

For Sound /j/ Spelled –dge in Two-Syllable Words, print each of the following words on index cards, using one card per word: *budget, badger, gadget, bridges,* and *fidget.*

〔 Offline 〕 ⑮ minutes

FOCUS: Sound /j/ Spelled *–dge*

Work **together** with students to complete offline Sight Words, Learn, and Try It activities.

Sight Words ●

Sight Word Fun

Help students learn the sight words *other*, *together*, and *people*, and up to two additional sight words they have yet to master.

1. Gather the sight word cards *other*, *together*, and *people*, and up to two additional sight word cards.

2. Choose one sight word card to begin.

   Say: Look at this word and take a picture of it in your mind. When you think you can spell the word yourself, turn the card over and use your letter tiles to spell the word.

3. After students spell the word, have them check the card to see if they spelled the word correctly.

   Say: Read aloud the word you spelled with the letter tiles.

4. Repeat the activity with the remaining sight words.

TIP Sight words can be very difficult for some students. Let students work at their own pace and really master these words.

> **Objectives**
> - Read sight words.
> - Spell sight words.

Learn ●

Sound /j/ Spelled *–dge* in One-Syllable Words

Help students learn the sound /j/ spelled *–dge* in one-syllable words.

1. Gather the index cards you prepared.

2. Place the following letter tiles on students' whiteboard: *d, e, f, g,* and *u*.

3. **Say:** The letter *g* can have the sound /j/ when it is followed by the letters *e, i,* or *y*. Today we'll talk about how the sound /j/ can also be made by the letters *dge*. Sometimes when you hear the sound /j/ at the end of a word, the sound /j/ is spelled by the letters *dge*. Let's learn some one-syllable words that end in the sound /j/ that are spelled with the letters *dge*.

> **Objectives**
> - Identify and use *–dge* for the sound /j/.
> - Identify syllables in words.
> - Identify individual sounds in words.
> - Read aloud grade-level text with appropriate automaticity, prosody, accuracy, and rate.

4. Make the word *fudge* on students' whiteboard and point to it.

   Say: The letters *dge* usually follow a short vowel sound. In this word, the letter *u* makes the sound /ŭ/. Let's touch and say the sounds.

5. Have students

   ▸ Touch and say *fudge*.
   ▸ Say and write the word *fudge*.
   ▸ Say the sound for the letters *dge*. /j/
   ▸ Say what letters spell the sound /j/. *dge*

6. Have students read the index cards with the following one-syllable words: *edge, ledge, wedge, badge, dodge, bridge, ridge,* and *smudge*.

7. Redirect students if they misread *–dge*, reminding them that the letters *dge* make the sound /j/. If they continue to have difficulty reading the words on the index cards, work with them to build the words with letter tiles and have them touch and say the words.

Sound /j/ Spelled *–dge* in Two-Syllable Words

Help students learn the sound /j/ spelled *–dge* in two-syllable words.

1. Gather the index cards you prepared.

2. Place the index card for the word *budget* in front of students.

   Say: This word is *budget*. We read the letters *dge* as the sound /j/, but we also read the letter *e* in the second syllable.

3. Have students fist tap the syllables in *budget. budg / et*

4. **Say:** In the word *budget*, the letter *e* has two jobs: It makes one sound in the second syllable, and it also works with the letters *dg* to make the sound /j/.

5. Have students fist tap on the table as they say the syllables in each word on the index cards:

   ▸ *badger badg / er*
   ▸ *gadget gadg / et*
   ▸ *bridges bridg / es*
   ▸ *fidget fidg / et*

Try It

Finish the Job

Have students complete page PH 46 in *K¹² PhonicsWorks Advanced Activity Book* for more practice with the sound /j/ spelled *–dge*. Have students choose a word from the box that best completes the sentence and write the word. Have them read the sentence aloud.

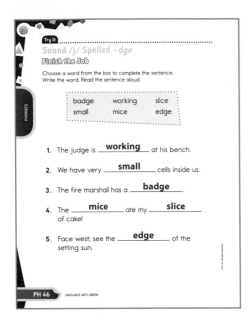

Objectives
- Identify and use *–dge* for the sound /j/.
- Identify complete sentences.
- Read aloud grade-level text with appropriate automaticity, prosody, accuracy, and rate.
- Decode words by applying grade-level word analysis skills.
- Write words by applying grade-level phonics knowledge.

 **15 minutes**

REVIEW: Sound /j/ Spelled *–dge*

Students will work online independently to

▸ Practice the sound /j/ spelled *–dge*.

▸ Practice decoding text by reading a story.

Help students locate the online activities and provide support as needed.

Offline Alternative

No computer access? Have students spell words that have the sound /j/ spelled *dge*, such as *ledge* and *smudge*.

Objectives
- Identify and use *–dge* for the sound /j/.
- Identify syllables in words.
- Identify individual sounds in words.
- Read aloud grade-level text with appropriate automaticity, prosody, accuracy, and rate.
- Decode words by applying grade-level word analysis skills.

Practice Spellings for Soft *c* and Soft *g*

Lesson Overview

[Offline]	**FOCUS:** Practice Spellings for Soft *c* and Soft *g*	**15** minutes

Sight Words	Sight Word Fun
Practice	Review Soft and Hard *c* Words
	Review Soft and Hard *g* Words
	Review Hard and Soft *c* and *g*
Try It	"Fudge for Madge"

[Online]	**REVIEW:** Spellings for Soft *c* and Soft *g*	**15** minutes

[Materials]

Supplied
- *K¹² PhonicsWorks Readers Advanced 8*, pp. 22–29

Also Needed
- sight words box
- index cards (17)
- index cards – all hard and soft *c* and *g* words used in this unit

Advance Preparation

For Review Soft and Hard *c* Words, print the following words on index cards, using one card per word: *rice, mice, slice, space, cab, cite, cube, clap,* and *crust.* Keep the cards in order.

For Review Soft and Hard *g* Words, print the following words on index cards, using one card per word: *magic, gym, gentle, bulge, get, gripe, gap,* and *gift.* Keep the cards in order.

For Review Hard and Soft *c* and *g*, gather the index cards with the hard and soft *c* and *g* words from this unit.

⟦ Offline ⟧ ⑮ minutes

FOCUS: Practice Spellings for Soft *c* and Soft *g*

Work **together** with students to complete offline Sight Words, Practice, and Try It activities.

Sight Words ....

Sight Word Fun

Help students learn the sight words *other*, *together*, and *people*, and up to two additional sight words they have yet to master.

1. Gather the sight word cards *other*, *together*, and *people*, and up to two additional sight word cards.

2. Choose one sight word card to begin.

   Say: Look at this word and take a picture of it in your mind. When you think you can spell the word yourself, turn the card over and use your letter tiles to spell the word.

3. After students spell the word, have them check the card to see if they spelled the word correctly.

   Say: Read aloud the word you spelled with the letter tiles.

4. Repeat the activity with the remaining sight words.

TIP Sight words can be very difficult for some students. Let students work at their own pace and really master these words.

> **Objectives**
> - Read sight words.
> - Spell sight words.

Practice

Review Soft and Hard *c* Words

Have students sort words by the sound made by the letter *c*.

1. Gather the index cards you prepared.

2. **Say:** When *c* has the sound /k/, it is called a hard *c*. When *c* has the sound /s/, it is called a soft *c*.

3. Place the word *rice* in front of students.

   Say: You are going to sort words into two piles. I will show you a word. You will read the word on the card and tell me whether the word has a soft or hard *c*. You will put the soft *c* words in one pile and the hard *c* words in another. I'll do the first one for you. This word is *rice*. *Rice* has a soft *c*. Now it's your turn.

4. Have students read and sort the remaining words:

   ▸ **Soft *c* Words:** *mice, slice, space, cite*
   ▸ **Hard *c* Words**: *cab, cube, clap, crust*

Review Soft and Hard *g* Words

Have students sort words by the sound made by the letter *g*.

1. Gather the index cards you prepared.

2. **Say:** When *g* has the sound /g/, it is called a hard *g*. When *g* has the sound /j/, it is called a soft *g*.

3. Place the word *magic* in front of students.

   Say: You are going to sort words into two piles. I will show you a word. You will read the word on the card and tell me whether the word has a soft or hard *g*. You will put the soft *g* words in one pile and the hard *g* words in another. I'll do the first one for you. This word is *magic*. *Magic* has a soft *g*. Now it's your turn.

4. Have students read and sort the remaining words:

   ▸ **Soft *g* Words:** *gym, gentle, bulge*
   ▸ **Hard *g* Words**: *get, gripe, gap, gift*

Review Hard and Soft *c* and *g*

Have students practice reading words with hard and soft *c* and *g*.

1. Gather the index cards with the hard and soft *c* and *g* words from this unit. Mix up the cards and put them in a stack on the table.

2. Have students draw a card, read the word, and place it in one of the following piles: soft *c*, hard *c*, soft *g*, and hard *g*.

3. Select three words at random and dictate them to students.

4. Have them check their spelling against the spelling on the card.

Objectives

- Identify and use *c* for the sound /s/.
- Identify and use *g* for the sound /j/.
- Identify the sound, given the letter *c*.
- Identify the sound, given the letter *g*.
- Identify individual sounds in words.
- Read aloud grade-level text with appropriate automaticity, prosody, accuracy, and rate.
- Write words by applying grade-level phonics knowledge.
- Follow three-step directions.

Try It

"Fudge for Madge"

Have students read "Fudge for Madge" on page 22 of *K¹² PhonicsWorks Readers Advanced 8.*

Students should read the story silently once or twice before reading the story aloud. When students miss a word that can be sounded out, point to it and give them three to six seconds to try the word again. If students still miss the word, tell them the word so the flow of the story isn't interrupted.

After reading the story, make a list of all the words students missed, and go over those words with them. You may use letter tiles to show students how to read the words.

Objectives

- Read aloud grade-level text with appropriate automaticity, prosody, accuracy, and rate.
- Decode words by applying grade-level word analysis skills.

[Online] ⏲ **minutes**

REVIEW: Spellings for Soft *c* and Soft *g*

Students will work online independently to

▸ Practice spellings for soft *c* and soft *g*.

Help students locate the online activities and provide support as needed.

Offline Alternative

No computer access? Gather the hard and soft *c* and *g* words from this unit. Have students read the words and sort the cards into one of four piles: soft *c*, hard *c*, soft *g*, and hard *g*.

Objectives

- Identify and use *c* for the sound /s/.
- Identify and use *g* for the sound /j/.
- Identify the sound, given the letter *c*.
- Identify the sound, given the letter *g*.
- Identify individual sounds in words.

Unit Checkpoint

Lesson Overview

🖥	**⟦Online⟧**	**REVIEW:** Spellings for Soft *c* and Soft *g* Sounds	**15** minutes
📄	**⟦Offline⟧**	**UNIT CHECKPOINT:** Spellings for Soft *c* and Soft *g* Sounds	**15** minutes

⟦Materials⟧

Supplied

- *K¹² PhonicsWorks Advanced Assessments,* pp. PH 133–138

Objectives

- Identify individual sounds in words.
- Identify the sound, given the letter *g*.
- Identify the sound, given the letter *c*.
- Identify and use *–dge* for the sound /j/.
- Identify and use c for the sound /s/.
- Given the letter, identify the most common sound.
- Given the sound, identify the most common letter or letters.
- Read instructional-level text with 90% accuracy.
- Read aloud grade-level text with appropriate automaticity, prosody, accuracy, and rate.
- Write words by applying grade-level phonics knowledge.
- Write sight words.
- Read sight words.

⟦Online⟧ **15** minutes

REVIEW: **Spellings for Soft *c* and Soft *g* Sounds**

Students will review spellings for soft *c* and soft *g* sounds to prepare for the Unit Checkpoint. Help students locate the online activities and provide support as needed.

⟦ Offline ⟧ ⏱ 15 minutes

UNIT CHECKPOINT: Spellings for Soft *c* and Soft *g* Sounds

Explain that students are going to show what they have learned about sounds, letters, and words.

1. Give students the Unit Checkpoint pages for the Spellings for Soft *c* and Soft *g* Sounds unit and print the Unit Checkpoint Answer Key, if you'd like.

2. Use the instructions below to help administer the Checkpoint to students. On the Answer Key or another sheet of paper, note student answers to oral response questions to help with scoring the Checkpoint later.

3. Use the Answer Key to score the Checkpoint, and then enter the results online.

Part 1. Circle Words with Sound /j/ Have students circle the words in which the *g* spells the sound /j/.

Part 2. Circle Words with Sound /s/ Have students circle the words in which the *c* spells the sound /s/.

Part 3. Read Sight Words Have students read each sight word aloud. Note any words they read incorrectly.

Part 4. Writing Read each sentence to students. Have them repeat and write the sentence.

25. *Vance put the fudge on the ledge to cool.*

26. *Gene and Nancy went to the dance.*

27. *Madge ran the race at the gym.*

Part 5. Read Aloud Listen to students read the sentences aloud. Count and note the number of words they read correctly.

Part 6. Read Words Have students read each word aloud. Note any words they read incorrectly.

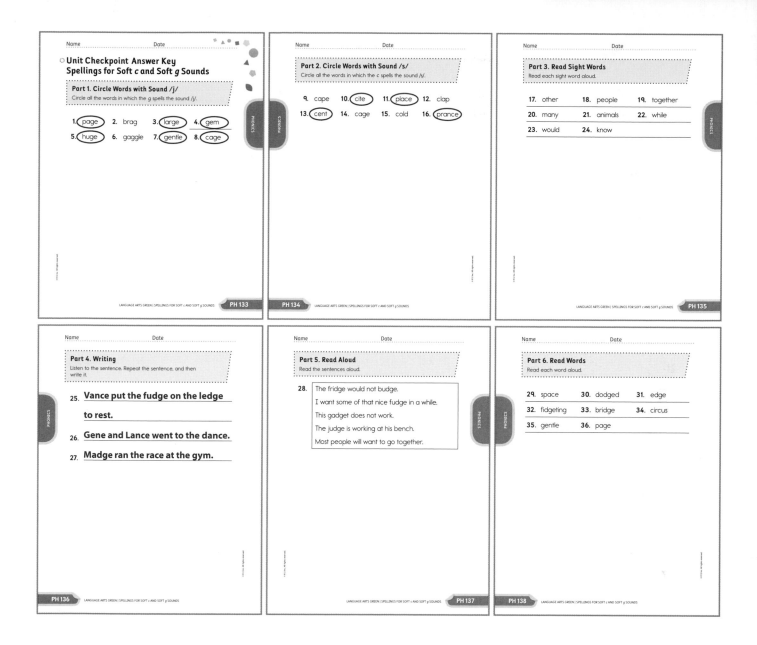

Name .... **Date** ....

Unit Checkpoint Answer Key
Spellings for Soft *c* and Soft *g* Sounds

Part 1. Circle Words with Sound /j/
Circle all the words in which the *g* spells the sound /j/.

1. (page) 2. brag 3. (large) 4. (gem)
5. (huge) 6. gaggle 7. (gentle) 8. (cage)

PHONICS

PH 133
LANGUAGE ARTS GREEN | SPELLINGS FOR SOFT *c* AND SOFT *g* SOUNDS

Name .... **Date** ....

Part 2. Circle Words with Sound /s/
Circle all the words in which the *c* spells the sound /s/.

9. cape 10. (cite) 11. (place) 12. clap
13. (cent) 14. cage 15. cold 16. (prance)

PH 134
LANGUAGE ARTS GREEN | SPELLINGS FOR SOFT *c* AND SOFT *g* SOUNDS

Name .... **Date** ....

Part 3. Read Sight Words
Read each sight word aloud.

17. other   18. people   19. together
20. many   21. animals 22. while
23. would   24. know

PHONICS

PH 135
LANGUAGE ARTS GREEN | SPELLINGS FOR SOFT *c* AND SOFT *g* SOUNDS

Name .... **Date** ....

Part 4. Writing
Listen to the sentence. Repeat the sentence, and then write it.

25. **Vance put the fudge on the ledge to rest.**

26. **Gene and Lance went to the dance.**

27. **Madge ran the race at the gym.**

PHONICS

PH 136   LANGUAGE ARTS GREEN | SPELLINGS FOR SOFT *c* AND SOFT *g* SOUNDS

Name .... **Date** ....

Part 5. Read Aloud
Read the sentences aloud.

28.
> The fridge would not budge.
> I want some of that nice fudge in a while.
> This gadget does not work.
> The judge is working at his bench.
> Most people will want to go together.

PHONICS

PH 137
LANGUAGE ARTS GREEN | SPELLINGS FOR SOFT *c* AND SOFT *g* SOUNDS

Name .... **Date** ....

Part 6. Read Words
Read each word aloud.

29. space   30. dodged   31. edge
32. fidgeting 33. bridge 34. circus
35. gentle 36. page

PHONICS

PH 138
LANGUAGE ARTS GREEN | SPELLINGS FOR SOFT *c* AND SOFT *g* SOUNDS

Introduce Spellings for Sound /ā/

Unit Overview

In this unit, students will
- ▸ Learn the sight words *above*, *here*, and *move*.
- ▸ Learn the spellings *a*, *ai*, *ay*, *eigh*, and *a-e* for the sound /ā/.
- ▸ Read and write sentences.
- ▸ Read a story silently and aloud.

Lesson Overview

⧉ [Offline]	**FOCUS:** Introduce Spellings for Sound /ā/	**15** minutes

Sight Words	Introduce Sight Words
Learn	Introduce Spellings for Sound /ā/
	Review Spellings for Sound /ā/
Try It	Investigator

🖥 [Online]	**REVIEW:** Spellings for Sound /ā/	**15** minutes

[Materials]

Supplied
- *K¹² PhonicsWorks Advanced Activity Book,* p. PH 47
- whiteboard, Learning Coach
- whiteboard, student
- Tile Kit

Also Needed
- sight words box
- dictation notebook

 **15** minutes

FOCUS: Introduce Spellings for Sound /ā/

Work **together** with students to complete offline Sight Words, Learn, and Try It activities.

Sight Words

Introduce Sight Words

Help students learn the sight words *above*, *here*, and *move*.

1. Gather the sight word cards *above*, *here*, and *move*.

2. Show students the *above* card.

3. **Say:** This is the word *above*. We see this word so often that we want to be able to read and spell it quickly without thinking about it. Look closely at the word *above*. Spell the word *above* aloud. Take a picture of the word *above* in your mind. When you think you can spell *above* yourself, turn the card over and use your letter tiles to spell the word *above*. Check the card to see if you spelled the word *above* correctly. Read aloud the word you spelled with the letter tiles.

4. Repeat the activity with the remaining sight words.

5. Chart students' progress on the back of each card.

   ▸ Divide the back of the card into two columns.
   ▸ Label the first column "Read" and the second column "Spell."
   ▸ Record the dates that students read or spell the word correctly. When students can read and spell the word correctly three times in a row, they have mastered the word. You may want to put a star or sticker on their card when they have mastered that word.

6. Add the cards to students' sight words box.

TIP Sight words can be very difficult for some students. Let students work at their own pace and really master these words, as they occur frequently in reading and writing.

> **Objectives**
> - Read sight words.
> - Spell sight words.

Learn •••

Introduce Spellings for Sound /ā/

Help students learn the spellings *a, ai, ay, eigh,* and *a-e* for the sound /ā/.

1. Place the following letter tiles on students' whiteboard: *a, ai, ay, b, c, d, e, eigh, k, n, or, r,* and *t.*

2. Make the word *bake* in the middle of students' whiteboard and point to it.

   Say: Today we are going to learn the five spellings for the sound /ā/. You already know one of them. Sometimes the long *a* sound is made by the letter *a* and a silent *e*. Let's touch and say the word *bake*.

3. Make the word *acorn* and point to it.

   Say: Now let's look at the next word. This is the word *acorn*. In the word *acorn,* the long *a* sound is made by the letter *a* all by itself.

   ► Touch and say *acorn*.
   ► Where is the sound /ā/ in this word? beginning
   ► Which letter or letters make this sound? *a*

4. Make the word *rain* and point to it.

   Say: This word is *rain*. In the word *rain,* the long *a* sound is made by the letters *ai*.

   ► Touch and say *rain*.
   ► Where is the sound /ā/ in this word? middle
   ► Which letter or letters make this sound? *ai*

5. Make the word *day* and point to it.

   Say: This word is *day*. In the word *day,* the long *a* sound is made by the letters *ay*.

   ► Touch and say *day*.
   ► Where is the sound /ā/ in this word? end
   ► Which letter or letters make this sound? *ay*

6. Make the word *eight* and point to it.

   Say: The last word is *eight*. In the word *eight,* the long *a* sound is made by the letters *eigh*.

   ► Touch and say *eight*.
   ► Where is the sound /ā/ in this word? beginning
   ► Which letter or letters make this sound? *eigh*

TIP Refer to the *K¹² PhonicsWorks* video for a demonstration of how to teach different spellings for long vowel sounds.

Objectives

- Identify individual sounds in words.
- Identify and use the sound /ā/.
- Identify the letters, given the sound /ā/.
- Identify and use /ā/ spelling patterns.
- Identify and use silent *e*.
- Read aloud grade-level text with appropriate automaticity, prosody, accuracy, and rate.
- Write words by applying grade-level phonics knowledge.

Review Spellings for Sound /ā/

Help students review the spellings *a, ai, ay, eigh*, and *a-e* for the sound /ā/.

1. Gather the dictation notebook and pencil.

2. Place the following letter tiles at the top of students' whiteboard: *a, ai, ay, eigh*, and *a-e*.

3. Write the following words on your whiteboard: *acorn, rain, day, eight*, and *bake*.

4. **Say:** Count the number of ways there are to spell the long vowel sound /ā/.

   ► Touch and say the spellings for sound /ā/. *a, ai, ay, eigh, a-e*
   ► Look at the words on the board and read them.
   ► Say how the sound is spelled in each word. *a* in *acorn, ai* in *rain, ay* in *day, eigh* in *eight, a-e* in *bake*
   ► Take a picture in your mind of the five ways of spelling the sound /ā/.

5. **Say:** I am going to hide the words and the spellings on the board. Your job is to remember each way of spelling the sound /ā/ and write them in your notebook.

6. After students have finished writing the spellings in their notebook, have them check their answer against the spellings on the board.

TIP If students cannot remember one or more of the spellings for the sound /ā/, tell them the guide word for that spelling (*a* as in *acorn, ai* as in *rain, ay* as in *day, eigh* as in *eight, a-e* as in *bake*).

Try It

Investigator

Have students complete page PH 47 in *K¹² PhonicsWorks Advanced Activity Book* for more practice with spellings for the sound /ā/. Have students read each word aloud, going down each column, and then read each word again, going across each row. Have them read the questions and circle the answers.

Try It
Introduce Spellings for Sound /ā/
Investigator

Read each word aloud, going down each column.
Then read each word again, going across each row.

a–e	ai	ay	eigh	a
lace	rain	play	eight	acorn
plate	chain	way	weight	David
made	train	say	weigh	raven
tape	brain	stay	sleigh	label
page	sail	day	freight	data
snake	paint	spray	neigh	major
lane	main	pay		fable
cane	braid	tray		basic
place	pail	May		April
grape	faint	gray		bacon

Circle the answer.

1. Where do you see *ai* in words? (middle) end
2. Where do you see *ay* in words? middle (end)
3. Which spelling has more words? (ai) eigh

LANGUAGE ARTS GREEN   **PH 47**

Objectives

- Identify and use the sound /ā/.
- Identify the letters, given the sound /ā/.
- Identify and use /ā/ spelling patterns.
- Decode words by applying grade-level word analysis skills.

〖Online〗 ⑮ minutes

REVIEW: **Spellings for Sound /ā/**

Students will work online independently to

- ▶ Practice spellings for the sound /ā/.
- ▶ Practice decoding text by reading a story.

Help students locate the online activities and provide support as needed.

Offline Alternative

No computer access? Have students spell words that have the spellings *a*, *ai*, *ay*, *eigh*, and *a-e* for the sound /ā/, such as *sang*, *nail*, *day*, *weigh*, and *base*.

Objectives

- Identify and use the sound /ā/.
- Identify the letters, given the sound /ā/.
- Identify and use /ā/ spelling patterns.
- Identify and use silent *e*.
- Read aloud grade-level text with appropriate automaticity, prosody, accuracy, and rate.
- Decode words by applying grade-level word analysis skills.

Practice Spellings for Sound /ā/ (A)

Lesson Overview

[Offline] **FOCUS:** Practice Spellings for Sound /ā/ — **15** minutes

Sight Words	Sight Word Fun
Practice	Word Chains
Try It	"Gail Makes the Best of a Mess"

[Online] **REVIEW:** Spellings for Sound /ā/ — **15** minutes

Materials

Supplied
- *K¹² PhonicsWorks Readers Advanced 8,* pp. 30–38
- whiteboard, student
- Tile Kit

Also Needed
- sight words box

[Offline] ⏱ 15 minutes

FOCUS: Practice Spellings for Sound /ā/

Work **together** with students to complete offline Sight Words, Practice, and Try It activities.

Sight Words ●●●

Sight Word Fun

Help students learn the sight words *above*, *here*, and *move*, and up to two additional sight words they have yet to master.

1. Gather the sight word cards *above*, *here*, and *move*, and up to two additional sight word cards.

2. Choose one sight word card to begin.

   Say: Look at this word and take a picture of it in your mind. When you think you can spell the word yourself, turn the card over and use your letter tiles to spell the word.

3. After students spell the word, have them check the card to see if they spelled the word correctly.

   Say: Read aloud the word you spelled with the letter tiles.

4. Repeat the activity with the remaining sight words.

   TIP Sight words can be very difficult for some students. Let students work at their own pace and really master these words.

> **Objectives**
> - Read sight words.
> - Spell sight words.

Practice ●●

Word Chains

Have students build words by adding and changing letters to help them recognize and use the spellings *a*, *ai*, *ay*, *eigh*, and *a-e* for the sound /ā/.

1. Place the following letter tiles at the top of students' whiteboard: *a, ai, ay, b, c, d, e, eigh, k, l, m, n, p, r, s, t,* and *w*.

2. **Say:** You will spell words in several short word chains today. There will be one chain for each of the spellings of the sound /ā/ that you know. How many spellings do you know for the sound /ā/? five

> **Objectives**
> - Identify the new word when one sound is changed in a word.
> - Identify individual sounds in words.
> - Identify and use the sound /ā/.
> - Identify the letters, given the sound /ā/.
> - Identify and use /ā/ spelling patterns.
> - Identify and use silent *e*.

3. **Say:** I'll do the first word. The word is *cake.*

   ▶ I will pull down the letters for the sounds /k/, /ā/, and /k/ to spell the word *cake.*

   ▶ I will touch and say *cake.* To change *cake* to *bake,* I will think about which sound is changed from the word *cake* to *bake.* I will need to replace the letter *c* with the letter *b.*

   ▶ Touch and say the word *bake.* Now it's your turn to change *bake* to *lake.* You can spell *lake* by making only one change. Touch and say the new word.

4. Redirect students if they select the incorrect letter for any sound.

   Say: That letter is for the sound [incorrect sound]. We want the letter for the sound [target sound]. What letter makes that sound? Answers will vary.

5. Redirect students if they name the sound incorrectly.

   Say: To change the word [first word] to [target word], we need the letter for the sound [target sound].

   Show students how to make the change. Have them touch and say the new word after they move the letters.

6. Follow this procedure to make the following groups of word chains:

   ▶ *rain, main, pain, plain*
   ▶ *play, day, say, stay*
   ▶ *able, cable, table, stable*
   ▶ *eight, weight, weigh, neigh*

7. For every new word, have students add, replace, or remove only one letter tile. Remind students that in these word chains only one sound—and only one letter tile—will change when the word changes.

TIP If students cannot remember one or more spellings, give them the guide word for that spelling (*a* as in *acorn, ai* as in *rain, ay* as in *day, eigh* as in *eight, a-e* as in *bake*).

Try It ••

"Gail Makes the Best of a Mess"
Have students read "Gail Makes the Best of a Mess" on page 30 of *K¹² PhonicsWorks Readers Advanced 8.*

Students should read the story silently once or twice before reading the story aloud. When students miss a word that can be sounded out, point to it and give them three to six seconds to try the word again. If students still miss the word, tell them the word so the flow of the story isn't interrupted.

After reading the story, make a list of all the words students missed, and go over those words with them. You may use letter tiles to show students how to read the words.

 **15 minutes**

REVIEW: Spellings for Sound /ā/

Students will work online independently to

▶ Practice spellings for the sound /ā/.

Help students locate the online activities and provide support as needed.

Offline Alternative

No computer access? Have students spell words that have the spellings *a*, *ai*, *ay*, *eigh*, and *a-e* for the sound /ā/, such as *tank*, *braid*, *hay*, *weigh*, and *date*.

Practice Spellings for Sound /ā/ (B)

Lesson Overview

[Offline] **FOCUS:** Practice Spellings for Sound /ā/ — **15** minutes

Sight Words	Sight Word Fun
Practice	Word Chains
Try It	Investigator
	Dictation: Write Sentences

[Online] **REVIEW:** Spellings for Sound /ā/ — **15** minutes

Materials

Supplied
- *K¹² PhonicsWorks Advanced Activity Book,* p. PH 48
- whiteboard, Learning Coach
- whiteboard, student
- Tile Kit

Also Needed
- sight words box
- dictation notebook

〔 Offline 〕 ⏱ 15 minutes

FOCUS: Practice Spellings for Sound /ā/

Work **together** with students to complete offline Sight Words, Practice, and Try It activities.

Sight Words ···

Sight Word Fun

Help students learn the sight words *above*, *here*, and *move*, and up to two additional sight words they have yet to master.

1. Gather the sight word cards *above*, *here*, and *move*, and up to two additional sight word cards.

2. Choose one sight word card to begin.

   Say: Look at this word and take a picture of it in your mind. When you think you can spell the word yourself, turn the card over and use your letter tiles to spell the word.

3. After students spell the word, have them check the card to see if they spelled the word correctly.

   Say: Read aloud the word you spelled with the letter tiles.

4. Repeat the activity with the remaining sight words.

TIP Sight words can be very difficult for some students. Let students work at their own pace and really master these words.

> **Objectives**
> - Read sight words.
> - Spell sight words.

Practice ···

Word Chains

Have students build words by adding and changing letters to help them recognize and use the spellings *a*, *ai*, *ay*, *eigh*, and *a-e* for the sound /ā/.

1. Place the following letter tiles at the top of students' whiteboard: *a*, *ai*, *ay*, *b*, *c*, *d*, *e*, *eigh*, *f*, *k*, *le*, *m*, *n*, *p*, *r*, *t*, and *w*.

2. **Say:** You will spell words in several short word chains today. There will be one chain for each of the spellings of the sound /ā/ that you know. How many spellings do you know for the sound /ā/? five

> **Objectives**
> - Identify the new word when one sound is changed in a word.
> - Identify individual sounds in words.
> - Identify and use the sound /ā/.
> - Identify the letters, given the sound /ā/.
> - Identify and use /ā/ spelling patterns.
> - Identify and use silent *e*.

3. **Say:** I'll do the first word. The word is *table*.

    ▸ I will pull down the letters for the sounds /t/, /ā/, /b/, and /l/ to spell the word *table*.

    ▸ I will touch and say *table*. To change *table* to *fable*, I will think about which sound is changed from the word *table* to *fable*. I will need to replace the letter *t* with the letter *f*.

    ▸ Touch and say the word *fable*. Now it's your turn to change *fable* to *cable*. You can spell *cable* by making only one change. Touch and say the new word.

4. Redirect students if they select the incorrect letter for any sound.

    Say: That letter is for the sound [incorrect sound]. We want the letter for the sound [target sound]. What letter makes that sound? Answers will vary.

5. Redirect students if they name the sound incorrectly.

    Say: To change the word [first word] to [target word], we need the letter for the sound [target sound].

    Show students how to make the change. Have them touch and say the new word after they move the letters.

6. Follow this procedure to make the following groups of word chains:

    ▸ *train, rain, brain, drain*
    ▸ *eight, weight, weigh*
    ▸ *may, ray, pray, tray*
    ▸ *tape, cape, cake, make*

7. For every new word, have students add, replace, or remove only one letter. Remind students that in these word chains only one sound—and only one letter tile—will change when the word changes.

TIP If students cannot remember one or more spellings, give them the guide word for that spelling (*a* as in *acorn*, *ai* as in *rain*, *ay* as in *day*, *eigh* as in *eight*, *a-e* as in *bake*).

Try It

Investigator

Have students complete page PH 48 in *K¹² PhonicsWorks Advanced Activity Book* for more practice with spellings for the sound /ā/. Have students read each word aloud. Have them decide the location of the sound /ā/ in the word and write the word in the correct column.

Objectives

- Identify and use the sound /ā/.
- Identify the letters, given the sound /ā/.
- Identify and use /ā/ spelling patterns.
- Write words by applying grade-level phonics knowledge.
- Follow three-step directions.

Dictation: Write Sentences

Use sentences to help students identify individual sounds in words.

1. Gather a pencil and the dictation notebook. Say the sentence, *Sit on the old chair.* Then give these directions to students:

   ▸ Repeat the sentence.
   ▸ Write the sentence in your notebook.
   ▸ Read the sentence aloud.

2. When students have finished, write the following sentence on your whiteboard: *Sit on the old chair.*

3. Have them compare their answer to your correct version.

4. Repeat this procedure with the following sentences: *Is Kim eight? The rain is so much fun! I get my paycheck today.*

   ▸ If students make an error and don't see it, help them correct their mistake by having them finger stretch the sounds in the word they missed.
   ▸ If students are having difficulty selecting the correct letters or sounds, review those letters or sounds that are confusing them.
   ▸ If students have difficulty with first, middle, and last sounds, have them finger stretch the sounds in words.

[Online] ⏱ 15 minutes

REVIEW: Spellings for Sound /ā/

Students will work online independently to

▶ Practice spellings for the sound /ā/.
▶ Practice decoding text by reading a story.

Help students locate the online activities and provide support as needed.

Offline Alternative

No computer access? Have students spell words that have the spellings *a, ai, ay, eigh,* and *a-e* for the sound /ā/, such as *rang, fail, pay, neigh,* and *gate*.

Objectives

- Identify and use the sound /ā/.
- Identify the letters, given the sound /ā/.
- Identify and use /ā/ spelling patterns.
- Identify and use silent *e*.
- Read aloud grade-level text with appropriate automaticity, prosody, accuracy, and rate.
- Decode words by applying grade-level word analysis skills.

Practice Spellings for Sound /ā/ (C)

Lesson Overview

〖 Offline 〗	**FOCUS:** Practice Spellings for Sound /ā/	**15** minutes
Sight Words	Sight Word Fun	
Practice	Sort Spellings for Sound /ā/	
Try It	"Kay and Vance Work Hard"	
〖 Online 〗	**REVIEW:** Spellings for Sound /ā/	**15** minutes

Materials

Supplied
- *K¹² PhonicsWorks Readers Advanced 9*, pp. 1–6

Also Needed
- sight words box
- index cards (15)

Advance Preparation

For Sort Spellings for Sound /ā/, print each of the following words on index cards, using one card per word: *acorn, sang, bank, rain, braid, fail, May, clay, spray, eight, sleigh, weight, name, rake,* and *made.*

 **15 minutes**

FOCUS: Practice Spellings for Sound /ā/

Work **together** with students to complete offline Sight Words, Practice, and Try It activities.

Sight Words •••

Sight Word Fun

Help students learn the sight words *above*, *here*, and *move*, and up to two additional sight words they have yet to master.

1. Gather the sight word cards *above*, *here*, and *move*, and up to two additional sight word cards.

2. Choose one sight word card to begin.

   Say: Look at this word and take a picture of it in your mind. When you think you can spell the word yourself, turn the card over and use your letter tiles to spell the word.

3. After students spell the word, have them check the card to see if they spelled the word correctly.

   Say: Read aloud the word you spelled with the letter tiles.

4. Repeat the activity with the remaining sight words.

   TIP Sight words can be very difficult for some students. Let students work at their own pace and really master these words.

> **Objectives**
> - Read sight words.
> - Spell sight words.

Practice •••

Sort Spellings for Sound /ā/

Help students practice identifying words that have the spellings *a*, *ai*, *ay*, *eigh*, and *a-e* for the sound /ā/.

1. Gather the index cards you prepared. Mix the cards well and place them in a stack face down on the table.

2. Gather the dictation notebook. Draw five columns and label them *a*, *ai*, *ay*, *eigh*, and *a-e* to represent the five different ways to spell the sound /ā/.

3. **Say:** You are going to sort words by the five spellings for the sound /ā/. You will take a card from the pile and read it to me. Then you will think about the spelling for the sound /ā/ in the word and write that word in the correct column. I'll do the first one for you.

> **Objectives**
> - Identify individual sounds in words.
> - Identify and use the sound /ā/.
> - Identify the letters, given the sound /ā/.
> - Identify and use /ā/ spelling patterns.
> - Identify and use silent *e*.

4. Demonstrate the following for students:

  ▸ Draw a card from the pile.
  ▸ Read the word aloud.
  ▸ Write the word in the correct column for the spelling for sound /ā/.

5. Have students continue the procedure with the remaining words:

  ▸ **Spelling _a_ Words:** _acorn, sang, bank_
  ▸ **Spelling _ai_ Words:** _rain, braid, fail_
  ▸ **Spelling _ay_ Words:** _May, clay, spray_
  ▸ **Spelling _eigh_ Words:** _eight, sleigh, weight_
  ▸ **Spelling _a-e_ Words:** _name, rake, made_

Try It

"Kay and Vance Work Hard"

Have students read "Kay and Vance Work Hard" on page 1 of _K¹² PhonicsWorks Readers Advanced 9._

Students should read the story silently once or twice before reading the story aloud. When students miss a word that can be sounded out, point to it and give them three to six seconds to try the word again. If students still miss the word, tell them the word so the flow of the story isn't interrupted.

After reading the story, make a list of all the words students missed, and go over those words with them. You may use letter tiles to show students how to read the words.

Objectives

- Read aloud grade-level text with appropriate automaticity, prosody, accuracy, and rate.
- Decode words by applying grade-level word analysis skills.

 **15 minutes**

REVIEW: Spellings for Sound /ā/

Students will work online independently to

▸ Practice spellings for the sound /ā/.

Help students locate the online activities and provide support as needed.

Offline Alternative

No computer access? Have students spell words that have the spellings *a*, *ai*, *ay*, *eigh*, and *a-e* for the sound /ā/, such as *sank*, *afraid*, *say*, *sleigh*, and *age*.

> ⭐ **Objectives**
> - Identify individual sounds in words.
> - Identify and use the sound /ā/.
> - Identify the letters, given the sound /ā/.
> - Identify and use /ā/ spelling patterns.
> - Identify and use silent *e*.

Unit Checkpoint

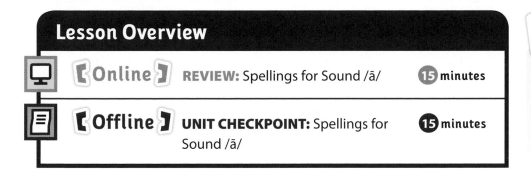

Lesson Overview

🖥️	**【Online 】** REVIEW: Spellings for Sound /ā/	**15** minutes
📄	**【Offline 】** UNIT CHECKPOINT: Spellings for Sound /ā/	**15** minutes

Objectives

- Identify individual sounds in words.
- Identify and use the sound /ā/.
- Identify the letters, given the sound /ā/.
- Identify and use /ā/ spelling patterns.
- Identify and use silent e.
- Read instructional-level text with 90% accuracy.
- Read aloud grade-level text with appropriate automaticity, prosody, accuracy, and rate.
- Write words by applying grade-level phonics knowledge.
- Write sight words.
- Read sight words.

Materials

Supplied

- *K¹² PhonicsWorks Advanced Assessments,* pp. PH 139–144

【Online 】 🕙 15 minutes

REVIEW: **Spellings for Sound /ā/**

Students will review spellings for the sound /ā/ to prepare for the Unit Checkpoint. Help students locate the online activities and provide support as needed.

【 Offline 】 ⓯ minutes

UNIT CHECKPOINT: Spellings for Sound /ā/

Explain that students are going to show what they have learned about sounds, letters, and words.

1. Give students the Unit Checkpoint pages for the Spellings for Sound /ā/ unit and print the Unit Checkpoint Answer Key, if you'd like.

2. Use the instructions below to help administer the Checkpoint to students. On the Answer Key or another sheet of paper, note student answers to oral response questions to help with scoring the Checkpoint later.

3. Use the Answer Key to score the Checkpoint, and then enter the results online.

Part 1. Circle Words with Sound /ā/ Have students circle the words with the sound /ā/.

Part 2. Many Spellings, One Sound. Have students circle the five ways to spell the sound /ā/.

Part 3. Read Sight Words Have students read each sight word aloud. Note any words they read incorrectly.

Part 4. Writing Read each sentence to students. Have them repeat and write the sentence.

25. *Jay and Gail will be late.*

26. *The sleigh ride was fun!*

27. *The clay plate has six acorns on it.*

Part 5. Read Aloud Listen to students read the sentences aloud. Count and note the number of words they read correctly.

Part 6. Read Nonsense Words Have students read each nonsense word aloud. Note any words they read incorrectly.

Part 7. Read Words Have students read each word aloud. Note any words they read incorrectly.

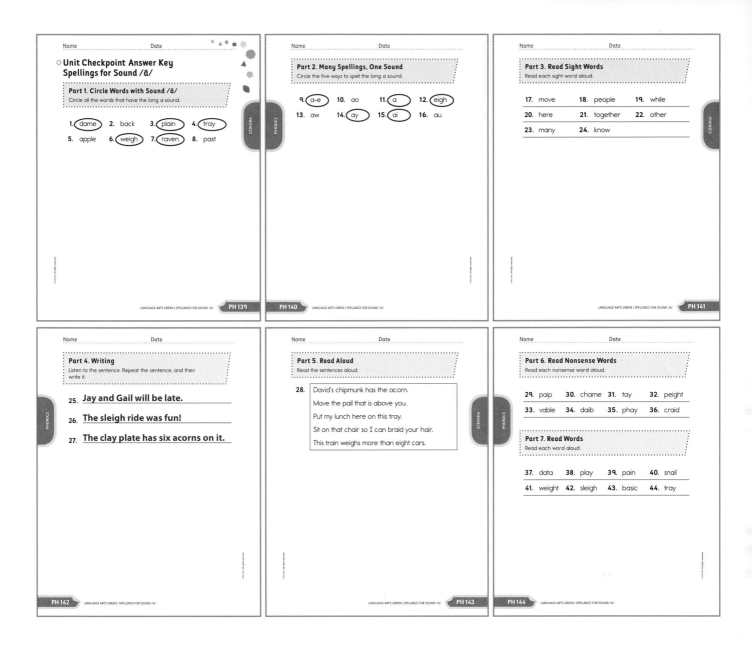

Unit Checkpoint Answer Key
Spellings for Sound /ā/

Part 1. Circle Words with Sound /ā/
Circle all the words that have the long a sound.

1. (dame) 2. back 3. (plain) 4. (tray)
5. apple 6. (weigh) 7. (raven) 8. past

Part 2. Many Spellings, One Sound
Circle the five ways to spell the long a sound.

9. (a-e) 10. ao 11. (a) 12. (eigh)
13. aw 14. (ay) 15. (ai) 16. au

Part 3. Read Sight Words
Read each sight word aloud.

17. move 18. people 19. while
20. here 21. together 22. other
23. many 24. know

Part 4. Writing
Listen to the sentence. Repeat the sentence, and then write it.

25. **Jay and Gail will be late.**
26. **The sleigh ride was fun!**
27. **The clay plate has six acorns on it.**

Part 5. Read Aloud
Read the sentences aloud.

28.
David's chipmunk has the acorn.
Move the pail that is above you.
Put my lunch here on this tray.
Sit on that chair so I can braid your hair.
This train weighs more than eight cars.

Part 6. Read Nonsense Words
Read each nonsense word aloud.

29. paip 30. chame 31. tay 32. peight
33. vable 34. daib 35. phay 36. craid

Part 7. Read Words
Read each word aloud.

37. data 38. play 39. pain 40. snail
41. weight 42. sleigh 43. basic 44. tray

Introduce Spellings for Sound /ī/

Unit Overview

In this unit, students will
- ▶ Review sight words.
- ▶ Learn the spellings *i*, *ie*, *y*, *igh*, and *i-e* for the sound /ī/.
- ▶ Read and write sentences.
- ▶ Read stories silently and aloud.

[Materials]

Supplied
- *K¹² PhonicsWorks Advanced Activity Book*, p. PH 49
- whiteboard, Learning Coach
- whiteboard, student
- Tile Kit

Also Needed
- sight words box
- dictation notebook

Lesson Overview

[Offline] FOCUS: Introduce Spellings for Sound /ī/		15 minutes
Sight Words	Review Sight Words	
Learn	Introduce Spellings for Sound /ī/	
	Review Spellings for Sound /ī/	
Try It	Investigator	
[Online] REVIEW: Spellings for Sound /ī/		15 minutes

[Offline] ⏱ minutes

FOCUS: Introduce Spellings for Sound /ī/

Work **together** with students to complete offline Sight Words, Learn, and Try It activities.

Sight Words

Review Sight Words

Help students learn to recognize sight words.

1. Gather all the sight word cards students have yet to master from their sight words box. Stack the cards on the table face down.

2. Have students pick a word and read it to you.

3. If they read it quickly and correctly, put the card in one stack. If they hesitate or do not read the word correctly, put it in another stack. The second stack should have words that they will review again.

4. Take the stack of words that students read correctly and dictate each word to them. They may choose to either write the word or spell it aloud.

5. If students spell the word correctly, put the card in the first stack because they have mastered the word. If they misspell the word, add it to the stack of cards to review again.

6. Chart students' progress on the back of each card.

   ▶ Divide the back of the card into two columns.
   ▶ Label the first column "Read" and the second column "Spell."
   ▶ Record the dates that students read or spell the word correctly. When students can read and spell the word correctly three times in a row, they have mastered the word. You may want to put a star or sticker on their card when they have mastered that word.

TIP Even if students can read and spell all the words correctly, it is still beneficial for them to review sight words. Choose as many additional words as you would like for each subsequent activity.

Learn

Introduce Spellings for Sound /ī/

Help students learn the spellings *i, ie, y, igh,* and *i-e* for the sound /ī/.

1. Place the following letter tiles on students' whiteboard: *e, f, h, i, ie, igh, k, l, p, t,* and *y.*

2. Make the word *kite* in the middle of students' whiteboard and point to it.

   Say: Today we are going to learn the five spellings for the sound /ī/. You already know one of them. Sometimes the long *i* sound is made by the letter *i* and a silent *e*, separated by a consonant. Let's touch and say the word *kite.*

3. Make the word *hi* and point to it.

   Say: Now let's look at the next word. This is the word *hi*. In the word *hi*, the long *i* sound is made by the letter *i* all by itself.

   ▶ Touch and say *hi.*
   ▶ Where is the sound /ī/ in this word? end
   ▶ Which letter or letters make this sound? *i*

4. Make the word *pie* and point to it.

   Say: This word is *pie*. In the word *pie*, the long *i* sound is made by the letters *ie.*

   ▶ Touch and say *pie.*
   ▶ Where is the sound /ī/ in this word? end
   ▶ Which letter or letters make this sound? *ie*

5. Make the word *light* and point to it.

   Say: This word is *light*. In the word *light*, the long *i* sound is made by the letters *igh.*

   ▶ Touch and say *light.*
   ▶ Where is the sound /ī/ in this word? middle
   ▶ Which letter or letters make this sound? *igh*

6. Make the word *fly* and point to it.

   Say: The last word is *fly*. In the word *fly*, the long *i* sound is made by the letter *y.*

   ▶ Touch and say *fly.*
   ▶ Where is the sound /ī/ in this word? end
   ▶ Which letter or letters make this sound? *y*

TIP Refer to the *K¹² PhonicsWorks* video for a demonstration of how to teach different spellings for long vowel sounds.

Objectives
- Identify individual sounds in words.
- Identify and use the sound /ī/.
- Identify the letters, given the sound /ī/.
- Identify and use /ī/ spelling patterns.
- Identify and use silent *e*.
- Write words by applying grade-level phonics knowledge.

Review Spellings for Sound /ī/

Help students review the spellings *i*, *ie*, *y*, *igh*, and *i-e* for the sound /ī/.

1. Gather the dictation notebook and pencil.

2. Place the following letter tiles at the top of students' whiteboard: *i*, *ie*, *y*, *igh*, and *i-e*.

3. Write the following words on your whiteboard: *hi*, *pie*, *fly*, *light*, and *kite*.

4. **Say:** Count the number of ways there are to spell the long vowel sound /ī/.

   ▸ Touch and say the spellings for the sound /ī/. *i, ie, y, igh, i-e*
   ▸ Look at the words on the board and read them.
   ▸ Say how the sound is spelled in each word *i* in *hi*, *ie* in *pie*, *y* in *fly*, *igh* in *light*, *i-e* in *kite*
   ▸ Take a picture in your mind of the five ways of spelling the sound /ī/.

5. **Say:** I am going to hide the words and the spellings on the board. Your job is to remember each way of spelling the sound /ī/ and write the spellings in your notebook.

6. After students have finished writing the spellings in their notebook, have them check their answers against the spellings on the board.

TIP If students cannot remember one or more of the spellings for the sound /ī/, tell them the guide word for that spelling (*i*, as in *hi*; *ie,* as in *pie*; *y*, as in *fly*; *igh*, as in *light*; *i-e*, as in *kite*).

Try It

Investigator

Have students complete page PH 49 in *K¹² PhonicsWorks Advanced Activity Book* for more practice with spellings for the sound /ī/. Have students read each word aloud going down each column, and then read each word again going across each row. Have them read the questions and circle the answers.

> **Try It**
> Introduce Spellings for Sound /ī/
> **Investigator**
>
> Read down each column, and then read across each row.
>
> | i-e | igh | i | y | ie |
> |------|----------|--------|-----|-----|
> | dine | sigh | hi | fly | tie |
> | hive | light | wild | cry | pie |
> | prize | sight | child | shy | die |
> | size | night | mild | try | lie |
> | kite | might | kind | dry | fie |
> | pile | fight | find | fry | |
> | line | fright | mind | spy | |
> | bike | lightning | behind | why | |
> | spike | right | title | my | |
>
> Circle the answer.
>
> 1. What letter usually follows *igh*?   (t)   b
> 2. Where is *y* in these words?   middle   (end)
> 3. Where is *ie* in these words?   middle   (end)
>
> LANGUAGE ARTS GREEN   **PH 49**

Objectives

- Identify and use the sound /ī/.
- Identify the letters, given the sound /ī/.
- Identify and use /ī/ spelling patterns.
- Identify and use silent *e*.

[Online] ⑮ minutes

REVIEW: Spellings for Sound /ī/

Students will work online independently to

▶ Practice spellings for the sound /ī/.

▶ Practice decoding text by reading a story.

Help students locate the online activities and provide support as needed.

Offline Alternative

No computer access? Have students spell words that have the spellings *i*, *ie*, *y*, *igh*, and *i-e* for the sound /ī/, such as *mind*, *tie*, *by*, *bright*, and *dime*.

Practice Spellings for Sound /ī/ (A)

Lesson Overview

Offline	FOCUS: Practice Spellings for Sound /ī/	15 minutes

Sight Words	Use Words in Sentences
Practice	Word Chains
Try It	"Marge's Plane Ride"

Online	REVIEW: Spellings for Sound /ī/	15 minutes

Materials

Supplied
- *K¹² PhonicsWorks Readers Advanced 9*, pp. 7–12
- whiteboard, student
- Tile Kit

Also Needed
- sight words box

[Offline] 🕐 minutes

FOCUS: Practice Spellings for Sound /ī/

Work **together** with students to complete offline Sight Words, Practice, and Try It activities.

Sight Words ....

Use Words in Sentences

Help students use sight words in sentences.

1. Gather all the sight word cards students have yet to master from their sight words box. Spread the sight word cards on the table.

2. **Say:** Let's use sight words in sentences.

3. Have students

   ▸ Touch each card and read the word on it.
   ▸ Make up a sentence using the word.
   ▸ Put the card in a pile after using the word in a sentence.
   ▸ Go through the pile of cards and read each sight word again.
   ▸ Spell each word.

TIP If students have difficulty with any of the sight words, place those cards in a pile to review again.

> **Objectives**
> • Read sight words.
> • Spell sight words.

Practice

Word Chains

Have students build words by adding and changing letters to help them recognize and use the spellings *i*, *ie*, *y*, *igh*, and *i-e* for the sound /ī/.

1. Place the following letter tiles at the top of students' whiteboard: *a, b, c, d, e, f, h, i, ie, igh, k, l, m, n, p, r, s, t,* and *y.*

2. **Say:** You will spell words in several short word chains today. There will be one chain for each of the spellings of the sound /ī/ that you know. How many spellings do you know for the sound /ī/? five

3. **Say:** I'll do the first word. The word is *cry.*

   ▶ I will pull down the letters for the sounds /k/, /r/, and /ī/ to spell the word *cry.*

   ▶ I will touch and say *cry.* To change *cry* to *try,* I will think about which sound is changed from the word *cry* to *try.* I will need to replace the letter *c* with the letter *t.*

   ▶ Touch and say the word *try.* Now it's your turn to change *try* to *dry.* You can spell *dry* by making only one change. Touch and say the new word.

4. Redirect students if they select the incorrect letter for any sound.

   Say: That letter is for the sound [incorrect sound]. We want the letter for the sound [target sound]. What letter makes that sound? Answers will vary.

5. Redirect students if they name the sound incorrectly.

   Say: To change the word [first word] to [target word], we need the letter for the sound [target sound].

   Show students how to make the change. Have them touch and say the new word after they move the letters.

6. Follow this procedure to make the following groups of word chains:

   ▶ *lie, tie, pie, die*
   ▶ *kind, mind, rind, find, bind,*
   ▶ *bright, right, light, fight, sight, sigh*
   ▶ *hike, bike, like, lake, take, tame, time, lime, lame, blame*

7. For every new word, have students add, replace, or remove only one letter tile. Remind students that in these word chains only one sound—and only one letter tile—will change when the word changes.

TIP If students cannot remember one or more of the spellings for the sound /ī/, give them the guide word for that spelling (*i,* as in *hi; ie,* as in *pie; y,* as in *fly; igh,* as in *light; i-e,* as in *kite*).

Objectives

- Identify the new word when one sound is changed in a word.
- Identify individual sounds in words.
- Identify and use the sound /ī/.
- Identify the letters, given the sound /ī/.
- Identify and use /ī/ spelling patterns.
- Identify and use silent *e.*

Try It •

"Marge's Plane Ride"

Have students read "Marge's Plane Ride" on page 7 of *K¹² PhonicsWorks Readers Advanced 9*.

Students should read the story silently once or twice before reading the story aloud. When students miss a word that can be sounded out, point to it and give them three to six seconds to try the word again. If students still miss the word, tell them the word so the flow of the story isn't interrupted.

After reading the story, make a list of all the words students missed, and go over those words with them. You may use letter tiles to show students how to read the words.

 **15 minutes**

REVIEW: Spellings for Sound /ī/

Students will work online independently to

▸ Practice spellings for the sound /ī/.

Help students locate the online activities and provide support as needed.

Offline Alternative

No computer access? Have students spell words that have the spellings *i*, *ie*, *y*, *igh*, and *i-e* for the sound /ī/, such as *hi*, *lie*, *dry*, *sight*, and *hide*.

Practice Spellings for Sound /ī/ (B)

Lesson Overview

Offline **FOCUS:** Practice Spellings for Sound /ī/ — **15** minutes

Sight Words	Sight Word Concentration
Practice	Word Chains
Try It	Finish the Job

Online **REVIEW:** Spellings for Sound /ī/ — **15** minutes

Materials

Supplied
- *K¹² PhonicsWorks Advanced Activity Book*, p. PH 50
- whiteboard, student
- Tile Kit

Also Needed
- sight words box

Advance Preparation

Gather two sets of the sight word cards that students have yet to master.

[Offline] 🕒 15 minutes

FOCUS: Practice Spellings for Sound /ī/

Work **together** with students to complete offline Sight Words, Practice, and Try It activities.

Sight Words ●

Sight Word Concentration

Help students review sight words.

1. Gather the two sets of sight word cards.

2. Scramble both sets of sight word cards and place them face down on the table or floor.

3. Turn over two cards at a time; take turns with students. If the cards match, the person turning over the matching cards reads the word and uses it in a sentence. If the cards don't match, the person turns them back over.

4. Remove and save the matching cards.

5. Continue the activity until all the cards are paired.

6. Have students read all the words.

7. Take the stack of words that students read correctly and dictate each word to them.

8. Have students write each word or spell it aloud.

TIP If students have difficulty with any sight words, let them work at their own pace to really master these words.

> **Objectives**
> - Read sight words.
> - Spell sight words.
> - Write sight words.

Practice ●

Word Chains

Have students build words by adding and changing letters to help them recognize and use the spellings *i*, *ie*, *y*, *igh*, and *i-e* for the sound /ī/.

1. Place the following letter tiles at the top of students' whiteboard: *c, ch, d, e, f, h, i, ie, igh, k, l, m, n, p, r, s, sh, t, w,* and *y*.

2. **Say:** You will spell words in several short word chains today. There will be one chain for each of the spellings of the sound /ī/ that you know. How many spellings do you know for the sound /ī/? five

> **Objectives**
> - Identify and use the sound /ī/.
> - Identify the letters, given the sound /ī/.
> - Identify and use /ī/ spelling patterns.
> - Identify and use silent *e*.

3. **Say:** I'll do the first word. The word is *high*.

   ▸ I will pull down the letters for the sounds /h/ and /ī/ to spell the word *high*.

   ▸ I will touch and say *high*. To change *high* to *sigh*, I will think about which sound is changed from the word *high* to *sigh*. I will need to replace the letter *h* with the letter *s*.

   ▸ Touch and say the word *sigh*. Now it's your turn to change *sigh* to *sight*. You can spell *sight* by making only one change. Touch and say the new word.

4. Redirect students if they select the incorrect letter for any sound.

   Say: That letter is for the sound [incorrect sound]. We want the letter for the sound [target sound]. What letter makes that sound? Answers will vary.

5. Redirect students if they name the sound incorrectly.

   Say: To change the word [first word] to [target word], we need the letter for the sound [target sound].

   Show students how to make the change. Have them touch and say the new word after they move the letters.

6. Follow this procedure to make the following groups of word chains:

   ▸ *spy, sky, sly, fly*
   ▸ *kind, mind, mild, wild, child*
   ▸ *mine, pine, shine, line*
   ▸ *cried, tried, tied, lied*

7. For every new word, have students add, replace, or remove only one letter tile. Remind students that in these word chains only one sound—and only one letter tile—will change when the word changes.

TIP If students cannot remember one or more of the spellings for the sound /ī/, give them the guide word for that spelling (*i*, as in *hi*; *ie*, as in *pie*; *y*, as in *fly*; *igh*, as in *light*; *i-e*, as in *kite*).

Try It

Finish the Job

Have students complete page PH 50 in *K¹² PhonicsWorks Advanced Activity Book* for more practice with the spellings for the sound /ī/. Have students read each sentence aloud, choose a word from the box, and write the word that best completes each sentence. Have them read the new sentences aloud.

Try It
Practice Spellings for Sound /ī/ (B)
Finish the Job

Choose a word from the box to complete the sentence.
Write the word. Read the sentence aloud.

bright	fight	child
sight	might	sign

1. The ___sign___ said, "Stop."

2. A sunrise is a splendid ___sight___.

3. Why did the cats begin to ___fight___?

4. Let's get away from the ___bright___ lights.

5. The nice ___child___ has gone to help.

6. Mom ___might___ bake a pie tonight.

PH 50 LANGUAGE ARTS GREEN

Objectives

- Read aloud grade-level text with appropriate automaticity, prosody, accuracy, and rate.
- Write words by applying grade-level phonics knowledge.
- Identify complete sentences.
- Identify and use the sound /ī/.
- Identify the letters, given the sound /ī/.
- Identify and use /ī/ spelling patterns.
- Identify and use silent *e*.

⟦ Online ⟧ 🔟 minutes

REVIEW: Spellings for Sound /ī/

Students will work online independently to

▶ Practice spellings for the sound /ī/.
▶ Practice decoding text by reading a story.

Help students locate the online activities and provide support as needed.

Offline Alternative

No computer access? Have students spell words that have the spellings *i*, *ie*, *y*, *igh*, and *i-e* for the sound /ī/, such as *child*, *pie*, *sky*, *right*, and *pine*.

Objectives

- Identify and use the sound /ī/.
- Identify the letters, given the sound /ī/.
- Identify and use /ī/ spelling patterns.
- Identify and use silent *e*.
- Read aloud grade-level text with appropriate automaticity, prosody, accuracy, and rate.
- Decode words by applying grade-level word analysis skills.

Practice Spellings for Sound /ī/ (C)

Lesson Overview

[Offline] **FOCUS:** Practice Spellings for Sound /ī/ — **15** minutes

Sight Words	Pick a Pair
Practice	Sort Spellings for Sound /ī/
Try It	"Bess and Jess"
	Dictation: Write Sentences

[Online] **REVIEW:** Spellings for Sound /ī/ — **15** minutes

Materials

Supplied
- *K¹² PhonicsWorks Readers Advanced 9*, pp. 13–18
- whiteboard, Learning Coach
- Tile Kit

Also Needed
- sight words box
- dictation notebook
- index cards (15)

Advance Preparation

For Sort Spellings for Sound /ī/, print each of the following words on index cards, using one card per word: *hi, iris, pie, tied, vied, fly, sky, spry, high, night, sight, right, bike, dime,* and *glide.*

⟦ Offline ⟧ ⑮ minutes

FOCUS: Practice Spellings for Sound /ī/

Work **together** with students to complete offline Sight Words, Practice, and Try It activities.

Sight Words ···

Pick a Pair

Play a card game with students for more practice with sight words.

1. Gather the sight word cards that students are reviewing. Choose two words and place the cards on the table.

2. Ask questions to help students identify each word. For example, if the words are *or* and *one*, you could ask, "Which word names a number?" If the words are *on* and *but*, you could ask, "Which word is the opposite of *off*?"

3. Continue the activity until students identify all the words.

4. Take the stack of words that students read correctly and dictate each word to them.

5. Have students write each word or spell it aloud.

Objectives
- Read sight words.
- Spell sight words.
- Write sight words.

Practice ··

Sort Spellings for Sound /ī/

Help students practice identifying words that have the spellings *i, ie, y, igh,* and *i-e* for the sound /ī/.

1. Gather the index cards you prepared. Mix the cards well and place them in a stack face down on the table.

2. Gather the dictation notebook. Draw five columns and label them *i, ie, y, igh,* and *i-e* to represent the five different ways to spell the sound /ī/.

3. **Say:** You are going to sort words by the five spellings for the sound /ī/. You will take a card from the pile and read it to me. Then you will think about the spelling for the sound /ī/ in the word and write that word in the correct column. I'll do the first one for you.

Objectives
- Identify individual sounds in words.
- Identify and use the sound /ī/.
- Identify the letters, given the sound /ī/.
- Identify and use /ī/ spelling patterns.
- Identify and use silent *e*.

4. Demonstrate the following for students:

 ► Draw a card from the pile.
 ► Read the word aloud.
 ► Write the word in the correct column for the spelling for the sound /ī/.

5. Have students continue the procedure with the remaining words:

 ► **Spelling *i* words:** *hi, iris*
 ► **Spelling *ie* words:** *pie, tied, vied*
 ► **Spelling *y* words:** *fly, sky, spry*
 ► **Spelling *igh* words:** *high, night, sight, right*
 ► **Spelling *i-e* words:** *bike, dime, glide*

Try It

"Bess and Jess"

Have students read "Bess and Jess" on page 13 of *K¹² PhonicsWorks Readers Advanced 9*.

Students should read the story silently once or twice before reading the story aloud. When students miss a word that can be sounded out, point to it and give them three to six seconds to try the word again. If students still miss the word, tell them the word so the flow of the story isn't interrupted.

After reading the story, make a list of all the words students missed, and go over those words with them. You may use letter tiles to show students how to read the words.

Dictation: Write Sentences

Use sentences to help students identify individual sounds in words.

1. Gather a pencil and the dictation notebook. Say the sentence, *I went on a hike.* Then give these directions to students:

 ► Repeat the sentence.
 ► Write the sentence in your notebook.
 ► Read the sentence aloud.

2. When students have finished, write the following sentence on your whiteboard: *I went on a hike.*

3. Have them compare their answer to your correct version.

4. Repeat this procedure with the following sentences: *Did you get it right? Tom is kind. My bike is wet. Mom likes pie.*

 ► If students make an error and don't see it, help them correct their mistake by having them finger stretch the sounds in the word they missed.
 ► If students are having difficulty selecting the correct letters or sounds, review those letters or sounds that are confusing them.
 ► If students have difficulty with first, middle, and last sounds, have them finger stretch the sounds in words.

Objectives

• Read aloud grade-level text with appropriate automaticity, prosody, accuracy, and rate.
• Decode words by applying grade-level word analysis skills.
• Write words by applying grade-level phonics knowledge.
• Follow three-step directions.

 **15 minutes**

REVIEW: **Spellings for Sound /ī/**

Students will work online independently to

▶ Practice spellings for the sound /ī/.

Help students locate the online activities and provide support as needed.

Offline Alternative

No computer access? Have students spell words that have the spellings *i*, *ie*, *y*, *igh*, and *i-e* for the sound /ī/, such as *mild*, *lied*, *fry*, *night*, and *ripe*.

Objectives
- Identify individual sounds in words.
- Identify and use the sound /ī/.
- Identify the letters, given the sound /ī/.
- Identify and use /ī/ spelling patterns.
- Identify and use silent *e*.

Unit Checkpoint

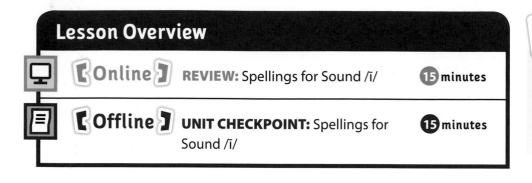

Lesson Overview

[Online] **REVIEW:** Spellings for Sound /ī/ — **15** minutes

[Offline] **UNIT CHECKPOINT:** Spellings for Sound /ī/ — **15** minutes

Materials

Supplied

- *K¹² PhonicsWorks Advanced Assessments,* pp. PH 145–150

Objectives

- Identify individual sounds in words.
- Identify and use the sound /ī/.
- Identify the letters, given the sound /ī/.
- Identify and use /ī/ spelling patterns.
- Identify and use silent *e*.
- Read instructional-level text with 90% accuracy.
- Read aloud grade-level text with appropriate automaticity, prosody, accuracy, and rate.
- Write words by applying grade-level phonics knowledge.
- Write sight words.
- Read sight words.

[Online] **15** minutes

REVIEW: Spellings for Sound /ī/

Students will review spellings for the sound /ī/ to prepare for the Unit Checkpoint. Help students locate the online activities and provide support as needed.

[Offline] 🕔 minutes

UNIT CHECKPOINT: Spellings for Sound /ī/

Explain that students are going to show what they have learned about sounds, letters, and words.

1. Give students the Unit Checkpoint pages for the Spellings for Sound /ī/ unit and print the Unit Checkpoint Answer Key, if you'd like.

2. Use the instructions below to help administer the Checkpoint to students. On the Answer Key or another sheet of paper, note student answers to oral response questions to help with scoring the Checkpoint later.

3. Use the Answer Key to score the Checkpoint, and then enter the results online.

Part 1. Circle Words with Sound /ī/ Have students circle the words with the sound /ī/.

Part 2. Many Spellings, One Sound Have students circle the five ways to spell the sound /ī/.

Part 3. Read Sight Words Have students read each sight word aloud. Note any words they read incorrectly.

Part 4. Writing Read each sentence to students. Have them repeat and write the sentence.

25. *It is five miles to Sky Light Lake.*

26. *The child has nine stamps.*

27. *Will you tie the ribbon for me?*

Part 5. Read Aloud Listen to students read the sentences aloud. Count and note the number of words they read correctly.

Part 6. Read Nonsense Words Have students read each nonsense word aloud. Note any words they read incorrectly.

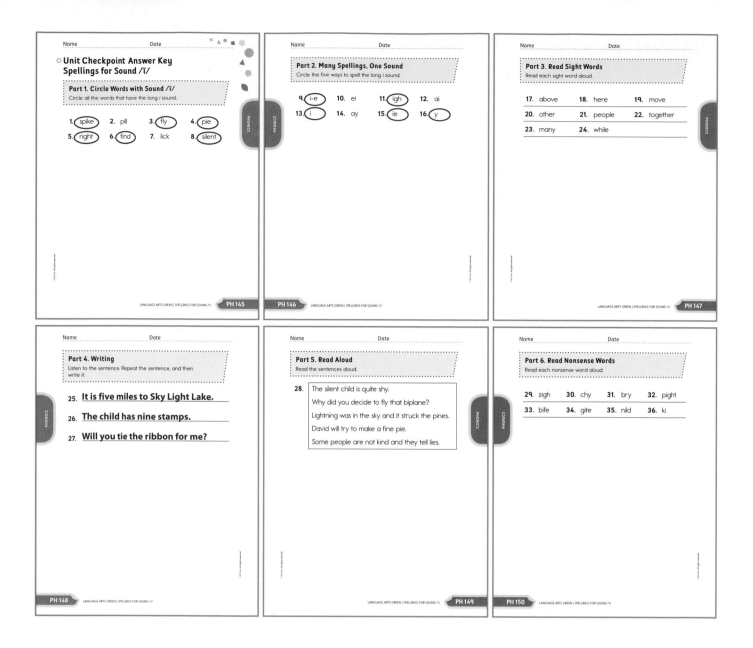

Name _____ **Date** _____

○ Unit Checkpoint Answer Key
Spellings for Sound /ī/

Part 1. Circle Words with Sound /ī/
Circle all the words that have the long i sound.

1. (spike) 2. pill 3. (fly) 4. (pie)
5. (right) 6. (find) 7. lick 8. (silent)

Name _____ **Date** _____

Part 2. Many Spellings, One Sound
Circle the five ways to spell the long i sound.

9. (i-e) 10. ei 11. (igh) 12. ai
13. (i) 14. ay 15. (ie) 16. (y)

Name _____ **Date** _____

Part 3. Read Sight Words
Read each sight word aloud.

17. above 18. here 19. move
20. other 21. people 22. together
23. many 24. while

Name _____ **Date** _____

Part 4. Writing
Listen to the sentence. Repeat the sentence, and then write it.

25. **It is five miles to Sky Light Lake.**
26. **The child has nine stamps.**
27. **Will you tie the ribbon for me?**

Name _____ **Date** _____

Part 5. Read Aloud
Read the sentences aloud.

28.
> The silent child is quite shy.
> Why did you decide to fly that biplane?
> Lightning was in the sky and it struck the pines.
> David will try to make a fine pie.
> Some people are not kind and they tell lies.

Name _____ **Date** _____

Part 6. Read Nonsense Words
Read each nonsense word aloud.

29. zigh 30. chy 31. bry 32. pight
33. bife 34. gite 35. nild 36. ki

Introduce Spellings for Sound /ō/

Unit Overview

In this unit, students will

- Learn the sight words *these*, *against*, and *now*.
- Learn the spellings *o*, *oa*, *ow*, *oe*, and *o-e* for the sound /ō/.
- Read and write sentences.
- Read a story silently and aloud.

Lesson Overview

[Offline] FOCUS: Introduce Spellings for Sound /ō/		**15** minutes
Sight Words	Introduce Sight Words	
Learn	Introduce Spellings for Sound /ō/	
	Review Spellings for Sound /ō/	
Try It	Investigator	
[Online] REVIEW: Spellings for Sound /ō/		**15** minutes

[Offline] 🕒 15 minutes

FOCUS: Introduce Spellings for Sound /ō/

Work **together** with students to complete offline Sight Words, Learn, and Try It activities.

Sight Words •

Introduce Sight Words

Help students learn the sight words *these*, *against*, and *now*.

1. Gather the sight word cards *these*, *against*, and *now*.

2. Show students the *these* card.

3. **Say:** This is the word *these*. We see this word so often that we want to be able to read and spell it quickly without thinking about it. Look closely at the word *these*. Spell the word *these* aloud. Take a picture of the word *these* in your mind. When you think you can spell *these* yourself, turn the card over and use your letter tiles to spell the word *these*. Check the card to see if you spelled the word *these* correctly. Read aloud the word you spelled with the letter tiles.

4. Repeat the activity with the remaining sight words.

5. Chart students' progress on the back of each card.

   ▶ Divide the back of the card into two columns.
   ▶ Label the first column "Read" and the second column "Spell."
   ▶ Record the dates that students read or spell the word correctly. When students can read and spell the word correctly three times in a row, they have mastered the word. You may want to put a star or sticker on their card when they have mastered that word.

6. Add the cards to students' sight words box.

TIP Sight words can be very difficult for some students. Let students work at their own pace and really master these words, as they occur frequently in reading and writing.

Objectives
- Read sight words.
- Spell sight words.

Learn ••

Introduce Spellings for Sound /ō/

Help students learn the spellings *o*, *oa*, *ow*, *oe*, and *o-e* for the sound /ō/.

1. Place the following letter tiles on students' whiteboard: *b*, *e*, *g*, *h*, *m*, *n*, *o*, *oa*, *oe*, *ow*, *s*, and *t*.

2. Make the word *home* in the middle of students' whiteboard and point to it.

   Say: Today we are going to learn the five spellings for the sound /ō/. You already know one of them. Sometimes the long *o* sound is made by the letter *o* and a silent *e*, separated by a consonant. Let's touch and say the word *home*.

3. Make the word *go* and point to it.

   Say: Now let's look at the next word. This is the word *go*. In the word *go*, the long *o* sound is made by the letter *o* all by itself.

   ▸ Touch and say *go*.
   ▸ Where is the sound /ō/ in this word? end
   ▸ Which letter or letters make this sound? *o*

4. Make the word *boat* and point to it.

   Say: This word is *boat*. In the word *boat*, the long *o* sound is made by the letters *oa*.

   ▸ Touch and say *boat*.
   ▸ Where is the sound /ō/ in this word? middle
   ▸ Which letter or letters make this sound? *oa*

5. Make the word *snow* and point to it.

   Say: This word is *snow*. In the word *snow*, the long *o* sound is made by the letters *ow*.

   ▸ Touch and say *snow*.
   ▸ Where is the sound /ō/ in this word? end
   ▸ Which letter or letters make this sound? *ow*

6. Make the word *toe* and point to it.

   Say: The last word is *toe*. In the word *toe*, the long *o* sound is made by the letters *oe*.

   ▸ Touch and say *toe*.
   ▸ Where is the sound /ō/ in this word? end
   ▸ Which letter or letters make this sound? *oe*

TIP Refer to the *K¹² PhonicsWorks* video for a demonstration of how to teach different spellings for long vowel sounds.

Objectives
- Identify individual sounds in words.
- Identify and use the sound /ō/.
- Identify the letters, given the sound /ō/.
- Identify and use /ō/ spelling patterns.
- Identify and use *ow* for the sound /ō/.
- Identify and use silent *e*.
- Write words by applying grade-level phonics knowledge.

Review Spellings for Sound /ō/

Help students review the spellings *o, oa, ow, oe,* and *o-e* for the sound /ō/.

1. Gather the dictation notebook and pencil.

2. Place the following letter tiles at the top of students' whiteboard: *o, oa, ow, oe,* and *o-e.*

3. Write the following words on your whiteboard: *go, boat, snow, toe,* and *home.*

4. **Say:** Count the number of ways there are to spell the long vowel sound /ō/.

   ▸ Touch and say the spellings for sound /ō/. *o, oa, ow, oe, o-e*
   ▸ Look at the words on the board and read them.
   ▸ Say how the sound is spelled in each word. *o* in *go, oa* in *boat, ow* in *snow, oe* in *toe, o-e* in *home*
   ▸ Take a picture in your mind of the five ways of spelling the sound /ō/.

5. **Say:** I am going to hide the words and the spellings on the board. Your job is to remember each way of spelling the sound /ō/ and write the spellings in your notebook.

6. After students have finished writing the spellings in their notebook, have them check their answers against the spellings on the board.

TIP If students cannot remember one or more of the spellings for the sound /ō/, tell them the guide word for that spelling (*o,* as in *go; oa,* as in *boat; ow,* as in *snow; oe,* as in *toe; o-e,* as in *home*).

Try It

Investigator

Have students complete page PH 51 in *K¹² PhonicsWorks Advanced Activity Book* for more practice with spellings for the sound /ō/. Have students read each word aloud going down each column, and then read each word again going across each row. Have them read the questions and circle the answers.

Objectives

- Identify and use the sound /ō/.
- Identify the letters, given the sound /ō/.
- Identify and use /ō/ spelling patterns.
- Identify and use *ow* for the sound /ō/.
- Identify and use silent *e.*

Try It

Introduce Spellings for Sound /ō/

Investigator

Read down each column, and then read across each row.

o–e	oa	ow	oe	o
home	boat	row	toe	go
joke	float	tow	doe	so
rope	boast	snow	hoe	both
scope	coal	grow	woe	old
stone	croak	show	oboe	fold
pole	road	flow	foe	cold
alone	goat	bow		most
phone	throat	glow		sold
cone	soak	slow		told

Circle the answer.

1. Where is *ow* in these words?   middle   (end)

2. Where is *oa* in these words?   (middle)   end

⌈Online⌉ ⑮ minutes

REVIEW: Spellings for Sound /ō/

Students will work online independently to

▶ Practice spellings for the sound /ō/.
▶ Practice decoding text by reading a story.

Help students locate the online activities and provide support as needed.

Offline Alternative

No computer access? Have students spell words that have the spellings *o*, *oa*, *ow*, *oe*, and *o-e* for the sound /ō/, such as *no*, *load*, *tow*, *roe*, and *robe*.

Objectives

- Identify and use the sound /ō/.
- Identify the letters, given the sound /ō/.
- Identify and use /ō/ spelling patterns.
- Identify and use *ow* for the sound /ō/.
- Identify and use silent *e*.
- Read aloud grade-level text with appropriate automaticity, prosody, accuracy, and rate.
- Decode words by applying grade-level word analysis skills.

Practice Spellings for Sound /ō/ (A)

Lesson Overview

[Offline] **FOCUS:** Practice Spellings for Sound /ō/   **15** minutes

Sight Words	Sight Word Fun
Practice	Word Chains
Try It	"Bo the Goat"

[Online] **REVIEW:** Spellings for Sound /ō/   **15** minutes

Materials

Supplied
- *K¹² PhonicsWorks Readers Advanced 9*, pp. 19–25
- whiteboard, student
- Tile Kit

Also Needed
- sight words box

⟦ Offline ⟧ ⑮ minutes

FOCUS: Practice Spellings for Sound /ō/

Work **together** with students to complete offline Sight Words, Practice, and Try It activities.

Sight Words •

Sight Word Fun

Help students learn the sight words *these, against,* and *now,* and up to two additional sight words they have yet to master.

1. Gather the sight word cards *these, against,* and *now,* and up to two additional sight word cards.

2. Choose one sight word card to begin.

   Say: Look at this word and take a picture of it in your mind. When you think you can spell the word yourself, turn the card over and use your letter tiles to spell the word.

3. After students spell the word, have them check the card to see if they spelled the word correctly.

   Say: Read aloud the word you spelled with the letter tiles.

4. Repeat the activity with the remaining sight words.

TIP Sight words can be very difficult for some students. Let them work at their own pace and really master these words.

Practice

Word Chains

Have students build words by adding and changing letters to help them recognize and use the spellings *o, oa, ow, oe,* and *o-e* for the sound /ō/.

1. Place the following letter tiles at the top of students' whiteboard: *b, c, d, e, f, g, h, l, m, n, o, oa, oe, ow, p, ph, r, s, sh, t,* and *th.*

2. **Say:** You will spell words in several short word chains today. There will be one chain for each of the spellings of the sound /ō/ that you know. How many spellings do you know for the sound /ō/? five

3. **Say:** I'll do the first word. The word is *float.*

   ▸ I will pull down the letters for the sounds /f/, /l/, /ō/, and /t/ to spell the word *float.*

   ▸ I will touch and say *float.* To change *float* to *bloat,* I will think about which sound is changed from the word *float* to *bloat.* I will need to replace the letter *f* with the letter *b.*

   ▸ Touch and say the word *bloat.* Now it's your turn to change *bloat* to *boat.* You can spell *boat* by making only one change. Touch and say the new word.

4. Redirect students if they select the incorrect letter for any sound.

   Say: That letter is for the sound [incorrect sound]. We want the letter for the sound [target sound]. What letter makes that sound? Answers will vary.

5. Redirect students if they name the sound incorrectly.

   Say: To change the word [first word] to [target word], we need the letter for the sound [target sound].

   Show students how to make the change. Have them touch and say the new word after they move the letters.

6. Follow this procedure to make the following groups of word chains:

   ▸ *boat, goat, goal*
   ▸ *toe, doe, foe, hoe*
   ▸ *post, most, molt, bolt, bold, cold, mold, sold*
   ▸ *show, row, throw, grow*
   ▸ *lone, bone, phone, cone, code, rode, mode*

7. For every new word, have students add, replace, or remove only one letter tile. Remind students that in these word chains only one sound—and only one letter tile—will change when the word changes.

TIP If students cannot remember one or more spellings, give them the guide word for that spelling (*o,* as in *go; oa,* as in *boat; ow,* as in *snow; oe,* as in *toe; o-e,* as in *home*).

Objectives

- Identify the new word when one sound is changed in a word.
- Identify individual sounds in words.
- Identify and use the sound /ō/.
- Identify the letters, given the sound /ō/.
- Identify and use /ō/ spelling patterns.
- Identify and use *ow* for the sound /ō/.
- Identify and use silent *e.*

"Bo the Goat"

Have students read "Bo the Goat" on page 19 of *K¹² PhonicsWorks Readers Advanced 9*.

Students should read the story silently once or twice before reading the story aloud. When students miss a word that can be sounded out, point to it and give them three to six seconds to try the word again. If students still miss the word, tell them the word so the flow of the story isn't interrupted.

After reading the story, make a list of all the words students missed, and go over those words with them. You may use letter tiles to show students how to read the words.

 **15 minutes**

REVIEW: Spellings for Sound /ō/

Students will work online independently to

▶ Practice spellings for the sound /ō/.

Help students locate the online activities and provide support as needed.

Offline Alternative

No computer access? Have students spell words that have the spellings *o, oa, ow, oe,* and *o-e* for the sound /ō/, such as *Mo, coal, grow, Joe,* and *hole*.

Objectives

- Read aloud grade-level text with appropriate automaticity, prosody, accuracy, and rate.
- Decode words by applying grade-level word analysis skills.

Objectives

- Identify individual sounds in words.
- Identify and use the sound /ō/.
- Identify the letters, given the sound /ō/.
- Identify and use /ō/. spelling patterns.
- Identify and use *ow* for the sound /ō/.
- Identify and use silent *e*.

Practice Spellings for Sound /ō/ (B)

Lesson Overview

[Offline] FOCUS: Practice Spellings for Sound /ō/		**15** minutes
Sight Words	Sight Word Fun	
Practice	Word Chains	
Try It	Tic Tac Toe	
[Online] REVIEW: Spellings for Sound /ō/		**15** minutes

Materials

Supplied
- *K¹² PhonicsWorks Advanced Activity Book*, p. PH 52
- whiteboard, student
- Tile Kit

Also Needed
- sight words box
- crayons

[Offline] 🕒 15 minutes

FOCUS: Practice Spellings for Sound /ō/

Work **together** with students to complete offline Sight Words, Practice, and Try It activities.

Sight Words ···

Sight Word Fun

Help students learn the sight words *these, against,* and *now,* and up to two additional sight words they have yet to master.

1. Gather the sight word cards *these, against,* and *now,* and up to two additional sight word cards.

2. Choose one sight word card to begin.

   Say: Look at this word and take a picture of it in your mind. When you think you can spell the word yourself, turn the card over and use your letter tiles to spell the word.

3. After students spell the word, have them check the card to see if they spelled the word correctly.

   Say: Read aloud the word you spelled with the letter tiles.

4. Repeat the activity with the remaining sight words.

TIP Sight words can be very difficult for some students. Let them work at their own pace and really master these words.

Objectives
• Read sight words.
• Spell sight words.

Practice

Word Chains

Have students build words by adding and changing letters to help them recognize and use the spellings *o, oa, ow, oe,* and *o-e* for the sound /ō/.

1. Place the following letter tiles at the top of students' whiteboard: *b, c, ch, d, e, f, g, h, i, J, l, l, m, o, oa, oe, ow, r, s, t,* and *y.*

2. **Say:** You will spell words in several short word chains today. There will be one chain for each of the spellings of the sound /ō/ that you know. How many spellings do you know for the sound /ō/? five

3. **Say:** I'll do the first word. The word is *cold.*

   ▸ I will pull down the letters for the sounds /k/, /ō/, /l/, and /d/ to spell the word *cold.*

   ▸ I will touch and say *cold.* To change *cold* to *sold,* I will think about which sound is changed from the word *cold* to *sold.* I will need to replace the letter *c* with the letter *s.*

   ▸ Touch and say the word *sold.* Now it's your turn to change *sold* to *gold.* You can spell *gold* by making only one change. Touch and say the new word.

4. Redirect students if they select the incorrect letter for any sound.

   Say: That letter is for the sound [incorrect sound]. We want the letter for the sound [target sound]. What letter makes that sound? Answers will vary.

5. Redirect students if they name the sound incorrectly.

   Say: To change the word [first word] to [target word], we need the letter for the sound [target sound].

   Show students how to make the change. Have them touch and say the new word after they move the letters.

6. Follow this procedure to make the following groups of word chains:

   ▸ *gold, bold, fold, mold, mild, child*
   ▸ *hollow, follow, fellow, yellow*
   ▸ *boat, goat, moat, coat, coach, roach, roam, road, load*
   ▸ *tore, store, sore, chore, more*
   ▸ *Joe, foe, doe, hoe*

7. For every new word, have students add, replace, or remove only one letter tile. Remind students that in these word chains only one sound—and only one letter tile—will change when the word changes.

TIP If students cannot remember one or more spellings, give them the guide word for that spelling (*o,* as in *go; oa,* as in *boat; ow,* as in *snow; oe,* as in *toe; o-e,* as in *home*).

Objectives

- Identify the new word when one sound is changed in a word.
- Identify individual sounds in words.
- Identify and use the sound /ō/.
- Identify the letters, given the sound /ō/.
- Identify and use /ō/ spelling patterns.
- Identify and use *ow* for the sound /ō/.
- Identify and use silent *e.*

Try It

Tic Tac Toe

Have students complete page PH 52 in *K¹² PhonicsWorks Advanced Activity Book* for more practice with spellings for the sound /ō/. Have students read each word aloud, find the five words in a row that rhyme, and color those boxes. Remind students that the row can be across, down, or diagonal.

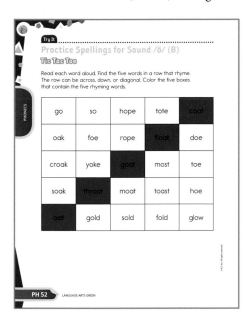

Objectives

- Identify and use the sound /ō/.
- Identify the letters, given the sound /ō/.
- Identify and use /ō/ spelling patterns.
- Identify and use *ow* for the sound /ō/.
- Identify and use silent *e*.
- Read aloud grade-level text with appropriate automaticity, prosody, accuracy, and rate.
- Decode words by applying grade-level word analysis skills.

[Online] 15 minutes

REVIEW: Spellings for Sound /ō/

Students will work online independently to

▶ Practice spellings for the sound /ō/.
▶ Practice decoding text by reading a story.

Help students locate the online activities and provide support as needed.

Offline Alternative

No computer access? Have students spell words that have the spellings *o*, *oa*, *ow*, *oe*, and *o-e* for the sound /ō/, such as *so*, *soak*, *mow*, *doe*, and *pole*.

Objectives

- Identify and use the sound /ō/.
- Identify the letters, given the sound /ō/.
- Identify and use /ō/ spelling patterns.
- Identify and use *ow* for the sound /ō/.
- Identify and use silent *e*.
- Read aloud grade-level text with appropriate automaticity, prosody, accuracy, and rate.
- Decode words by applying grade-level word analysis skills.

Practice Spellings for Sound /ō/ (C)

Lesson Overview

[Offline] FOCUS: Practice Spellings for Sound /ō/		**15** minutes

Sight Words	Sight Word Fun
Practice	Sort Spellings for Sound /ō/
Try It	"Joan Fishes with Her Father"
	Dictation: Write Sentences

[Online] REVIEW: Spellings for Sound /ō/   **15** minutes

Materials

Supplied
- *K¹² PhonicsWorks Readers Advanced 9*, pp. 26–31
- whiteboard, Learning Coach

Also Needed
- sight words box
- dictation notebook
- index cards (15)

Advance Preparation

For Sort Spellings for Sound /ō/, print each of the following words on index cards, using one card per word: *go, no, so, road, coat, croak, stow, slow, throw, toe, Joe, doe, bone, drove,* and *nose.*

[Offline] 🕐 minutes

FOCUS: Practice Spellings for Sound /ō/

Work **together** with students to complete offline Sight Words, Practice, and
Try It activities.

Sight Words ···

Sight Word Fun

Help students learn the sight words *these*, *against*, and *now*, and up to two additional
sight words they have yet to master.

1. Gather the sight word cards *these*, *against*, and *now*, and up to two additional
   sight word cards.

2. Choose one sight word card to begin.

   Say: Look at this word and take a picture of it in your mind. When you think
   you can spell the word yourself, turn the card over and use your letter tiles to
   spell the word.

3. After students spell the word, have them check the card to see if they spelled
   the word correctly.

   Say: Read aloud the word you spelled with the letter tiles.

4. Repeat the activity with the remaining sight words.

   TIP Sight words can be very difficult for some students. Let them work at their own
   pace and really master these words.

> **Objectives**
> - Read sight words.
> - Spell sight words.

Practice ··

Sort Spellings for Sound /ō/

Help students practice identifying words that have the spellings *o*, *oa*, *ow*, *oe*, and *o-e*
for the sound /ō/.

1. Gather the index cards you prepared. Mix the cards well and place them in a
   stack face down on the table.

2. Gather the dictation notebook. Draw five columns and label them *o*, *oa*, *ow*, *oe*,
   and *o-e* to represent the five different ways to spell the sound /ō/.

3. **Say:** You are going to sort words by the five spellings for the sound /ō/.
   You will take a card from the pile and read it to me. Then you will think
   about the spelling for the sound /ō/ in the word and write that word
   in the correct column. I'll do the first one for you.

> **Objectives**
> - Identify individual sounds
>   in words.
> - Identify and use the
>   sound /ō/.
> - Identify the letters, given the
>   sound /ō/.
> - Identify and use /ō/
>   spelling patterns.
> - Identify and use *ow* for the
>   sound /ō/.
> - Identify and use silent *e*.

4. Demonstrate the following for students:

- ► Draw a card from the pile.
- ► Read the word aloud.
- ► Write the word in the correct column for the spelling for the sound /ō/.

5. Have students continue the procedure with the remaining words:

- ► **Spelling *o* words:** *go, no, so*
- ► **Spelling *oa* words:** *road, coat, croak*
- ► **Spelling *ow* words:** *stow, slow, throw*
- ► **Spelling *oe* words:** *toe, Joe, doe*
- ► **Spelling *o-e* words:** *bone, drove, nose*

Try It

"Joan Fishes with Her Father"

Have students read "Joan Fishes with Her Father" on page 26 of *K¹² PhonicsWorks Readers Advanced 9*.

Students should read the story silently once or twice before reading the story aloud. When students miss a word that can be sounded out, point to it and give them three to six seconds to try the word again. If students still miss the word, tell them the word so the flow of the story isn't interrupted.

After reading the story, make a list of all the words students missed, and go over those words with them. You may use letter tiles to show students how to read the words.

Objectives

- Read aloud grade-level text with appropriate automaticity, prosody, accuracy, and rate.
- Decode words by applying grade-level word analysis skills.
- Write words by applying grade-level phonics knowledge.
- Follow three-step directions.

Dictation: Write Sentences

Use sentences to help students identify individual sounds in words.

1. Gather a pencil and the dictation notebook. Say the sentence, *Get the stone off my toe!* Then give these directions to students:

- ► Repeat the sentence.
- ► Write the sentence in your notebook.
- ► Read the sentence aloud.

2. When students have finished, write the following sentence on your whiteboard: *Get the stone off my toe!*

3. Have them compare their answer to your correct version.

4. Repeat this procedure with the following sentences: *Get the yellow coat. I like the snow. We will go in a rowboat.*

- ► If students make an error and don't see it, help them correct their mistake by having them finger stretch the sounds in the word they missed.
- ► If students are having difficulty selecting the correct letters or sounds, review those letters or sounds that are confusing them.
- ► If students have difficulty with first, middle, and last sounds, have them finger stretch the sounds in words.

[Online] ⑮ minutes

REVIEW: Spellings for Sound /ō/

Students will work online independently to

▶ Practice spellings for the sound /ō/.

Help students locate the online activities and provide support as needed.

Offline Alternative

No computer access? Have students spell words that have the spellings *o*, *oa*, *ow*, *oe*, and *o-e* for the sound /ō/, such as *go*, *toad*, *show*, *foe*, and *hope*.

Unit Checkpoint

Lesson Overview

🖥️	**〔Online〕**	**REVIEW:** Spellings for Sound /ō/	**15** minutes
📄	**〔Offline〕**	**UNIT CHECKPOINT:** Spellings for Sound /ō/	**15** minutes

〔 Materials 〕

Supplied
- *K¹² PhonicsWorks Advanced Assessments,* pp. PH 151–156

⭐ Objectives

- Identify individual sounds in words.
- Identify and use the sound /ō/.
- Identify the letters, given the sound /ō/.
- Identify and use /ō/ spelling patterns.
- Identify and use *ow* for the sound /ō/.
- Identify and use silent *e*.
- Read instructional-level text with 90% accuracy.
- Read aloud grade-level text with appropriate automaticity, prosody, accuracy, and rate.
- Write words by applying grade-level phonics knowledge.
- Write sight words.
- Read sight words.

〔Online〕 **15** minutes

REVIEW: Spellings for Sound /ō/

Students will review spellings for the sound /ō/ to prepare for the Unit Checkpoint. Help students locate the online activities and provide support as needed.

[Offline] ⑮ minutes

UNIT CHECKPOINT: Spellings for Sound /ō/

Explain that students are going to show what they have learned about sounds, letters, and words.

1. Give students the Unit Checkpoint pages for the Spellings for Sound /ō/ unit and print the Unit Checkpoint Answer Key, if you'd like.

2. Use the instructions below to help administer the Checkpoint to students. On the Answer Key or another sheet of paper, note student answers to oral response questions to help with scoring the Checkpoint later.

3. Use the Answer Key to score the Checkpoint, and then enter the results online.

Part 1. Circle Words with Sound /ō/ Have students circle the words with the sound /ō/.

Part 2. Many Spellings, One Sound Have students circle the five ways to spell the sound /ō/.

Part 3. Read Sight Words Have students read each sight word aloud. Note any words they read incorrectly.

Part 4. Writing Read each sentence to students. Have them repeat and write the sentence.

25. *Did Joe pet these goats?*

26. *The crows have a nest against the shed.*

27. *Can we go to Stone Cove now?*

Part 5. Read Aloud Listen to students read the sentences aloud. Count and note the number of words they read correctly.

Part 6. Read Nonsense Words Have students read each nonsense word aloud. Note any words they read incorrectly.

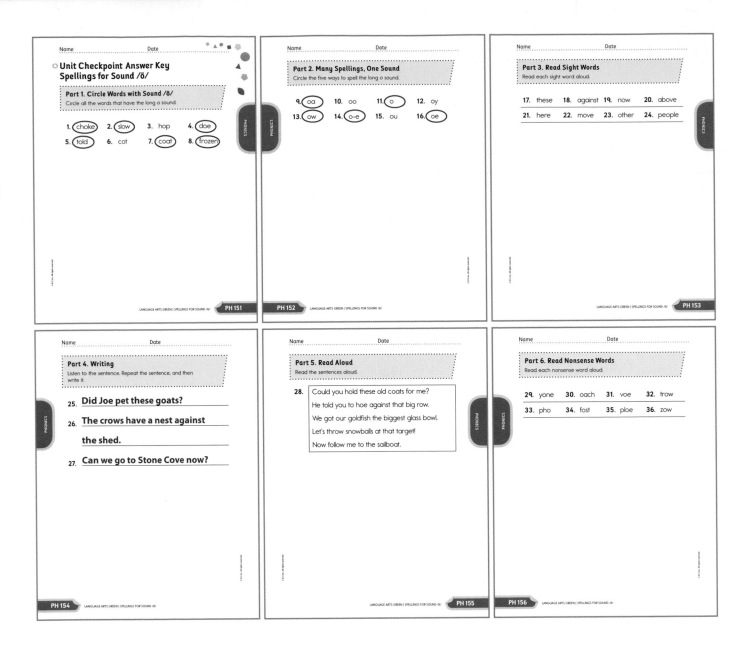

Name _____ Date _____

Unit Checkpoint Answer Key
Spellings for Sound /ō/

Part 1. Circle Words with Sound /ō/
Circle all the words that have the long o sound.

1. (choke) 2. (slow) 3. hop 4. (doe)
5. (told) 6. cot 7. (coat) 8. (frozen)

Name _____ Date _____

Part 2. Many Spellings, One Sound
Circle the five ways to spell the long o sound.

9. (oa) 10. oo 11. (o) 12. oy
13. (ow) 14. (o-e) 15. ou 16. (oe)

Name _____ Date _____

Part 3. Read Sight Words
Read each sight word aloud.

17. these 18. against 19. now 20. above
21. here 22. move 23. other 24. people

Name _____ Date _____

Part 4. Writing
Listen to the sentence. Repeat the sentence, and then write it.

25. **Did Joe pet these goats?**

26. **The crows have a nest against the shed.**

27. **Can we go to Stone Cove now?**

Name _____ Date _____

Part 5. Read Aloud
Read the sentences aloud.

28. Could you hold these old coats for me?
He told you to hoe against that big row.
We got our goldfish the biggest glass bowl.
Let's throw snowballs at that target!
Now follow me to the sailboat.

Name _____ Date _____

Part 6. Read Nonsense Words
Read each nonsense word aloud.

29. yone 30. oach 31. voe 32. trow
33. pho 34. fost 35. ploe 36. zow

Introduce Spellings for Sound /ē/

Unit Overview

In this unit, students will

- Learn the sight words *every*, *neighbor*, and *behind*.
- Learn the spellings *e*, *ea*, *ee*, *e-e*, *ie*, and *y* for the sound /ē/.
- Read and write sentences.
- Read stories silently and aloud.

Lesson Overview

	Offline FOCUS: Introduce Spellings for Sound /ē/	**15** minutes
Sight Words	Introduce Sight Words	
Learn	Introduce Spellings for Sound /ē/	
	Review Spellings for Sound /ē/	
Try It	Investigator	
	Online REVIEW: Spellings for Sound /ē/	**15** minutes

Materials

Supplied

- *K¹² PhonicsWorks Advanced Activity Book,* p. PH 53
- whiteboard, Learning Coach
- whiteboard, student
- Tile Kit

Also Needed

- sight words box
- dictation notebook

Offline 15 minutes

FOCUS: Introduce Spellings for Sound /ē/

Work **together** with students to complete offline Sight Words, Learn, and Try It activities.

Sight Words ....

Introduce Sight Words

Help students learn the sight words *every*, *neighbor*, and *behind*.

1. Gather the sight word cards *every*, *neighbor*, and *behind*.

2. Show students the *every* card.

3. **Say:** This is the word *every*. We see this word so often that we want to be able to read and spell it quickly without thinking about it. Look closely at the word *every*. Spell the word *every* aloud. Take a picture of the word *every* in your mind. When you think you can spell *every* yourself, turn the card over and use your letter tiles to spell the word *every*. Check the card to see if you spelled the word *every* correctly. Read aloud the word you spelled with the letter tiles.

4. Repeat the activity with the remaining sight words.

5. Chart students' progress on the back of each card.

   ▸ Divide the back of the card into two columns.
   ▸ Label the first column "Read" and the second column "Spell."
   ▸ Record the dates that students read or spell the word correctly. When students can read and spell the word correctly three times in a row, they have mastered the word. You may want to put a star or sticker on the card when they have mastered that word.

6. Add the cards to students' sight words box.

TIP Sight words can be very difficult for some students. Let students work at their own pace and really master these words, as they occur frequently in reading and writing.

Objectives
- Read sight words.
- Spell sight words.

Learn

· ·

Introduce Spellings for Sound /ē/

Help students learn the spellings *e, ea, ee, e-e, ie,* and *y* for the sound /ē/.

1. Place the following letter tiles on students' whiteboard: *ai, c, e, e, ea, ee, ie, m, n, p, P, r, s, t,* and *y*.

2. Make the word *Pete* in the middle of students' whiteboard and point to it.

   Say: Today we are going to learn the six spellings for the sound /ē/. You already know one of them. Sometimes the long *e* sound is made by the letter *e* and a silent *e*, separated by a consonant. Let's touch and say the word *Pete.*

3. Make the word *me* and point to it.

   Say: Now let's look at the next word. This is the word *me.* In the word *me,* the long *e* sound is made by the letter *e* all by itself.

   ▸ Touch and say *me.*
   ▸ Where is the sound /ē/ in this word? end
   ▸ Which letter or letters make this sound? *e*

4. Make the word *feet* and point to it.

   Say: This word is *feet.* In the word *feet,* the long *e* sound is made by the letters *ee.*

   ▸ Touch and say *feet.*
   ▸ Where is the sound /ē/ in this word? middle
   ▸ Which letter or letters make this sound? *ee*

5. Make the word *sea* and point to it.

   Say: This word is *sea.* In the word *sea,* the long *e* sound is made by the letters *ea.*

   ▸ Touch and say *sea.*
   ▸ Where is the sound /ē/ in this word? end
   ▸ Which letter or letters make this sound? *ea*

6. Make the word *piece* and point to it.

   Say: This word is *piece.* In the word *piece,* the long *e* sound is made by the letters *ie.*

   ▸ Touch and say *piece.*
   ▸ Where is the sound /ē/ in this word? middle
   ▸ Which letter or letters make this sound? *ie*

7. Make the word *rainy* and point to it.

   Say: The last word is *rainy.* In the word *rainy,* the long *e* sound is made by the letter *y.*

   ▸ Touch and say *rainy.*
   ▸ Where is the sound /ē/ in this word? end
   ▸ Which letter or letters make this sound? *y*

(TIP) Refer to the *K¹² PhonicsWorks* video for a demonstration of how to teach different spellings for long vowel sounds.

Objectives
- Identify individual sounds in words.
- Identify and use the sound /ē/.
- Identify the letters, given the sound /ē/.
- Identify and use /ē/ spelling patterns.
- Identify and use *ea* spelling patterns.
- Identify and use silent *e.*
- Write words by applying grade-level phonics knowledge.

Review Spellings for Sound /ē/

Help students review the spellings *e, ea, ee, e-e, ie,* and *y* for the sound /ē/.

1. Gather the dictation notebook and pencil.

2. Place the following letter tiles at the top of students' whiteboard: *e, ea, ee, e-e, ie,* and *y.*

3. Write the following words on your whiteboard: *me, sea, feet, Pete, piece,* and *rainy.*

4. **Say:** Count the number of ways there are to spell the long vowel sound /ē/.
   - Touch and say the spellings for the sound /ē/. *e, ea, ee, e-e, ie, y*
   - Look at the words on the board and read them.
   - Say how the sound /ē/ is spelled in each word. *e* in *me, ea* in *sea, ee* in *feet, e-e* in *Pete, ie* in *piece, y* in *rainy*
   - Take a picture in your mind of the six ways of spelling the sound /ē/.

5. **Say:** I am going to hide the words and the spellings on the board. Your job is to remember each way of spelling the sound /ē/ and write the spellings in your notebook.

6. After students have finished writing the spellings in their notebook, have them check their answers against the spellings on the board.

TIP If students cannot remember one or more of the spellings for the sound /ē/, tell them the guide word for that spelling (*e,* as in *me; ea,* as in *sea; ee,* as in *feet; e-e,* as in *Pete; ie,* as in *piece; y,* as in *rainy*).

Try It

Investigator

Have students complete page PH 53 in *K¹² PhonicsWorks Advanced Activity Book* for more practice with spellings for the sound /ē/. Have students read each word aloud going down each column, and then read each word again going across each row. Have them read the questions and circle the answers.

[Online] 🕐 minutes

REVIEW: Spellings for Sound /ē/

Students will work online independently to

- ▶ Practice spellings for the sound /ē/.
- ▶ Practice decoding text by reading a story.

Help students locate the online activities and provide support as needed.

Offline Alternative

No computer access? Have students spell words that have the spellings *e*, *ea*, *ee*, *e-e*, *ie*, or *y* for the sound /ē/, such as *be, bean, beet, Pete, niece,* and *candy*.

PHONICS

Practice Spellings for Sound /ē/ (A)

Lesson Overview

	〖Offline〗 FOCUS: Practice Spellings for Sound /ē/	⏱ **15** minutes
Sight Words	Sight Word Fun	
Practice	Word Chains	
Try It	"Sunny Days at the Creek"	
	〖Online〗 REVIEW: Spellings for Sound /ē/	⏱ **15** minutes

〖 Materials 〗

Supplied
- *K¹² PhonicsWorks Readers Advanced 9*, pp. 32–38
- whiteboard, student
- Tile Kit

Also Needed
- sight words box

[Offline] ⓛ⑤ minutes

FOCUS: Practice Spellings for Sound /ē/

Work **together** with students to complete offline Sight Words, Practice, and Try It activities.

Sight Words ···

Sight Word Fun

Help students learn the sight words *every*, *neighbor*, and *behind*, and up to two additional sight words they have yet to master.

1. Gather the sight word cards *every*, *neighbor*, and *behind*, and up to two additional sight word cards.

2. Choose one sight word card to begin.

   Say: Look at this word and take a picture of it in your mind. When you think you can spell the word yourself, turn the card over and use your letter tiles to spell the word.

3. After students spell the word, have them check the card to see if they spelled the word correctly.

   Say: Read aloud the word you spelled with the letter tiles.

4. Repeat the activity with the remaining sight words.

TIP Sight words can be very difficult for some students. Let them work at their own pace and really master these words.

> **Objectives**
> - Read sight words.
> - Spell sight words.

Practice ···

Word Chains

Have students build words by adding and changing letters to help them recognize and use the spellings *e*, *ea*, *ee*, *e-e*, *ie*, and *y* for the sound /ē/.

1. Place the following letter tiles at the top of students' whiteboard: *b*, *ch*, *e*, *e*, *ea*, *ee*, *f*, *h*, *ie*, *m*, *n*, *n*, *p*, *r*, *s*, *sh*, *t*, *th*, *u*, and *y*.

2. **Say:** You will spell words in several short word chains today. There will be one chain for each of the spellings of the sound /ē/ that you know. How many spellings do you know for the sound /ē/? six

3. **Say:** I'll do the first word. The word is *be*.

   ▶ I will pull down the letters for the sounds /b/ and /ē/ to spell the word *be*.
   ▶ I will touch and say *be*. To change *be* to *me*, I will think about which sound is changed from the word *be* to *me*. I will need to replace the letter *b* with the letter *m*.
   ▶ Touch and say the word *me*. Now it's your turn to change *me* to *he*. You can spell *he* by making only one change. Touch and say the new word.

> **Objectives**
> - Identify the new word when one sound is changed in a word.
> - Identify individual sounds in words.
> - Identify and use the sound /ē/.
> - Identify the letters, given the sound /ē/.
> - Identify and use /ē/ spelling patterns.
> - Identify and use *ea* spelling patterns.
> - Identify and use silent *e*.

4. Redirect students if they select the incorrect letter for any sound.

Say: That letter is for the sound [incorrect sound]. We want the letter for the sound [target sound]. What letter makes that sound? Answers will vary.

5. Redirect students if they name the sound incorrectly.

Say: To change the word [first word] to [target word], we need the letter for the sound [target sound].

Show students how to make the change. Have them touch and say the new word after they move the letters.

6. Follow this procedure to make the following groups of word chains:

   ▸ *pea, sea, seat, heat*
   ▸ *beet, meet, sheet, sheep*
   ▸ *these, theme*
   ▸ *thief, chief, brief*
   ▸ *bunny, funny, sunny, runny*

7. For every new word, have students add, replace, or remove only one letter tile. Remind students that in these word chains only one sound—and only one letter tile—will change when the word changes. Exception: Students will need to use two letter tiles for changing *chief* to *brief*.

TIP If students cannot remember one or more spellings, give them the guide word for that spelling (*e,* as in *me; ea,* as in *sea; ee,* as in *feet; e-e,* as in *Pete; ie,* as in *piece; y,* as in *rainy*).

Try It •••

"Sunny Days at the Creek"
Have students read "Sunny Days at the Creek" on page 32 of *K¹² PhonicsWorks Readers Advanced 9.*

Students should read the story silently once or twice before reading the story aloud. When students miss a word that can be sounded out, point to it and give them three to six seconds to try the word again. If students still miss the word, tell them the word so the flow of the story isn't interrupted.

After reading the story, make a list of all the words students missed, and go over those words with them. You may use letter tiles to show students how to read the words.

Objectives
- Read aloud grade-level text with appropriate automaticity, prosody, accuracy, and rate.
- Decode words by applying grade-level word analysis skills.

[Online] ⓕ minutes

REVIEW: Spellings for Sound /ē/

Students will work online independently to

▸ Practice spellings for the sound /ē/.

Help students locate the online activities and provide support as needed.

Offline Alternative

No computer access? Have students spell words that have the spellings *e*, *ea*, *ee*, *e-e*, *ie*, and *y* for the sound /ē/, such as *he*, *pea*, *weed*, *eve*, *chief*, and *sandy*.

Practice Spellings for Sound /ē/ (B)

Lesson Overview

📋	**【Offline 】 FOCUS:** Practice Spellings for Sound /ē/	**15** minutes

Sight Words	Sight Word Fun
Practice	Word Chains
Try It	Tic Tac Toe

🖥	**【Online 】 REVIEW:** Spellings for Sound /ē/	**15** minutes

Materials

Supplied
- *K¹² PhonicsWorks Advanced Activity Book,* p. PH 54
- whiteboard, student
- Tile Kit

Also Needed
- sight words box
- crayons

〔 Offline 〕 ⏱ 15 minutes

FOCUS: Practice Spellings for Sound /ē/

Work **together** with students to complete offline Sight Words, Practice, and Try It activities.

Sight Words ....

Sight Word Fun

Help students learn the sight words *every, neighbor,* and *behind,* and up to two additional sight words they have yet to master.

1. Gather the sight word cards *every, neighbor,* and *behind,* and up to two additional sight word cards.

2. Choose one sight word card to begin.

   Say: Look at this word and take a picture of it in your mind. When you think you can spell the word yourself, turn the card over and use your letter tiles to spell the word.

3. After students spell the word, have them check the card to see if they spelled the word correctly.

   Say: Read aloud the word you spelled with the letter tiles.

4. Repeat the activity with the remaining sight words.

TIP Sight words can be very difficult for some students. Let them work at their own pace and really master these words.

> **Objectives**
> - Read sight words.
> - Spell sight words.

Practice ....

Word Chains

Have students build words by adding and changing letters to help them recognize and use the spellings *e, ea, ee, e-e, ie,* and *y* for the sound /ē/.

1. Place the following letter tiles at the top of students' whiteboard: *a, b, c, d, d, e, e, ea, ee, f, ie, k, l, m, n, R, s, sh, t, th,* and *y*.

2. **Say:** You will spell words in several short word chains today. There will be one chain for each of the spellings of the sound /ē/ that you know. How many spellings do you know for the sound /ē/? six

3. **Say:** I'll do the first word. The word is *see*.

   ▶ I will pull down the letters for the sounds /s/ and /ē/ to spell the word *see*.

   ▶ I will touch and say *see*. To change *see* to *seem*, I will think about which sound is changed from the word *see* to *seem*. I will need to add the letter *m* to the end of the word.

   ▶ Touch and say the word *seem*. Now it's your turn to change *seem* to *seek*. You can spell *seek* by making only one change. Touch and say the new word.

> **Objectives**
> - Identify the new word when one sound is changed in a word.
> - Identify individual sounds in words.
> - Identify and use the sound /ē/.
> - Identify the letters, given the sound /ē/.
> - Identify and use /ē/ spelling patterns.
> - Identify and use *ea* spelling patterns.
> - Identify and use silent *e*.

4. Redirect students if they select the incorrect letter for any sound.

Say: That letter is for the sound [incorrect sound]. We want the letter for the sound [target sound]. What letter makes that sound? Answers will vary.

5. Redirect students if they name the sound incorrectly.

Say: To change the word [first word] to [target word], we need the letter for the sound [target sound].

Show students how to make the change. Have them touch and say the new word after they move the letters.

6. Follow this procedure to make the following groups of word chains:

   ► *me, he, she*
   ► *meat, beat, beam, team, tea, sea, seat, eat*
   ► *theme, these*
   ► *field, yield, shield*
   ► *candy, dandy, Randy, sandy*

7. For every new word, have students add, replace, or remove only one letter tile. Remind students that in these word chains only one sound—and only one letter tile—will change when the word changes.

TIP If students cannot remember one or more spellings, give them the guide word for that spelling (*e*, as in *me*; *ea*, as in *sea*; *ee*, as in *feet*; *e-e*, as in *Pete*; *ie*, as in *piece*; *y*, as in *rainy*.

Try It

Tic Tac Toe

Have students complete page PH 54 in *K¹² PhonicsWorks Advanced Activity Book* for more practice with the spellings for the sound /ē/. Have students read each word aloud, find the five words in a row that rhyme, and color those boxes. Remind them that the row can be across, down, or diagonal.

Objectives

- Identify and use the sound /ē/.
- Identify the letters, given the sound /ē/.
- Identify and use /ē/ spelling patterns.
- Identify words that rhyme.
- Identify and use *ea* spelling patterns.
- Identify and use silent *e*.

Try It
Practice Spellings for Sound /ē/ (B)
Tic Tac Toe

Read each word aloud. Find the five words in a row that rhyme.
The row can be across, down, or diagonal. Color the five boxes
that contain the five rhyming words.

tree	flea	bee	each	holly
three	see	glee	peach	jolly
sea	sheep	peep	teach	dear
dream	weep	thief	reach	Polly
steep	deep	Pete	beach	dolly

PH 54   LANGUAGE ARTS GREEN

[Online] ⓘ minutes

REVIEW: Spellings for Sound /ē/

Students will work online independently to

- ► Practice spellings for the sound /ē/.
- ► Practice decoding text by reading a story.

Help students locate the online activities and provide support as needed.

Offline Alternative

No computer access? Have students spell words that have the spellings *e*, *ea*, *ee*, *e-e*, *ie*, and *y* for the sound /ē/, such as *she*, *tea*, *seed*, *Gene*, *shield*, and *handy*.

Practice Spellings for Sound /ē/ (C)

Lesson Overview

〔Offline〕 FOCUS: Practice Spellings for Sound /ē/		**15** minutes
Sight Words	Sight Word Fun	
Practice	Sort Spellings for Sound /ē/	
Try It	"Becky's Funny Dream"	
	Dictation: Write Sentences	
〔Online〕 REVIEW: Spellings for Sound /ē/		**15** minutes

Materials

Supplied
- *K¹² PhonicsWorks Readers Advanced 10*, pp. 1–8
- whiteboard, Learning Coach

Also Needed
- sight words box
- dictation notebook
- index cards (18)

Advance Preparation

For Sort Spellings for Sound /ē/, print each of the following words on index cards, using one card per word: *me, we, be, clean, beak, dream, breed, feet, beep, eve, here, Pete, niece, piece, yield, sunny, story,* and *handy.*

[Offline] ⏱ **15** minutes

FOCUS: Practice Spellings for Sound /ē/

Work **together** with students to complete offline Sight Words, Practice, and Try It activities.

Sight Words ....

Sight Word Fun

Help students learn the sight words *every, neighbor,* and *behind,* and up to two additional sight words they have yet to master.

1. Gather the sight word cards *every, neighbor,* and *behind,* and up to two additional sight word cards.

2. Choose one sight word card to begin.

   Say: Look at this word and take a picture of it in your mind. When you think you can spell the word yourself, turn the card over and use your letter tiles to spell the word.

3. After students spell the word, have them check the card to see if they spelled the word correctly.

   Say: Read aloud the word you spelled with the letter tiles.

4. Repeat the activity with the remaining sight words.

   TIP Sight words can be very difficult for some students. Let them work at their own pace and really master these words.

> **Objectives**
> - Read sight words.
> - Spell sight words.

Practice ....

Sort Spellings for Sound /ē/

Help students practice identifying words that have the spellings *e, ea, ee, e-e, ie,* and *y* for the sound /ē/.

1. Gather the index cards you prepared. Mix the cards well and place them in a stack face down on the table.

2. Gather the dictation notebook. Draw six columns and label them *e, ea, ee, e-e, ie,* and *y* to represent the six different ways to spell the sound /ē/.

3. **Say:** You are going to sort words by the six spellings for the sound /ē/. You will take a card from the pile and read it to me. Then you will think about the spelling for the sound /ē/ in the word and write that word in the correct column. I'll do the first one for you.

> **Objectives**
> - Identify individual sounds in words.
> - Identify and use the sound /ē/.
> - Identify the letters, given the sound /ē/.
> - Identify and use /ē/ spelling patterns.
> - Identify and use *ea* spelling patterns.
> - Identify and use silent *e*.

4. Demonstrate the following for students:

  ▸ Draw a card from the pile.
  ▸ Read the word aloud.
  ▸ Write the word in the correct column for the spelling for sound /ē/.

5. Have students continue the procedure with the remaining words:

  ▸ **Spelling *e* words:** *me, we, be*
  ▸ **Spelling *ea* words:** *clean, beak, dream*
  ▸ **Spelling *ee* words:** *breed, feet, beep*
  ▸ **Spelling *e-e* words:** *eve, here, Pete*
  ▸ **Spelling *ie* words:** *niece, piece, yield*
  ▸ **Spelling *y* words:** *sunny, story, handy*

Try It

"Becky's Funny Dream"

Have students read "Becky's Funny Dream" on page 1 of *K¹² PhonicsWorks Readers Advanced 10*.

Students should read the story silently once or twice before reading the story aloud. When students miss a word that can be sounded out, point to it and give them three to six seconds to try the word again. If students still miss the word, tell them the word so the flow of the story isn't interrupted.

After reading the story, make a list of all the words students missed, and go over those words with them. You may use letter tiles to show students how to read the words.

Objectives

- Read aloud grade-level text with appropriate automaticity, prosody, accuracy, and rate.
- Decode words by applying grade-level word analysis skills.
- Write words by applying grade-level phonics knowledge.
- Follow three-step directions.

Dictation: Write Sentences

Use sentences to help students identify individual sounds in words.

1. Gather a pencil and the dictation notebook. Say the sentence, *I see you.* Then give these directions to students:

   ▶ Repeat the sentence.
   ▶ Write the sentence in your notebook.
   ▶ Read the sentence aloud.

2. When students have finished, write the following sentence on your whiteboard: *I see you.*

3. Have them compare their answer to your correct version.

4. Repeat this procedure with the following sentences: *The sick kitten was weak. Pick up the baby. Tim has big feet. Please heat up my lunch. The athlete won the game.*

   ▶ If students make an error and don't see it, help them correct their mistake by having them finger stretch the sounds in the word they missed.
   ▶ If students are having difficulty selecting the correct letters or sounds, review those letters or sounds that are confusing them.
   ▶ If students have difficulty with first, middle, and last sounds, have them finger stretch the sounds in words.

[Online] 15 minutes

REVIEW: Spellings for Sound /ē/

Students will work online independently to

▶ Practice spellings for the sound /ē/.

Help students locate the online activities and provide support as needed.

Offline Alternative

No computer access? Have students spell words that have the spellings *e, ea, ee, e-e, ie,* and *y* for the sound /ē/, such as *be, beam, free, Steve, yield,* and *funny.*

Objectives

- Identify individual sounds in words.
- Identify and use the sound /ē/.
- Identify the letters, given the sound /ē/.
- Identify and use /ē/ spelling patterns.
- Identify and use *ea* spelling patterns.
- Identify and use silent *e.*

Unit Checkpoint

Lesson Overview

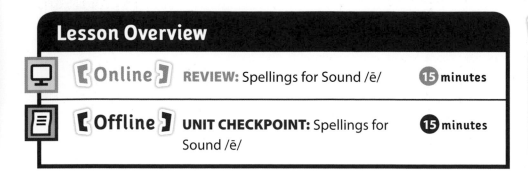

🖥	**〔Online〕**	**REVIEW:** Spellings for Sound /ē/	**15** minutes
📄	**〔Offline〕**	**UNIT CHECKPOINT:** Spellings for Sound /ē/	**15** minutes

〔Materials〕

Supplied

- *K¹² PhonicsWorks Advanced Assessments,* pp. PH 157–162

Objectives

- Identify individual sounds in words.
- Identify and use the sound /ē/.
- Identify the letters, given the sound /ē/.
- Identify and use /ē/ spelling patterns.
- Identify and use *ea* spelling patterns.
- Identify and use silent *e*.
- Read instructional-level text with 90% accuracy.

- Read aloud grade-level text with appropriate automaticity, prosody, accuracy, and rate.
- Write words by applying grade-level phonics knowledge.
- Write sight words.
- Read sight words.

〔Online〕 **15** minutes

REVIEW: **Spellings for Sound /ē/**

Students will review spellings for the sound /ē/ to prepare for the Unit Checkpoint. Help students locate the online activities and provide support as needed.

[Offline] 🕔 minutes

UNIT CHECKPOINT: Spellings for Sound /ē/

Explain that students are going to show what they have learned about sounds, letters, and words.

1. Give students the Unit Checkpoint pages for the Spellings for Sound /ē/ unit and print the Unit Checkpoint Answer Key, if you'd like.

2. Use the instructions below to help administer the Checkpoint to students. On the Answer Key or another sheet of paper, note student answers to oral response questions to help with scoring the Checkpoint later.

3. Use the Answer Key to score the Checkpoint, and then enter the results online.

Part 1. Circle Words with Sound /ē/ Have students circle the words with the sound /ē/.

Part 2. Many Spellings, One Sound Have students circle the six ways to spell the sound /ē/.

Part 3. Read Sight Words Have students read each sight word aloud. Note any words they read incorrectly.

Part 4. Writing Read each sentence to students. Have them repeat and write the sentence.

25. *Did Steve speak to the neighbor?*

26. *We need every piece.*

27. *Sandy hid the penny behind the vase.*

Part 5. Read Aloud Listen to students read the sentences aloud. Count and note the number of words they read correctly.

Part 6. Read Nonsense Words Have students read each nonsense word aloud. Note any words they read incorrectly.

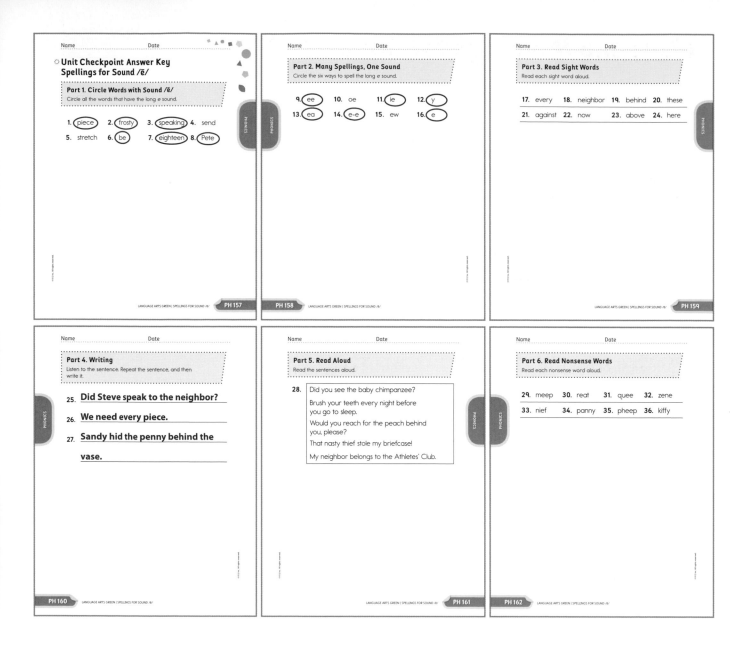

Unit Checkpoint Answer Key
Spellings for Sound /ē/

Part 1. Circle Words with Sound /ē/
Circle all the words that have the long e sound.

1. (piece)   2. (frosty)   3. (speaking)   4. send
5. stretch   6. (be)   7. (eighteen)   8. (Pete)

Part 2. Many Spellings, One Sound
Circle the six ways to spell the long e sound.

9. (ee)   10. oe   11. (ie)   12. (y)
13. (ea)   14. (e-e)   15. ew   16. (e)

Part 3. Read Sight Words
Read each sight word aloud.

17. every   18. neighbor   19. behind   20. these
21. against   22. now   23. above   24. here

Part 4. Writing
Listen to the sentence. Repeat the sentence, and then write it.

25. **Did Steve speak to the neighbor?**
26. **We need every piece.**
27. **Sandy hid the penny behind the vase.**

Part 5. Read Aloud
Read the sentences aloud.

28. Did you see the baby chimpanzee?
Brush your teeth every night before you go to sleep.
Would you reach for the peach behind you, please?
That nasty thief stole my briefcase!
My neighbor belongs to the Athletes' Club.

Part 6. Read Nonsense Words
Read each nonsense word aloud.

29. meep   30. reat   31. quee   32. zene
33. nief   34. panny   35. pheep   36. kiffy

PH 157 PH 158 PH 159 PH 160 PH 161 PH 162

Introduce Spellings for Sound /ū/

Unit Overview

In this unit, students will

- ▶ Review sight words.
- ▶ Learn the spellings *u*, *ue*, *ew*, and *u-e* for the sound /ū/.
- ▶ Read and write sentences.
- ▶ Read stories silently and aloud.

[Materials]

Supplied

- *K¹² PhonicsWorks Advanced Activity Book*, p. PH 55
- whiteboard, Learning Coach
- whiteboard, student
- Tile Kit

Also Needed

- sight words box
- dictation notebook

Lesson Overview

[**Offline**]	**FOCUS:** Introduce Spellings for Sound /ū/	**15** minutes

Sight Words	Review Sight Words
Learn	Introduce Spellings for Sound /ū/
	Review Spellings for Sound /ū/
Try It	Investigator

[**Online**]	**REVIEW:** Spellings for Sound /ū/	**15** minutes

 **15** minutes

FOCUS: Introduce Spellings for Sound /ū/

Work **together** with students to complete offline Sight Words, Learn, and Try It activities.

Sight Words

Review Sight Words

Help students learn to recognize sight words.

1. Gather all the sight word cards students have yet to master from their sight words box. Stack the cards on the table face down.

2. Have students pick a word and read it to you.

3. If they read it quickly and correctly, put the card in one stack. If they hesitate or do not read the word correctly, put it in another stack. The second stack should have words that they will review again.

4. Take the stack of words that students read correctly and dictate each word to them. They may choose to either write the word or spell it aloud.

5. If students spell the word correctly, put the card in the first stack because they have mastered the word. If they misspell the word, add it to the stack of cards to review again.

6. Chart students' progress on the back of each card.

   ▸ Divide the back of the card into two columns.
   ▸ Label the first column "Read" and the second column "Spell."
   ▸ Record the dates that students read or spell the word correctly. When students can read and spell the word correctly three times in a row, they have mastered the word. You may want to put a star or sticker on their card when they have mastered that word.

TIP Even if students can read and spell all the words correctly, it is still beneficial for them to review sight words. Choose as many additional words as you would like for each subsequent activity.

Objectives
- Read sight words.
- Spell sight words.
- Write sight words.

Learn

Introduce Spellings for Sound /ū/

Help students learn the spellings *u*, *ue*, *ew*, and *u-e* for the sound /ū/.

1. Place the following letter tiles on students' whiteboard: *b, c, e, ew, f, i, m, s, u,* and *ue*.

2. Make the word *cube* in the middle of students' whiteboard and point to it.

   Say: Today we are going to learn four spellings for the sound /ū/. You already know one of them. Sometimes the long *u* sound is made by the letter *u* and a silent *e*, separated by a consonant. Let's touch and say the word *cube*.

3. Make the word *cue* and point to it.

   Say: Now let's look at the next word. This is the word *cue*. In the word *cue*, the long *u* sound is made by the letters *ue*.

   ▶ Touch and say *cue*.
   ▶ Where is the sound /ū/ in this word? end
   ▶ Which letter or letters make this sound? *ue*

4. Make the word *few* and point to it.

   Say: This word is *few*. In the word *few*, the long *u* sound is made by the letters *ew*.

   ▶ Touch and say *few*.
   ▶ Where is the sound /ū/ in this word? end
   ▶ Which letter or letters make this sound? *ew*

5. Make the word *music* and point to it.

   Say: This word is *music*. In the word *music*, the long *u* sound is made by the letter *u* all by itself.

   ▶ Touch and say *music*.
   ▶ Where is the sound /ū/ in this word? middle
   ▶ Which letter or letters make this sound? *u*

TIP Refer to the *K¹² PhonicsWorks* video for a demonstration of how to teach different spellings for long vowel sounds.

Objectives

- Identify individual sounds in words.
- Identify and use the sound /ū/.
- Identify the letters, given the sound /ū/.
- Identify and use /ū/ spelling patterns.
- Identify and use silent *e*.

Review Spellings for Sound /ū/

Help students review the spellings *u*, *ue*, *ew*, and *u-e* for the sound /ū/.

1. Gather the dictation notebook and pencil.

2. Place the following letter tiles at the top of students' whiteboard: *u, ue, ew,* and *u-e*.

3. Write the following words on your whiteboard: *music, cue, few,* and *cube*.

4. **Say:** Count the number of ways there are to spell the long vowel sound /ū/.

   ▸ Touch and say the spellings for the sound /ū/. *u, ue, ew, u-e*
   ▸ Look at the words on the board and read them.
   ▸ Say how the sound is spelled in each word. *u* in *music*, *ue* in *cue*, *ew* in *few*, *u-e* in *cube*
   ▸ Take a picture in your mind of the four ways of spelling the sound /ū/.

5. **Say:** I am going to hide the words and the spellings on the board. Your job is to remember each way of spelling the sound /ū/ and write the spellings in your notebook.

6. After students have finished writing the spellings in their notebook, have them check their answers against the spellings on the board.

TIP If students cannot remember one or more of the spellings for the sound /ū/, tell them the guide word for that spelling (*u,* as in *music; ue,* as in *cue; ew,* as in *few; u-e,* as in *cube*).

Try It

Investigator

Have students complete page PH 55 in *K¹² PhonicsWorks Advanced Activity Book* for more practice with spellings for the sound /ū/. Have students read each word aloud going down each column, and then read each word again going across each row. Have them read the question and circle the answer.

Try It
Introduce Spellings for Sound /ū/
Investigator

Read down each column, and then read across each row.

u–e	u	ue
cube	music	hue
use	cupid	argue
mule	menu	rescue
cute	human	value
fume	bugle	continue
fuse	unicorn	
	unite	
	united	
	humid	

Circle the answer.

1. Where is *ue* in these words? middle (end)

LANGUAGE ARTS GREEN   **PH 55**

Objectives
- Identify and use the sound /ū/.
- Identify the letters, given the sound /ū/.
- Identify and use /ū/ spelling patterns.
- Identify and use silent *e*.
- Read aloud grade-level text with appropriate automaticity, prosody, accuracy, and rate.
- Decode words by applying grade-level word analysis skills.

[Online] ⑮ minutes

REVIEW: Spellings for Sound /ū/

Students will work online independently to

- ► Practice spellings for the sound /ū/.
- ► Practice decoding text by reading a story.

Help students locate the online activities and provide support as needed.

Offline Alternative

No computer access? Have students spell words that have the spellings *u*, *ue*, *ew*, and *u-e* for the sound /ū/, such as *unit*, *hue*, *fewest*, and *tube*.

Objectives

- Identify and use the sound /ū/.
- Identify the letters, given the sound /ū/.
- Identify and use /ū/ spelling patterns.
- Identify and use silent *e*.
- Read aloud grade-level text with appropriate automaticity, prosody, accuracy, and rate.
- Decode words by applying grade-level word analysis skills.

Introduce Spellings for Long Double *o* Sound

Lesson Overview

[Offline] FOCUS: Introduce Spellings for Long Double *o* Sound — **15** minutes

Sight Words	Use Words in Sentences
Learn	Introduce Spellings for Long Double *o* Sound
	Review Spellings for Long Double *o* Sound
Try It	"Sandy and Dean"

[Online] REVIEW: Spellings for Long Double *o* Sound — **15** minutes

[Materials]

Supplied

- *K¹² PhonicsWorks Readers Advanced 10,* pp. 9–16
- whiteboard, Learning Coach
- whiteboard, student
- Tile Kit

Also Needed

- sight words box
- dictation notebook

[Offline] 🕒 15 minutes

FOCUS: Introduce Spellings for Long Double *o* Sound
Work **together** with students to complete offline Sight Words, Learn, and Try It activities.

Sight Words ....

Use Words in Sentences
Help students use sight words in sentences.

1. Gather all the sight word cards students have yet to master from their sight words box. Spread the sight word cards on the table.

2. **Say:** Let's use sight words in sentences.

3. Have students

   ▸ Touch each card and read the word on it.
   ▸ Make up a sentence using the word.
   ▸ Put the card in a pile after using the word in a sentence.
   ▸ Go through the pile of cards and read each sight word again.
   ▸ Spell each word.

TIP If students have difficulty with any of the sight words, place those cards in a pile to review again.

> **Objectives**
> • Read sight words.
> • Spell sight words.

Learn ....

Introduce Spellings for Long Double *o* Sound
Help students learn the spellings *u, ue, ew, oo,* and *u-e* for the sound /o͞o/.

1. Place the following letter tiles on students' whiteboard: *a, b, e, ew, l, m, n, oo, r, t, u,* and *ue*.

2. Make the word *rule* in the middle of students' whiteboard and point to it.

   Say: Today we are going to learn five spellings for the sound /o͞o/. You already know one of them. Sometimes the long double *o* sound is made by the letter *u* and a silent *e*, separated by a consonant. Let's touch and say the word *rule*.

3. Make the word *tuna* and point to it.

   Say: Now let's look at the next word. This is the word *tuna*. In the word *tuna*, the long double *o* sound is made by the letter *u* all by itself.

   ▸ Touch and say *tuna* and point to it.
   ▸ Where is the sound /o͞o/ in this word? middle
   ▸ Which letter or letters make this sound? *u*

> **Objectives**
> • Identify individual sounds in words.
> • Identify and use the long double *o* sound.
> • Identify the letters, given the long double *o* sound.
> • Identify and use double *o* (oo) spelling patterns.
> • Identify and use silent *e*.
> • Write words by applying grade-level phonics knowledge.

4. Make the word *blue* and point to it.

Say: This word is *blue.* In the word *blue,* the long double *o* sound is made by the letters *ue.*

- ▸ Touch and say *blue* and point to it.
- ▸ Where is the sound /o͞o/ in this word? end
- ▸ Which letter or letters make this sound? *ue*

5. Make the word *moon* and point to it.

Say: This word is *moon.* In the word *moon,* the long double *o* sound is made by the letters *oo.*

- ▸ Touch and say *moon.*
- ▸ Where is the sound /o͞o/ in this word? middle
- ▸ Which letter or letters make this sound? *oo*

6. Make the word *new* and point to it.

Say: The last word is *new.* In the word *new,* the long double *o* sound is made by the letters *ew.*

- ▸ Touch and say *new.*
- ▸ Where is the sound /o͞o/ in this word? ending
- ▸ Which letter or letters make this sound? *ew*

TIP Refer to the *K¹² PhonicsWorks* video for a demonstration of how to teach different spellings for long vowel sounds.

Review Spellings for Long Double *o* Sound

Help students review the spellings *u, ue, ew, oo,* and *u-e* for the sound /o͞o/.

1. Gather the dictation notebook and pencil.

2. Place the following letter tiles at the top of students' whiteboard: *u, ue, ew, oo,* and *u-e.*

3. Write the following words on your whiteboard: *tuna, blue, stew, moon,* and *rule.*

4. **Say:** Count the number of ways there are to spell the sound /o͞o/.

- ▸ Touch and say the spellings for the sound /o͞o/. *u, ue, ew, oo, u-e*
- ▸ Look at the words on the board and read them.
- ▸ Say how the sound is spelled in each word. *u* in *tuna, ue* in *blue, ew* in *stew, oo* in *moon, u-e* in *rule*
- ▸ Take a picture in your mind of the five ways of spelling the sound /o͞o/.

5. **Say:** I am going to hide the words and the spellings on the board. Your job is to remember each way of spelling the sound /o͞o/ and write the spellings in your notebook.

6. After students have finished writing the spellings in their notebook, have them check their answer against the spellings on the board.

TIP If students cannot remember one or more of the spellings for the sound /o͞o/, tell them the guide word for that spelling (*u,* as in *tuna; ue,* as in *blue; ew,* in *stew; oo,* as in *moon; u-e,* as in *rule*).

Try It ••

"Sandy and Dean"

Have students read "Sandy and Dean" on page 9 of *K¹² PhonicsWorks Readers Advanced 10*.

Students should read the story silently once or twice before reading the story aloud. When students miss a word that can be sounded out, point to it and give them three to six seconds to try the word again. If students still miss the word, tell them the word so the flow of the story isn't interrupted.

After reading the story, make a list of all the words students missed, and go over those words with them. You may use letter tiles to show students how to read the words.

[Online] **15** minutes

REVIEW: Spellings for Long Double *o* Sound

Students will work online independently to

▸ Practice spellings for the sound /o͞o/.

Help students locate the online activities and provide support as needed.

___

Offline Alternative

No computer access? Have students spell words that have the spellings *u, ue, ew, oo,* and *u-e* for the sound /o͞o/, such as *luna, glue, chew, food,* and *June*.

Practice Spellings for Sounds /ū/ and Long Double *o* (A)

Lesson Overview

	Offline FOCUS: Practice Spellings for Sounds /ū/ and Long Double *o*	**15** minutes
Sight Words	Sight Word Concentration	
Practice	Practice Sounds /ū/ and Long Double *o*	
Try It	Rhyming Words	
	Online REVIEW: Spellings for Sounds /ū/ and Long Double *o*	**15** minutes

Materials

Supplied
- *K¹² PhonicsWorks Advanced Activity Book*, p. PH 56
- whiteboard, student
- Tile Kit

Also Needed
- sight words box

Advance Preparation

Gather two sets of all sight word cards that students have yet to master.

[**Offline**] **15** minutes

FOCUS: Practice Spellings for Sounds /ū/ and Long Double *o*

Work **together** with students to complete offline Sight Words, Practice, and Try It activities.

Sight Words ●●●

Sight Word Concentration

Help students review sight words.

1. Gather the two sets of sight word cards.

2. Scramble both sets of sight word cards and place them face down on the table or floor.

3. Turn over two cards at a time; take turns with students. If the cards match, the person turning over the matching cards reads the word and uses it in a sentence. If the cards don't match, the person turns them back over.

4. Remove and save the matching cards.

5. Continue the activity until all the cards are paired.

6. Have students read all the words.

7. Take the stack of words that students read correctly and dictate each word to them.

8. Have students write each word or spell it aloud.

TIP If students have difficulty with any sight words, let them work at their own pace to really master these words.

> **Objectives**
> - Read sight words.
> - Spell sight words.
> - Write sight words.

Practice Sounds /ū/ and Long Double *o*

Have students build words by adding and changing letters to help them recognize and use the spellings *u*, *ue*, *ew*, and *u-e* for the sound /ū/ and the spellings *ew* and *oo* for the sound /o͞o/.

1. Write the following words on students' whiteboard: *use* and *zoo*.

2. **Say:** I am going to say a word. You will listen to the word I say and tell me if the word has the sound /ū/ as in *use* or the sound /o͞o/ as in *zoo*. Point to the word *use* when you say the sound /ū/. Point to the word *zoo* when you say the sound /o͞o/. I'll do the first couple for you.

   ▸ The first word is *cue*. *Cue* has the sound /ū/ as in *use*.
   ▸ The next word is *moon*. *Moon* has the sound/o͞o/ as in *zoo*.

3. Say the following words. Have students say the sounds for /ū/ or /o͞o/and point to the example word.

   ▸ *loop* /o͞o/ as in *zoo*   ▸ *school* /o͞o/ as in *zoo*
   ▸ *spoon* /o͞o/ as in *zoo*   ▸ *scoop* /o͞o/ as in *zoo*
   ▸ *cube* /ū/ as in *use*   ▸ *cute* /ū/ as in *use*
   ▸ *cool* /o͞o/ as in *zoo*   ▸ *few* /ū/ as in *use*
   ▸ *fuse* /ū/ as in *use*   ▸ *unit* /ū/ as in *use*
   ▸ *rescue* /ū/ as in *use*   ▸ *menu* /ū/ as in *use*
   ▸ *threw* /o͞o/ as in *zoo*   ▸ *tool* /o͞o/ as in *zoo*
   ▸ *room* /o͞o/ as in *zoo*

Rhyming Words

Have students complete page PH 56 in *K¹² PhonicsWorks Advanced Activity Book* for more practice with the spellings for the sounds /ū/ and /o͞o/. Have students read each word aloud and write the *Y* in the Yes column if the two words rhyme or *N* in the No column if they do not rhyme.

Objectives
- Identify and use the sound /ū/.
- Identify and use the long double *o* sound.
- Identify individual sounds in words.

Objectives
- Identify words that rhyme.
- Identify and use the sound /ū/.
- Identify and use the long double *o* sound.
- Identify individual sounds in words.

⌈Online⌋ ⑮ minutes

REVIEW: Spellings for Sounds /ū/ and Long Double *o*

Students will work online independently to

► Practice spellings for the sounds /ū/ and /o͞o/.
► Practice decoding text by reading a story.

Help students locate the online activities and provide support as needed.

Offline Alternative

No computer access? Read the following words with the sound /o͞o/ and have students say the spellings: spelling *u: tuna, Ruth, truth*; spelling *ue: clue, glue*; spelling *ew: flew, chewing, brew*; spelling *oo: loop, spoon, cool, room, school, tool*; spelling *u-e: rude, dude, cube.* Then read the following words with the sound /ū/ and have students say the spellings: spelling *u: music, bugle, unicorn*; spelling *ue: cue, argue, fescue*; spelling *ew: few, mew, fewest*; spelling *u-e: cute, mule, rule.*

Objectives

- Identify and use the sound /ū/.
- Identify the letters, given the sound /ū/.
- Identify and use /ū/ spelling patterns.
- Identify and use the long double *o* sound.
- Identify the letters, given the long double *o* sound.
- Identify and use double *o* (oo) spelling patterns.
- Identify and use silent *e*.
- Read aloud grade-level text with appropriate automaticity, prosody, accuracy, and rate.
- Decode words by applying grade-level word analysis skills.

Practice Spellings for Sounds /ū/ and Long Double *o* (B)

Lesson Overview

📋	**[Offline]** FOCUS: Practice Spellings for Sounds /ū/ and Long Double *o*		**15** minutes
Sight Words	Pick a Pair		
Practice	Sort Spellings for Sound /ū/		
	Sort Spellings for Long Double *o* Sound		
Try It	"Ruben"		
	Dictation: Write Sentences		
🖥	**[Online]** REVIEW: Spellings for Sounds /ū/ and Long Double *o*		**15** minutes

[Materials]

Supplied

- *K¹² PhonicsWorks Readers Advanced 10*, pp. 17–23
- whiteboard, Learning Coach
- Tile Kit

Also Needed

- sight words box
- dictation notebook
- index cards (27)

Advance Preparation

For Sort Spellings for Sound /ū/, print each of the following words on index cards, using one card per word: *music, unit, humid, cue, hue, rescue, mew, few, fewest, cube, mule,* and *fume.*

For Sort Spellings for Long Double *o* Sound, print each of the following words on index cards, using one card per word: *tuna, lunar, truth, Sue, blue, due, brew, flew, new, bloom, room, moose, dude, ruse,* and *tune.*

[Offline] ⏱ 15 minutes

FOCUS: Practice Spellings for Sounds /ū/ and Long Double *o*

Work **together** with students to complete offline Sight Words, Practice, and Try It activities.

Sight Words ••

Pick a Pair

Play a card game with students for more practice with sight words.

1. Gather the sight word cards that students are reviewing. Choose two words and place the cards on the table.

2. Ask questions to help students identify each word. For example, if the words are *or* and *one*, you could ask, "Which word names a number?" If the words are *on* and *but*, you could ask, "Which word is the opposite of *off*?"

3. Continue the activity until students identify all the words.

4. Take the stack of words that students read correctly and dictate each word to them.

5. Have students write each word or spell it aloud.

> **Objectives**
> - Read sight words.
> - Write sight words.
> - Spell sight words.

Practice ••

Sort Spellings for Sound /ū/

Help students practice identifying words that have the spellings *u*, *ue*, *ew*, and *u-e* for the sound /ū/.

1. Gather the index cards that you prepared. Mix the cards well and place them in a stack face down on the table.

2. Gather the dictation notebook. Draw four columns and label them *u*, *ue*, *ew*, and *u-e* to represent the four different ways to spell the sound /ū/.

3. **Say:** You are going to sort words by the four spellings for the sound /ū/. You will take a card from the pile and read it to me. Then you will think about the spelling for the sound /ū/ in the word and write that word in the correct column. I'll do the first one for you.

4. Demonstrate the following for students:
   ▸ Draw a card from the pile.
   ▸ Read the word aloud.
   ▸ Write the word in the correct column for the spelling for the sound /ū/.

5. Have students continue the procedure with the remaining words:
   ▸ **Spelling *u* words:** *music, unit, humid*
   ▸ **Spelling *ue* words:** *cue, hue, rescue*
   ▸ **Spelling *ew* words:** *mew, few, fewest*
   ▸ **Spelling *u-e* words:** *cube, mule, fume*

> **Objectives**
> - Identify and use the sound /ū/.
> - Identify the letters, given the sound /ū/.
> - Identify and use /ū/ spelling patterns.
> - Identify and use the long double *o* sound.
> - Identify the letters, given the long double *o* sound.
> - Identify and use double *o* (oo) spelling patterns.
> - Identify and use silent *e*.
> - Identify individual sounds in words.

Sort Spellings for Long Double *o* Sound

Help students practice identifying words that have the spellings *u, ue, ew, oo,* and *u-e* for the sound /oo/.

1. Gather the index cards that you prepared. Mix the cards well and place them in a stack face down on the table.

2. Gather the dictation notebook. Draw five columns and label them *u, ue, ew, oo,* and *u-e* to represent the five different ways to spell the sound /oo/.

3. **Say:** You are going to sort words by the five spellings for the sound /oo/. You will take a card from the pile and read it to me. Then you will think about the spelling for the sound /oo/ in the word and write that word in the correct column. I'll do the first one for you.

4. Demonstrate the following for students:

    ‣ Draw a card from the pile.
    ‣ Read the word aloud.
    ‣ Write the word in the correct column for the spelling for the sound /oo/.

5. Have students continue the procedure with the remaining words:

    ‣ **Spelling *u* words:** *tuna, lunar, truth*
    ‣ **Spelling *ue* words:** *Sue, blue, due*
    ‣ **Spelling *ew* words:** *brew, flew, new*
    ‣ **Spelling *oo* words:** *bloom, room, moose*
    ‣ **Spelling *u-e* words:** *dude, ruse, tune*

Try It

"Ruben"

Have students read "Ruben" on page 17 of *K¹² PhonicsWorks Readers Advanced 10.*

Students should read the story silently once or twice before reading the story aloud. When students miss a word that can be sounded out, point to it and give them three to six seconds to try the word again. If students still miss the word, tell them the word so the flow of the story isn't interrupted.

After reading the story, make a list of all the words students missed, and go over those words with them. You may use letter tiles to show students how to read the words.

Objectives

- Read aloud grade-level text with appropriate automaticity, prosody, accuracy, and rate.
- Decode words by applying grade-level word analysis skills.
- Write words by applying grade-level phonics knowledge.
- Follow three-step directions.

Dictation: Write Sentences
Use sentences to help students identify individual sounds in words.

1. Gather a pencil and the dictation notebook. Say the sentence, *Use the new shampoo and toothpaste.* Then give these directions to students:

   ▸ Repeat the sentence.
   ▸ Write the sentence in your notebook.
   ▸ Read the sentence aloud.

2. When students have finished, write the following sentence on your whiteboard: *Use the new shampoo and toothpaste.*

3. Have them compare their answer to your correct version.

4. Repeat this procedure with the following sentences: *Ruth will go to the zoo. The bedroom walls are blue. That dude came to the rescue.*

   ▸ If students make an error and don't see it, help them correct their mistake by having them finger stretch the sounds in the word they missed.
   ▸ If students are having difficulty selecting the correct letters or sounds, review those letters or sounds that are confusing them.
   ▸ If students have difficulty with first, middle, and last sounds, have them finger stretch the sounds in words.

 **15 minutes**

REVIEW: Spellings for Sounds /ū/ and Long Double *o*

Students will work online independently to

▸ Practice spellings for the sounds /ū/ and /o͞o/.

Help students locate the online activities and provide support as needed.

Offline Alternative

No computer access? Read the following words with the sound /o͞o/ and have students say the spellings: spelling *u*: *luna, Ruth*; spelling *ue*: *true, blue*; spelling *ew*: *dew, blew, screw*; spelling *oo*: *loon, bloom, moon, doom, noon*; spelling *u-e*: *rule, flute, prune.* Then read the following words with the sound /ū/ and have students say the spellings: spelling *u*: *stupid, humid, unite*; spelling *ue*: *Sue, cruel, argue, rescue*; spelling *ew*: *few, mew, fewest*; spelling *u-e*: *fume, fuse, use.*

Objectives

- Identify and use the sound /ū/.
- Identify the letters, given the sound /ū/.
- Identify and use /ū/ spelling patterns.
- Identify and use the long double *o* sound.
- Identify the letters, given the long double *o* sound.
- Identify and use double *o* (oo) spelling patterns.
- Identify and use silent *e*.
- Identify individual sounds in words.

Unit Checkpoint

Lesson Overview

🖥	**〖Online〗**	**REVIEW:** Spellings for Sounds /ū/ and Long Double *o*	**15** minutes
📄	**〖Offline〗**	**UNIT CHECKPOINT:** Spellings for Sounds /ū/ and Long Double *o*	**15** minutes

〖Materials〗

Supplied

- *K¹² PhonicsWorks Advanced Assessments,* pp. PH 163–168

⭐ Objectives

- Identify individual sounds in words.
- Identify and use the sound /ū/.
- Identify the letters, given the sound /ū/.
- Identify and use /ū/ spelling patterns.
- Identify and use the long double *o* sound.
- Identify the letters, given the long double *o* sound.
- Identify and use double *o* (oo) spelling patterns.
- Identify and use silent *e*.
- Read instructional-level text with 90% accuracy.
- Read aloud grade-level text with appropriate automaticity, prosody, accuracy, and rate.
- Write words by applying grade-level phonics knowledge.
- Write sight words.
- Read sight words.

〖Online〗 **15** minutes

REVIEW: Spellings for Sounds /ū/ and Long Double *o*

Students will review spellings for the sounds /ū/ and /o͞o/ to prepare for the Unit Checkpoint. Help students locate the online activities and provide support as needed.

⌈ Offline ⌋ ⏱ minutes

UNIT CHECKPOINT: Spellings for Sounds /ū/ and Long Double *o*

Explain that students are going to show what they have learned about sounds, letters, and words.

1. Give students the Unit Checkpoint pages for the Spellings for Sounds /ū/ and Long Double *o* unit and print the Unit Checkpoint Answer Key, if you'd like.

2. Use the instructions below to help administer the Checkpoint to students. On the Answer Key or another sheet of paper, note student answers to oral response questions to help with scoring the Checkpoint later.

3. Use the Answer Key to score the Checkpoint, and then enter the results online.

Part 1. Circle Words with Sound /ū/ Have students circle the words with the sound /ū/.

Part 2. Circle Words with the Long Double *o* Sound Have students circle the words with the sound /o͞o/.

Part 3. Many Spellings, One Sound: /ū/ Have students circle the four ways to spell the sound /ū/.

Part 4. Many Spellings, One Sound: Long Double *o* Sound Have students circle the five ways to spell the sound /o͞o/.

Part 5. Writing Read each sentence to students. Have them repeat and write the sentence.

33. *Ruben made beef stew for lunch.*

34. *Jude had to use the fewest clues.*

35. *June threw the screws in the toolbox.*

Part 6. Read Aloud Listen to students read the sentences aloud. Count and note the number of words they read correctly.

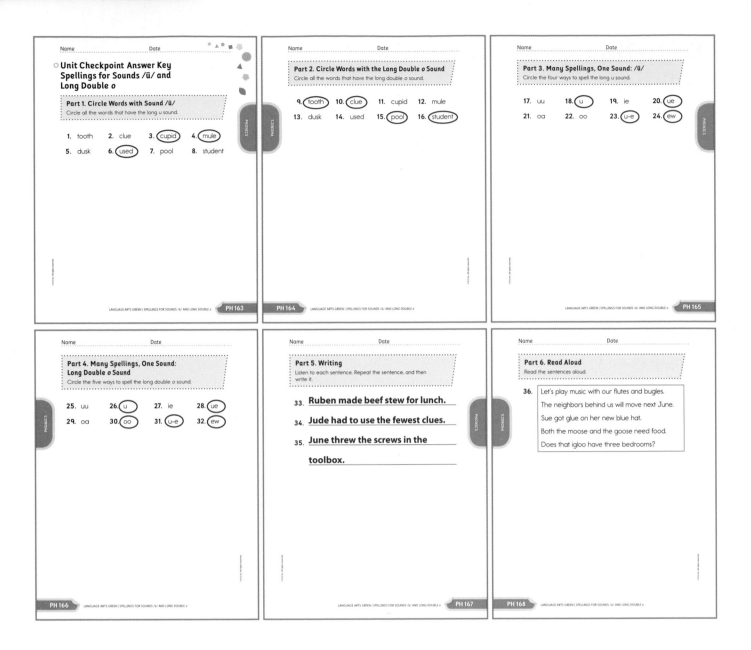

Name _____ **Date** _____

Unit Checkpoint Answer Key
Spellings for Sounds /ū/ and Long Double o

Part 1. Circle Words with Sound /ū/
Circle all the words that have the long u sound.

1. tooth   2. clue   3. (cupid)   4. (mule)
5. dusk   6. (used)   7. pool   8. student

Name _____ **Date** _____

Part 2. Circle Words with the Long Double o Sound
Circle all the words that have the long double o sound.

9. (tooth)   10. (clue)   11. cupid   12. mule
13. dusk   14. used   15. (pool)   16. (student)

Name _____ **Date** _____

Part 3. Many Spellings, One Sound: /ū/
Circle the four ways to spell the long u sound.

17. uu   18. (u)   19. ie   20. (ue)
21. oa   22. oo   23. (u-e)   24. (ew)

Name _____ **Date** _____

Part 4. Many Spellings, One Sound:
Long Double o Sound
Circle the five ways to spell the long double o sound.

25. uu   26. (u)   27. ie   28. (ue)
29. oa   30. (oo)   31. (u-e)   32. (ew)

Name _____ **Date** _____

Part 5. Writing
Listen to each sentence. Repeat the sentence, and then write it.

33. **Ruben made beef stew for lunch.**

34. **Jude had to use the fewest clues.**

35. **June threw the screws in the**
toolbox.

Name _____ **Date** _____

Part 6. Read Aloud
Read the sentences aloud.

36.
Let's play music with our flutes and bugles.
The neighbors behind us will move next June.
Sue got glue on her new blue hat.
Both the moose and the goose need food.
Does that igloo have three bedrooms?

Introduce Spellings for Short Double *o* Sound

Unit Overview

In this unit, students will

- ▸ Learn the sight words *once*, *come*, and *about*.
- ▸ Learn the *oo* spelling for the sound /o͞o/.
- ▸ Read and write sentences.
- ▸ Read a story silently and aloud.

Lesson Overview

〖 Offline 〗	**FOCUS:** Introduce Spellings for Short Double *o* Sound	**15** minutes

Sight Words	Introduce Sight Words
Learn	Introduce the *oo* Spelling for the Short Double *o* Sound
	Build Words
Try It	Investigator

〖 Online 〗	**REVIEW:** Spellings for Short Double *o* Sound	**15** minutes

〖 Materials 〗

Supplied

- *K¹² PhonicsWorks Advanced Activity Book,* p. PH 57
- whiteboard, student
- Tile Kit

Also Needed

- sight words box
- crayons

〔 Offline 〕 ⑮ minutes

FOCUS: Introduce Spellings for Short Double *o* Sound

Work **together** with students to complete offline Sight Words, Learn, and Try It activities.

Sight Words ....

Introduce Sight Words

Help students learn the sight words *once*, *come*, and *about*.

1. Gather the sight word cards *once*, *come*, and *about*.

2. Show students the *once* card.

3. **Say:** This is the word *once*. We see this word so often that we want to be able to read and spell it quickly without thinking about it. Look closely at the word *once*. Spell the word *once* aloud. Take a picture of the word *once* in your mind. When you think you can spell *once* yourself, turn the card over and use your letter tiles to spell the word *once*. Check the card to see if you spelled the word *once* correctly. Read aloud the word you spelled with the letter tiles.

4. Repeat the activity with the remaining sight words.

5. Chart students' progress on the back of each card.

   ▸ Divide the back of the card into two columns.
   ▸ Label the first column "Read" and the second column "Spell."
   ▸ Record the dates that students read or spell the word correctly. When students can read and spell the word correctly three times in a row, they have mastered the word. You may want to put a star or sticker on their card when they have mastered that word.

6. Add the cards to students' sight words box.

TIP Sight words can be very difficult for some students. Let students work at their own pace and really master these words, as they occur frequently in reading and writing.

Objectives
- Read sight words.
- Spell sight words.

Introduce the *oo* Spelling for the Short Double *o* Sound

Help students learn the *oo* spelling for the sound /o͝o/.

1. Place the following letter tiles on students' whiteboard: *b, k,* and *oo*.

2. Make the word *book* in the middle of students' whiteboard and point to it.

   Say: Today we are going to learn a spelling for the short double *oo* sound. The short double *oo* sound can be spelled with the letters *oo*, and it makes the sound /o͝o/. We use the *oo* letter tile to show this spelling for the sound /o͝o/.

   ▸ Touch and say *book*.
   ▸ What is the vowel sound in this word? /o͝o/
   ▸ Which letter or letters make this sound? *oo*

> **Objectives**
> - Identify and use double *o* (oo) spelling patterns.
> - Identify and use the short double *o* sound.
> - Blend sounds to create words.
> - Identify individual sounds in words.
> - Write words by applying grade-level phonics knowledge.

Build Words

Help students use letters and sounds to build words.

1. Place the following letter tiles at the top of students' whiteboard: *d, h, k, l, oo, s, sh, t,* and *w*.

2. Draw three horizontal lines across the middle of students' whiteboard to represent the sounds in a word.

3. **Say:** Let's use letters and sounds to build the word *look*.

4. Have students finger stretch the sounds in *look*.

5. Have students

   ▸ Identify the first, next, and last sounds in *look*.
   ▸ Choose the corresponding letter tile for each of the sounds.
   ▸ Move the letters to the correct lines on their whiteboard.

6. Guide students with these questions:

   ▸ What is the first sound in *look*? /l/
      Which line does the letter for that sound go on? the first one
   ▸ What is the next sound in *look*?/o͝o/
      Which line do the letters for that sound go on? the second one
   ▸ What's the last sound in *look*? /k/
      Which line does the letter for that sound go on? the last one

7. Redirect students if they select the incorrect letter.

   Say: That sound is in the word [word], and it is the [first, second, third] sound. We want the sound [target sound].

   Continue until students select the correct letter tile.

8. Have students touch and say the word.

9. Have them say the word as they use a dry-erase marker to write the word on the whiteboard.

10. Draw horizontal lines across the middle of students' whiteboard that represent the number of sounds in each word. Repeat the activity to build the following words:

- ▸ *hood* /h/ /o͝o/ /d/
- ▸ *shook* /sh/ /o͝o/ /k/
- ▸ *stood* /s/ /t/ /o͝o/ /d/
- ▸ *wood* /w/ /o͝o/ /d/

Try It

Investigator

Have students complete page PH 57 in *K¹² PhonicsWorks Advanced Activity Book* for more practice with the *oo* spelling for the sound /o͝o/. Have students read each word aloud. Have them circle the words with the sound /o͝o/, as in *book*, in yellow and the words with the sound /o͞o/, as in *moon*, in pink.

Try It

Introduce Spellings for Short Double *o* Sound

Investigator

Circle the words with the sound /o͝o/, as in book, yellow.
Circle the words with the sound /o͞o/, as in moon, pink.

book	**yellow** nook	moon	**yellow** took
yellow brook	**yellow** cook	**yellow** shook	**pink** food
yellow good	**pink** broom	**yellow** stood	**yellow** crook
pink boot	**yellow** hoof	**yellow** wood	**yellow** wooden
yellow look	**yellow** foot	**yellow** wool	**yellow** hook
pink balloon	**yellow** hood	**yellow** football	**pink** raccoon

Circle the answer.

1. Where is oo in these words?   middle   end

LANGUAGE ARTS GREEN   **PH 57**

Objectives

- Identify and use double *o* (oo) spelling patterns.
- Identify and use the short double *o* sound.

[Online] **15** minutes

REVIEW: Spellings for Short Double *o* Sound

Students will work online independently to

▶ Practice the *oo* spelling for the sound /o͝o/.

▶ Practice decoding text by reading a story.

Help students locate the online activities and provide support as needed.

Offline Alternative

No computer access? Have students name and spell words that have the *oo* spelling for the sound /o͝o/, such as *good* or *took*.

Objectives

- Identify and use double *o* (oo) spelling patterns.
- Identify and use the short double *o* sound.
- Read aloud grade-level text with appropriate automaticity, prosody, accuracy, and rate.
- Decode words by applying grade-level word analysis skills.

Practice Spellings for Double *o* Sounds (A)

Lesson Overview

[Offline] **FOCUS:** Practice Spellings for Double *o* Sounds — **15** minutes

Sight Words	Sight Word Fun
Practice	Two-Syllable Words with the Short Double *o* Sound
	Word Chains
Try It	"Brandy Helps Make a Sweet Treat"

[Online] **REVIEW:** Spellings for Double *o* Sounds — **15** minutes

[Materials]

Supplied
- *K¹² PhonicsWorks Readers Advanced 10,* pp. 24–30
- whiteboard, Learning Coach
- whiteboard, student
- small whiteboards (2)
- Tile Kit

Also Needed
- sight words box

[Offline] ⏱ 15 minutes

FOCUS: Practice Spellings for Double *o* Sounds

Work **together** with students to complete offline Sight Words, Practice, and Try It activities.

Sight Words ··

Sight Word Fun

Help students learn the sight words *once*, *come*, and *about*, and up to two additional sight words they have yet to master.

1. Gather the sight word cards *once*, *come*, and *about*, and up to two additional sight word cards.

2. Choose one sight word card to begin.

   Say: Look at this word and take a picture of it in your mind. When you think you can spell the word yourself, turn the card over and use your letter tiles to spell the word.

3. After students spell the word, have them check the card to see if they spelled the word correctly.

   Say: Read aloud the word you spelled with the letter tiles.

4. Repeat the activity with the remaining sight words.

   TIP Sight words can be very difficult for some students. Let them work at their own pace and really master these words.

> **Objectives**
> - Read sight words.
> - Spell sight words.

Practice ··

Two-Syllable Words with the Short Double *o* Sound

Have students practice making two-syllable words with the sound /o͝o/. Grab your whiteboard, two small whiteboards, and the dry-erase marker.

1. **Say:** Let's spell words that have the sound /o͝o/ spelled *oo*. Each word will have two syllables. The first word is *football*.

   - ► Fist tap the syllables in the word. *foot / ball*
   - ► Write the first syllable on a small whiteboard. *foot*
   - ► Write the second syllable on another small whiteboard. *ball*
   - ► Push the two small whiteboards together and read the word aloud.
   - ► Turn the small whiteboards face down and write the word on your whiteboard.
   - ► Turn the small whiteboards face up and check the spelling.

2. Have students follow this procedure to make the following words:

   - ► *bookcase book / case*
   - ► *hardwood hard / wood*
   - ► *footstep foot / step*
   - ► *textbook text / book*

> **Objectives**
> - Identify the number of syllables in a word.
> - Identify syllables in words.
> - Identify and use double *o* (oo) spelling patterns.
> - Identify and use the short double *o* sound.
> - Identify and use the long double *o* sound.
> - Identify individual sounds in words.
> - Identify the new word when one sound is changed in a word.

Word Chains

Have students build words by adding and changing letters to help them recognize and use individual sounds in words.

1. Place the following letter tiles at the top of students' whiteboard: *b, c, ch, ew, f, l, n, o, oo, s, S, u,* and *ue.*

2. **Say:** I am going to build the first word in a chain. The word is *chew.*

   ▶ I will pull down the letters for the sounds /ch/ and /ew/ to spell the word *chew.*

   ▶ I will touch and say *chew.* To change *chew* to *few,* I will think about which sound is changed from the word *chew* to *few.* I will need to replace the *ch* letter tile with the letter *f.*

   ▶ Touch and say the word *few.* Now it's your turn to change *few* to *flew.* You can spell *flew* by making only one change. Touch and say the new word.

3. Redirect students if they select the incorrect letter for any sound.

   Say: That letter is for the sound [incorrect sound]. We want the letter for the sound [target sound]. What letter makes that sound? Answers will vary.

4. Redirect students if they name the sound incorrectly.

   Say: To change the word [first word] to [target word], we need the letter for the sound [target sound].

   Show students how to make the change. Have them touch and say the new word after they move the letters.

5. Follow this procedure to make the following words: *blew, blue, clue, cue, Sue, sun, soon.*

6. For every new word, have students add, replace, or remove only one letter tile.

   TIP For the proper name word, replace the lowercase letter with a capital letter. Remember to change back to the lowercase letter for the next word in the chain.

Try It ••

"Brandy Helps Make a Sweet Treat"

Have students read "Brandy Helps Make a Sweet Treat" on page 24 of *K¹² PhonicsWorks Readers Advanced 10.*

Students should read the story silently once or twice before reading the story aloud. When students miss a word that can be sounded out, point to it and give them three to six seconds to try the word again. If students still miss the word, tell them the word so the flow of the story isn't interrupted.

After reading the story, make a list of all the words students missed, and go over those words with them. You may use letter tiles to show students how to read the words.

Objectives
- Read aloud grade-level text with appropriate automaticity, prosody, accuracy, and rate.
- Decode words by applying grade-level word analysis skills.

[Online] ⑮ minutes

REVIEW: Spellings for Double *o* Sounds

Students will work online independently to

▸ Practice the *oo* spelling for the sounds /o͝o/ and /o͞o/.

Help students locate the online activities and provide support as needed.

Offline Alternative

No computer access? Have students spell words with the *oo* spelling for the sounds /o͝o/ and /o͞o/, such as *woof*, *book*, and *look* for the sound /o͝o/ and *gloom*, *spoon*, and *moon* for the sound /o͞o/.

⭐ Objectives

- Identify individual sounds in words.
- Identify and use the short double *o* sound.
- Identify and use the long double *o* sound.
- Identify and use double *o* (oo) spelling patterns.

Practice Spellings for Double *o* Sounds (B)

Lesson Overview

Offline	**FOCUS:** Practice Spellings for Double *o* Sounds	**15** minutes

Sight Words	Sight Word Fun
Practice	Read for Fluency
	Sort Long and Short Double *o* Sounds
	Build Words
Try It	Clues

Online	**REVIEW:** Spellings for Double *o* Sounds	**15** minutes

[Materials]

Supplied
- *K¹² PhonicsWorks Advanced Activity Book*, p. PH 58
- whiteboard, student
- Tile Kit

Also Needed
- sight words box
- dictation notebook
- index cards (43)

Advance Preparation

For Read for Fluency, print each of the following words on index cards, using one card per word: *food, feel, fail, full, foot, pine, pain, pipe, green, grain, grin, groom, dance, fence, chance, since, mean, moan, mine, moon, mood, book, beak, bike,* and *buck.*

For Sort Long and Short Double *o* Sounds, print each of the following words on index cards, using one card per word: *brook, cook, good, hood, hook, look, shook, took, stood, wood, boom, boost, cool, hoop, pool, spoon, tool,* and *zoom.*

【 Offline 】 ⏱ minutes

FOCUS: Practice Spellings for Double *o* Sounds

Work **together** with students to complete offline Sight Words, Practice, and Try It activities.

Sight Words ··

Sight Word Fun

Help students learn the sight words *once, come,* and *about,* and up to two additional sight words they have yet to master.

1. Gather the sight word cards *once, come,* and *about,* and up to two additional sight word cards.

2. Choose one sight word card to begin.

   Say: Look at this word and take a picture of it in your mind. When you think you can spell the word yourself, turn the card over and use your letter tiles to spell the word.

3. After students spell the word, have them check the card to see if they spelled the word correctly.

   Say: Read aloud the word you spelled with the letter tiles.

4. Repeat the activity with the remaining sight words.

(TIP) Sight words can be very difficult for some students. Let them work at their own pace and really master these words.

> **Objectives**
> - Read sight words.
> - Spell sight words.

Practice ··

Read for Fluency

Have students practice reading words to become fluent.

1. Gather the index cards you prepared. Shuffle the cards, and place them face down in a stack on the table.

2. Have students pick a word and read it to you.

3. If students read it quickly and correctly, put the card in one stack. If they hesitate or do not read the word correctly, put it in another stack. The second stack should have words that they will review again.

4. After students read all 25 words, have them read the difficult words again. Continue the procedure until they read all the words without hesitating.

> **Objectives**
> - Read aloud grade-level text with appropriate automaticity, prosody, accuracy, and rate.
> - Identify and use double *o* (oo) spelling patterns.
> - Identify and use the short double *o* sound.
> - Identify and use the long double *o* sound.
> - Blend sounds to create words.
> - Identify individual sounds in words.
> - Write words by applying grade-level phonics knowledge.

Sort Long and Short Double *o* Sounds

Help students practice identifying words that have the sounds /o͝o/ and /o͞o/.

1. Gather the index cards you prepared and the following double *o* words from the Read for Fluency activity: *food, foot, book, groom, mood,* and *moon.* Mix the cards well, and place them face down in a stack on the table.

2. Gather the dictation notebook. Draw two columns and label them /o͝o/, for the short double *o* sound words, and /o͞o/, for the long double *o* sound words.

3. **Say:** You are going to sort short and long double *o* sound words. You will take a card from the pile and read it to me. Then you will say if the word has the short double *o* sound /o͝o/ or the long double *o* sound /o͞o/. You will write that word in the correct column. I'll do the first one for you.

4. Demonstrate the following for students:
   ▸ Draw a card from the pile.
   ▸ Read the word aloud.
   ▸ Write the word in the correct column for the sound.

5. Have students continue the procedure with the remaining words.
   ▸ /o͝o/ **Words:** *book, brook, cook, foot, good, hood, hook, look, shook, took, stood, wood*
   ▸ /o͞o/ **Words:** *boom, boost, cool, food, groom, hoop, mood, moon, pool, spoon, tool, zoom*

Build Words

Help students use letters and sounds to build words.

1. Place the following letter tiles at the top of students' whiteboard: *b, d, k, m, oo, p, r, s, sh, t, th,* and *w.*

2. Draw four horizontal lines across the middle of students' whiteboard to represent the sounds in a word.

3. **Say:** Let's use letters and sounds to build the word *brook.*

4. Have students finger stretch the sounds in *brook.*

5. Have students
   ▸ Identify the first, next, and last sounds in *brook.*
   ▸ Choose the corresponding letter tile for each of the sounds.
   ▸ Move the letters to the correct lines on their whiteboard.

6. Guide students with these questions:

   ► What is the first sound in *brook*? /b/
     Which line does the letter for that sound go on? the first one
   ► What is the next sound in *brook*? /r/
     Which line does the letter for that sound go on? the second one
   ► What is the next sound in *brook* /ŏŏ/
     Which line do the letters for that sound go on? the third one
   ► What's the last sound in *brook*? /k/
     Which line does the letter for that sound go on? the last one

7. Redirect students if they select the incorrect letter.

   Say: That sound is in the word [word], and it is the [first, second, third, fourth] sound. We want the sound [target sound].

   Continue until students select the correct letter tile.

8. Have students touch and say the word.

9. Have them say the word as they use a dry-erase marker to write the word on the whiteboard.

10. Draw horizontal lines across the middle of students' whiteboard that represent the number of sounds in each word. Repeat the activity to build the following words:

    ► *stood* /s/ /t/ /ŏŏ/ /d/
    ► *shook* /sh/ /ŏŏ/ /k/
    ► *swoop* /s/ /w/ /ōō/ /p/
    ► *tooth* /t/ /ōō/ /th/
    ► *broom* /b/ /r/ /ōō/ /m/

Try It ●

Clues

Have students complete page PH 58 in *K¹² PhonicsWorks Advanced Activity Book* for more practice with spellings for the sound /o͝o/. Have students read each clue aloud. Have them find the word from the box that matches the clue and write that word next to the clue.

Try It ....

Practice Spellings for Double *o* Sounds (B)

Clues

Read the clue aloud. Find the word in the box that matches the clue, and write it next to the clue.

notebook	cookbook
hook	football
hood	shook

	Clue	What Is It?
1.	Used for catching fish	hook
2.	Used to play game	football
3.	Used for taking notes	notebook
4.	Trembled and quaked	shook
5.	Part of some coats	hood
6.	Tells how to prepare foods	cookbook

PH 58   LANGUAGE ARTS GREEN

Objectives

- Identify and use double *o* (oo) spelling patterns.
- Identify and use the short double *o* sound.
- Read aloud grade-level text with appropriate automaticity, prosody, accuracy, and rate.
- Decode words by applying grade-level word analysis skills.
- Write words by applying grade-level phonics knowledge.

【Online】 ⑮ minutes

REVIEW: Spellings for Double *o* Sounds

Students will work online independently to

▶ Practice the *oo* spelling for the sounds /o͝o/ and /o͞o/.
▶ Practice decoding text by reading a story.

Help students locate the online activities and provide support as needed.

Offline Alternative

No computer access? Have students spell words with the *oo* spelling for the sounds /o͝o/ and /o͞o/, such as *stood*, *hood*, and *wood* for the sound /o͝o/ and *spook*, *broom*, and *hoot* for the sound /o͞o/.

Objectives

- Identify individual sounds in words.
- Identify and use double *o* (oo) spelling patterns.
- Identify and use the short double *o* sound.
- Identify and use the long double *o* sound.
- Read aloud grade-level text with appropriate automaticity, prosody, accuracy, and rate.
- Decode words by applying grade-level word analysis skills.

Practice Spellings for Double *o* Sounds (C)

Lesson Overview

[Offline] **FOCUS:** Practice Spellings for Double *o* Sounds		**15** minutes

Sight Words	Sight Word Fun

Practice	Sort Spellings for Long Double *o* Sound
	Build Words

Try It	"Joe"

[Online] **REVIEW:** Spellings for Double *o* Sounds		**15** minutes

Materials

Supplied
- *K¹² PhonicsWorks Readers Advanced 11*, pp. 1–6
- whiteboard, student

Also Needed
- sight words box
- dictation notebook
- index cards (10)

Advance Preparation

For Sort Spellings for Long Double *o* Sound, print each of the following words on index cards, using one card per word: *flew, stew, blue, tune, moon, pool, June, hoop, glue,* and *threw*.

[Offline] 15 minutes

FOCUS: Practice Spellings for Double *o* Sounds

Work **together** with students to complete offline Sight Words, Practice, and Try It activities.

Sight Words

Sight Word Fun

Help students learn the sight words *once, come,* and *about,* and up to two additional sight words they have yet to master.

1. Gather the sight word cards *once, come,* and *about,* and up to two additional sight word cards.

2. Choose one sight word card to begin.

   Say: Look at this word and take a picture of it in your mind. When you think you can spell the word yourself, turn the card over and use your letter tiles to spell the word.

3. After students spell the word, have them check the card to see if they spelled the word correctly.

   Say: Read aloud the word you spelled with the letter tiles.

4. Repeat the activity with the remaining sight words.

   TIP Sight words can be very difficult for some students. Let them work at their own pace and really master these words.

> **Objectives**
> * Read sight words.
> * Spell sight words.

Practice

Sort Spellings for Long Double *o* Sound

Help students practice identifying words that have the spellings *ue, ew, oo,* and *u-e* for the sound /$\overline{oo}$/.

1. Gather the index cards you prepared. Mix the cards well, and place them in a stack face down on the table.

2. Gather the dictation notebook. Draw four columns and label them *ue, ew, oo,* and *u-e* to represent four different ways to spell the sound /$\overline{oo}$/.

3. **Say:** You are going to sort words by the four spellings for the sound /$\overline{oo}$/. You will take a card from the pile and read it to me. Then you will think about the spelling for the sound /$\overline{oo}$/ in the word and write that word in the correct column. I'll do the first one for you.

> **Objectives**
> * Read aloud grade-level text with appropriate automaticity, prosody, accuracy, and rate.
> * Identify and use double *o* (oo) spelling patterns.
> * Identify and use the short double *o* sound.
> * Identify and use the long double *o* sound.
> * Blend sounds to create words.
> * Identify individual sounds in words.
> * Write words by applying grade-level phonics knowledge.

4. Demonstrate the following for students:

  ‣ Draw a card from the pile.
  ‣ Read the word aloud.
  ‣ Write the word in the correct column for the spelling for sound /o͞o/.

5. Have students continue the procedure with the remaining words:

  ‣ **Spelling *ue* Words:** *blue, glue*
  ‣ **Spelling *ew* Words:** *flew, stew, threw*
  ‣ **Spelling *oo* Words:** *moon, pool, hoop*
  ‣ **Spelling *u-e* Words:** *June, tune*

Build Words

Help students use letters and sounds to build words.

1. Place the following letter tiles at the top of students' whiteboard: *c, ch, d, e, ew, k, n, oo, p, r, s, t, u,* and *ue.*

2. Draw two horizontal lines across the middle of students' whiteboard to represent the sounds in a word.

3. **Say:** Let's use letters and sounds to build the word *chew.*

4. Have students finger stretch the sounds in *chew.*

5. Have students

  ‣ Identify the first and last sounds in *chew.*
  ‣ Choose the corresponding letter tile for each of the sounds.
  ‣ Move the letters to the correct lines on their whiteboard.

6. Guide students with these questions:

  ‣ What is the first sound in *chew*? /ch/
    Which line do the letters for that sound go on? the first one
  ‣ What is the last sound in *chew*? /o͞o/
    Which line do the letters for that sound go on? the last one

7. Redirect students if they select the incorrect letter.

   Say: That sound is in the word [word], and it is the [first, second] sound. We want the sound [target sound].

   Continue until students select the correct letter tile.

8. Have students touch and say the word.

9. Have them say the word as they use a dry-erase marker to write the word on the whiteboard.

10. Draw horizontal lines across the middle of students' whiteboard that represent the number of sounds in each word. Repeat the activity to build the following words:

- *stood* /s/ /t/ /o͝o/ /d/
- *stoop* /s/ /t/ /o͞o/ /p/
- *true* /t/ /r/ /o͞o/
- *prune* /p/ /r/ /o͞o/ /n/
- *cook* /k/ /o͝o/ /k/

Try It

"Joe"
Have students read "Joe" on page 1 of *K¹² PhonicsWorks Readers Advanced 11*.

Students should read the story silently once or twice before reading the story aloud. When students miss a word that can be sounded out, point to it and give them three to six seconds to try the word again. If students still miss the word, tell them the word so the flow of the story isn't interrupted.

After reading the story, make a list of all the words students missed, and go over those words with them. You may use letter tiles to show students how to read the words.

Objectives
- Read aloud grade-level text with appropriate automaticity, prosody, accuracy, and rate.
- Decode words by applying grade-level word analysis skills.

[Online] 15 minutes

REVIEW: Spellings for Double *o* Sounds
Students will work online independently to

- Practice spellings for the sounds /o͝o/ and /o͞o/.

Help students locate the online activities and provide support as needed.

Offline Alternative

No computer access? Have students spell words with the *oo* spelling for the sound /o͝o/, such as *cook*, *hook*, and *soot*, and have them spell words with the *oo*, *u-e*, *ue*, and *ew* spellings for the sound /o͞o/, such as *boot*, *flute*, *glue*, and *blew*.

Objectives
- Identify individual sounds in words.
- Identify and use double *o* (oo) spelling patterns.
- Identify and use the short double *o* sound.
- Identify and use the long double *o* sound.

Unit Checkpoint

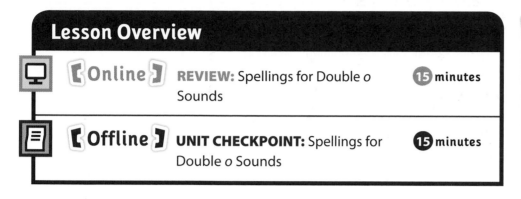

Lesson Overview

| 🖥️ | **[Online]** | **REVIEW:** Spellings for Double *o* Sounds | **15** minutes |
| 📄 | **[Offline]** | **UNIT CHECKPOINT:** Spellings for Double *o* Sounds | **15** minutes |

[Materials]

Supplied
- *K¹² PhonicsWorks Advanced Assessments,* pp. PH 169–174

⭐ Objectives

- Identify individual sounds in words.
- Identify and use double *o* (oo) spelling patterns.
- Identify and use the short double *o* sound.
- Identify and use the long double *o* sound.
- Read instructional-level text with 90% accuracy.
- Read aloud grade-level text with appropriate automaticity, prosody, accuracy, and rate.
- Write words by applying grade-level phonics knowledge.
- Write sight words.
- Read sight words.

[Online] 15 minutes

REVIEW: Spellings for Double *o* Sounds

Students will review spellings for sounds /o͝o/ and /o͞o/ to prepare for the Unit Checkpoint. Help students locate the online activities and provide support as needed.

[Offline] 🕒 15 minutes

UNIT CHECKPOINT: Spellings for Double *o* Sounds

Explain that students are going to show what they have learned about sounds, letters, and words.

1. Give students the Unit Checkpoint pages for the Spellings for Double *o* Sounds unit and print the Unit Checkpoint Answer Key, if you'd like.

2. Use the instructions below to help administer the Checkpoint to students. On the Answer Key or another sheet of paper, note student answers to oral response questions to help with scoring the Checkpoint later.

3. Use the Answer Key to score the Checkpoint, and then enter the results online.

Part 1. Circle Words with the Short Double *o* Sound Have students circle the words with the sound /o͝o/.

Part 2. Circle Words with the Long Double *o* Sound Have students circle the words with the sound /o͞o/.

Part 3. Count Sounds Have students read each word aloud, count the number of sounds in each word, and write that number.

Part 4. Writing Read each sentence to students. Have them repeat and write the sentence.

23. *Is there a rule about picking the new blooms?*

24. *I once drew on a huge balloon.*

25. *June's new book about the zoo is good.*

26. *My neighbor has a cool blue car.*

Part 5. Read Aloud Listen to students read the sentences aloud. Count and note the number of words they read correctly.

Part 6. Read Sight Words Have students read each sight word aloud. Note any words they read incorrectly.

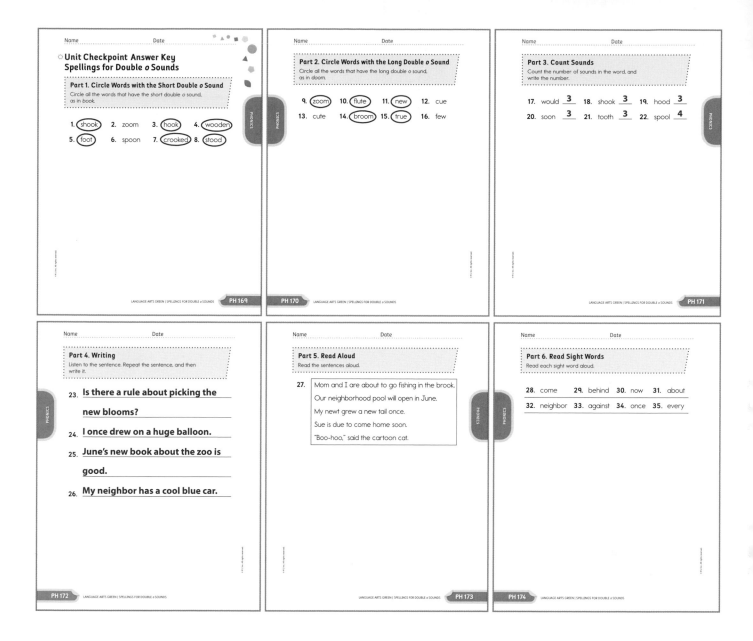

Review Long Vowels and Double *o* Sounds (A)

Unit Overview

In this unit, students will
- Learn the sight words *please*, *follow*, and *saw*.
- Review long vowels and double *o* sounds.
- Read and write sentences.
- Read a story silently and aloud.

[Materials]

Supplied
- *K¹² PhonicsWorks Advanced Activity Book*, p. PH 59
- whiteboard, Learning Coach
- whiteboard, student
- Tile Kit

Also Needed
- sight words box
- dictation notebook
- index cards (41)

Lesson Overview

[Offline] FOCUS: Review Long Vowels and Double *o* Sounds — **15** minutes

Sight Words	Introduce Sight Words
Practice	Sort Long Vowel Sounds
	Introduce Homophones
	Homophone Concentration
Try It	Hunt for Information
	Dictation: Write Sentences

[Online] REVIEW: Long Vowels and Double *o* Sounds — **15** minutes

Advance Preparation

For Sort Long Vowel Sounds, print each of the following words on index cards, using one card per word: *stay, sleigh, fray, trade, April, seed, clean, sight, my, fly, open, goat, tote, mow, show, clue, cue, stew, flew, few, prune, tune, use, cute,* and *unit.*

For Introduce Homophones and Homophone Concentration, print each of the following words on index cards, using one card per word: *weigh, way, maid, made, reed, read, seem, seam, high, hi, rode, road, toe, tow, blue,* and *blew.*

[Offline] 15 minutes

FOCUS: Review Long Vowels and Double *o* Sounds

Work **together** with students to complete offline Sight Words, Practice, and Try It activities.

Sight Words ....

Introduce Sight Words

Help students learn the sight words *please, follow,* and *saw.*

1. Gather the sight word cards *please, follow,* and *saw.*

2. Show students the *please* card.

3. **Say:** This is the word *please*. We see this word so often that we want to be able to read and spell it quickly without thinking about it. Look closely at the word *please*. Spell the word *please* aloud. Take a picture of the word *please* in your mind. When you think you can spell *please* yourself, turn the card over and use your letter tiles to spell the word *please*. Check the card to see if you spelled the word *please* correctly. Read aloud the word you spelled with the letter tiles.

4. Repeat the activity with the remaining sight words.

5. Chart students' progress on the back of each card.

   ▸ Divide the back of the card into two columns.
   ▸ Label the first column "Read" and the second column "Spell."
   ▸ Record the dates that students read or spell the word correctly. When students can read and spell the word correctly three times in a row, they have mastered the word. You may want to put a star or sticker on their card when they have mastered that word.

6. Add the cards to students' sight words box.

(TIP) Sight words can be very difficult for some students. Let students work at their own pace and really master these words, as they occur frequently in reading and writing.

Objectives
- Read sight words.
- Spell sight words.

Practice

Sort Long Vowel Sounds

Help students practice identifying words that have the sounds /ā/, /ē/, /ī/, /ō/, /ū/, and /o͞o/.

1. Gather the index cards you prepared. Mix the cards well, and place them in a stack face down on the table.

2. Gather the dictation notebook. Draw six columns and label them /ā/, /ē/, /ī/, /ō/, /ū/, and /o͞o/ to represent the long vowel sounds.

3. **Say:** You are going to sort words by the long vowel sounds /ā/, /ē/, /ī/, /ō/, /ū/, and /o͞o/. You will take a card from the pile and read it to me. Then you will think about the sound for the long vowel in the word and write that word in the correct column. I'll do the first one for you.

4. Demonstrate the following for students

   ▸ Draw a card from the pile.
   ▸ Read the word aloud.
   ▸ Write the word in the correct column for the long vowel sounds.

5. Have students continue the procedure with the remaining words.

   ▸ /ā/ **Words:** *stay, sleigh, fray, trade, April*
   ▸ /ē/ **Words:** *seed, clean*
   ▸ /ī/ **Words:** *sight, my, fly*
   ▸ /ō/ **Words:** *open, goat, tote, mow, show*
   ▸ /ū/ **Words:** *cue, few, use, cute, unit*
   ▸ /o͞o/ **Words:** *clue, stew, flew, prune, tune*

Introduce Homophones

Help students learn about homophones. Homophones are words that sound the same but they have different meanings and spellings.

1. Gather the index cards you prepared. Keep the homophone word pairs together.

2. Place the following cards face up in front of students and point to them: *blue* and *blew*.

   Say: These two words are called **homophones**. Homophones are words that sound the same but they are spelled differently and have different meanings. Let's finger stretch the sounds in these two words. /b/ /l/ /ū/

3. Point to the word *blue*.

   Say: This spelling for the word *blue* means the color *blue*. A sentence using this word is, "The sky is *blue*."

Objectives

- Identify individual sounds in words.
- Identify long vowel sounds.
- Identify and use the long double *o* sound.
- Identify and use double *o* (oo) spelling patterns.
- Identify the correct homophone to complete a sentence.

---

4. Point to the word *blew*.

   Say: This spelling for the word *blew* means something you did. A sentence using this word is, "Sam *blew* out the candles."

5. Place the next pair of words face up in front of students. Have them

   ▸ Finger stretch the sounds in the words.
   ▸ Touch and say each word.
   ▸ Say what each word means.
   ▸ Make up a sentence using each word.

6. Continue the activity with the rest of the homophone pairs.

Homophone Concentration

Help students review homophones.

1. Gather the index cards you prepared. Scramble the cards, and place them face down on the table or floor.

2. Turn over two cards at a time; take turns with students. If the cards are a homophone pair, the person turning over the pair reads the words. If the cards aren't a homophone pair, the person turns them back over.

3. Remove and save the homophone pairs.

4. Continue the activity until all the cards are paired.

5. Have students read all the words.

6. Dictate each word to students. Use each word in a sentence so students will know which homophone to write.

7. Have students write each pair of words in their dictation notebook.

Try It

Hunt for Information

Have students complete page PH 59 in *K¹² PhonicsWorks Advanced Activity Book* for more practice with long vowels and the double *o* sounds. Have students read the story aloud. Have them choose a word from the story that best completes each sentence. Have students read each sentence aloud to determine if it makes sense.

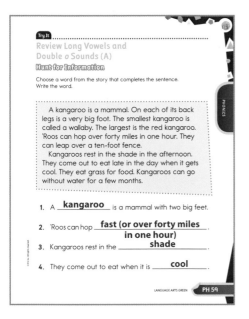

Objectives

- Identify and use double *o* (oo) spelling patterns.
- Identify long vowel sounds.
- Read aloud grade-level text with appropriate automaticity, prosody, accuracy, and rate.
- Write words by applying grade-level phonics knowledge.
- Follow three-step directions.

Dictation: Write Sentences

Use sentences to help students identify individual sounds in words.

1. Gather a pencil and the dictation notebook. Say the sentence, *Look at that clean pool.* Then give these directions to students:

   ▸ Repeat the sentence.
   ▸ Write the sentence in your notebook.
   ▸ Read the sentence aloud.

2. When students have finished, write the following sentence on your whiteboard: *Look at that clean pool.*

3. Have them compare their answer to your correct version.

4. Repeat this procedure with the following sentences: *Sue has a new clue for us. I will hand you each screw.*

   ▸ If students make an error and don't see it, help them correct their mistake by having them finger stretch the sounds in the word they missed.
   ▸ If students are having difficulty selecting the correct letters or sounds, review those letters or sounds that are confusing them.
   ▸ If students have difficulty with first, middle, and last sounds, have them finger stretch the sounds in words.

 **15 minutes**

REVIEW: Long Vowels and Double *o* Sounds

Students will work online independently to

► Practice long vowels and sounds /o͝o/ and /o͞o/.
► Practice decoding text by reading a story.

Help students locate the online activities and provide support as needed.

Offline Alternative

No computer access? Say each long vowel word to students and have them tell you the spelling for the vowel sound in the word: *acorn, a*; *rain, ai*; *day, ay*; *eight, eigh*; *bake, a-e*; *hi, i*; *pie, ie*; *fly, y*; *light, igh*; *kite, i-e*; *go, o*; *boat, oa*; *snow, ow*; *toe, oe*; *home, o-e*; *me, e*; *feet, ee*; *Pete, e-e*; *sea, ea*; *piece, ie*; *rainy, y*; *music, u*; *cue, ue*; *few, ew*; and *cube, u-e*. Say each double *o* sound word to students and have them tell you the spelling for the vowel sound in the word: sound /o͞o/ words: *tuna, u*; *blue, ue*; *stew, ew*; *moon, oo*; *rule, u-e*; sound /o͝o/ words: *book* and *brook*.

Objectives

- Identify and use double *o* (oo) spelling patterns.
- Identify and use the long double *o* sound.
- Identify long vowel sounds.
- Read aloud grade-level text with appropriate automaticity, prosody, accuracy, and rate.
- Decode words by applying grade-level word analysis skills.

Review Long Vowels and Double *o* Sounds (B)

Lesson Overview

Offline	FOCUS: Review Long Vowels and Double *o* Sounds	15 minutes

Sight Words	Sight Word Fun
Practice	Quick Word Review
	Build Compound Words
Try It	"Gail"

Online	REVIEW: Long Vowels and Double *o* Sounds	15 minutes

Materials

Supplied
- *K¹² PhonicsWorks Readers Advanced 11*, pp. 7–12
- whiteboard, Learning Coach
- whiteboard, student
- small whiteboards (2)
- Tile Kit

Also Needed
- sight words box
- index cards (40)

Advance Preparation

For Quick Word Review, print each of the following words on index cards, using one card per word: *like, alike, use, amuse, try, cute, cue, rescue, due, spice, rice, twice, rise, arise, revise, bite, invite, quite, cry, why, shy, tune, tuna, tuba, student, cool, fool, moon, soon, spoon, book, cook, wood, took, foot, shook, stood, brook, broom,* and *room.*

〔Offline〕 🕐 minutes

FOCUS: Review Long Vowels and Double *o* Sounds

Work **together** with students to complete offline Sight Words, Practice, and Try It activities.

Sight Words ●

Sight Word Fun

Help students learn the sight words *please, follow,* and *saw,* and up to two additional sight words they have yet to master.

1. Gather the sight word cards *please, follow,* and *saw,* and up to two additional sight word cards.

2. Choose one sight word card to begin.

   Say: Look at this word and take a picture of it in your mind. When you think you can spell the word yourself, turn the card over and use your letter tiles to spell the word.

3. After students spell the word, have them check the card to see if they spelled the word correctly.

   Say: Read aloud the word you spelled with the letter tiles.

4. Repeat the activity with the remaining sight words.

   TIP Sight words can be very difficult for some students. Let them work at their own pace and really master these words.

> **Objectives**
> - Read sight words.
> - Spell sight words.

Practice ●

Quick Word Review

Have students practice reading words quickly to build fluency.

1. Gather the index cards you prepared.

2. Give students the stack of cards, and have them read as many words as possible in one minute.

3. If students finish the stack in less than one minute, have them start over.

4. Have students read the stack of words three times.

> **Objectives**
> - Read aloud grade-level text with appropriate automaticity, prosody, accuracy, and rate.
> - Identify long vowel sounds.
> - Identify individual sounds in words.
> - Identify and use double *o* (oo) spelling patterns.
> - Identify and use the short double *o* sound.
> - Identify and use the long double *o* sound.
> - Identify the number of syllables in a word.
> - Identify syllables in words.

Build Compound Words

Have students practice making compound words. Grab two small whiteboards and the dry-erase marker.

1. **Say:** Let's spell compound words, which are words made from two smaller words. The first word is *inside*. We can figure out how to spell the word *inside* by listening for the two smaller words.

   ► Fist tap the two small words in the compound word. *in / side*
   ► Write the first word on a small whiteboard. *in*
   ► Write the second word on another small whiteboard. *side*
   ► Push the small whiteboards together and read both words aloud, quickly and smoothly.
   ► Read the compound word aloud.
   ► Turn the small whiteboards face down and write the word on students' whiteboard.
   ► Turn the small whiteboards face up and check the spelling.

2. Have students follow this procedure to make the following words:

   ► *beside be / side*   ► *footprint foot / print*
   ► *snowflake snow / flake*   ► *footpath foot / path*
   ► *snowball snow / ball*   ► *footstool foot / stool*
   ► *baseball base / ball*   ► *cookbook cook / book*
   ► *football foot / ball*   ► *notebook note / book*

TIP Have students use the words *side*, *snow*, *ball*, *foot*, and *book* multiple times to save time building the words.

Try It ....

"Gail"

Have students read "Gail" on page 7 of *K¹² PhonicsWorks Readers Advanced 11*.

   Students should read the story silently once or twice before reading the story aloud. When students miss a word that can be sounded out, point to it and give them three to six seconds to try the word again. If students still miss the word, tell them the word so the flow of the story isn't interrupted.

   After reading the story, make a list of all the words students missed, and go over those words with them. You may use letter tiles to show students how to read the words.

> **Objectives**
> - Read aloud grade-level text with appropriate automaticity, prosody, accuracy, and rate.
> - Decode words by applying grade-level word analysis skills.

⟦Online⟧ ⑮ minutes

REVIEW: Long Vowels and Double *o* Sounds

Students will work online independently to

▸ Practice long vowels and sounds /ŏŏ/ and /o͞o/.

Help students locate the online activities and provide support as needed.

Offline Alternative

No computer access? Say each long vowel word to students and have them tell you the spelling for the vowel sound in the word: *acre, a; paint, ai; say, ay; freight, eigh; take, a-e; mild, i; vie, ie; why, y; tight, igh; pipe, i-e; no, o; road, oa; slow, ow; Poe, oe; phone, o-e; we, e; beet, ee; eve, e-e; mean, ea; field, ie; funny, y; flu, u; rescue, ue; curfew, ew;* and *tube, u-e.* Say each double *o* sound word to students and have them tell you the spelling for the vowel sound in the word: sound /o͞o/ words: *luna, u; glue, ue; blew, ew; drool, oo; rude, u-e;* sound /ŏŏ/ words: *woof* and *look.*

> **Objectives**
>
> - Identify individual sounds in words.
> - Identify long vowel sounds.
> - Identify and use double *o* (oo) spelling patterns.
> - Identify and use the short double *o* sound.
> - Identify and use the long double *o* sound.

Review Long Vowels and Double *o* Sounds (C)

Lesson Overview

[Offline] FOCUS: Review Long Vowels and Double *o* Sounds		**15** minutes

Sight Words	Sight Word Fun
Practice	Sort Long and Short Double *o* Sounds
	Word Chains
Try It	By Sight

[Online] REVIEW: Long Vowels and Double *o* Sounds		**15** minutes

Materials

Supplied
- *K¹² PhonicsWorks Advanced Activity Book,* p. PH 60
- whiteboard, student
- Tile Kit

Also Needed
- sight words box
- index cards (32)

Advance Preparation

For Sort Long and Short Double *o* Sounds, print each of the following words on index cards, using one card per word: *book, brook, cook, hook, look, rook, shook, took, should, would, could, good, hood, wood, foot, soot, droop, stoop, troop, loop, fool, stool, cool, spool, room, zoom, boom, noon, spoon, loot, root,* and *tooth.*

〔 Offline 〕 🕐 15 minutes

FOCUS: Review Long Vowels and Double *o* Sounds

Work **together** with students to complete offline Sight Words, Practice, and Try It activities.

Sight Words ···

Sight Word Fun

Help students learn the sight words *please, follow,* and *saw,* and up to two additional sight words they have yet to master.

1. Gather the sight word cards *please, follow,* and *saw,* and up to two additional sight word cards.

2. Choose one sight word card to begin.

   Say: Look at this word and take a picture of it in your mind. When you think you can spell the word yourself, turn the card over and use your letter tiles to spell the word.

3. After students spell the word, have them check the card to see if they spelled the word correctly.

   Say: Read aloud the word you spelled with the letter tiles.

4. Repeat the activity with the remaining sight words.

(TIP) Sight words can be very difficult for some students. Let them work at their own pace and really master these words.

> **Objectives**
> - Read sight words.
> - Spell sight words.

Practice ···

Sort Long and Short Double *o* Sounds

Help students practice identifying words that have the sounds /ŏŏ/ and /ōō/.

1. Gather the index cards you prepared. Mix the cards well, and place them face down in a stack on the table.

2. **Say:** You are going to sort short and long double *o* sound words. You will take a card from the pile and read it to me. Then you will say if the word has the sound /ŏŏ/ or /ōō/. You will place the card in the pile with the words that have the same sound. I'll do the first one for you.

> **Objectives**
> - Read aloud grade-level text with appropriate automaticity, prosody, accuracy, and rate.
> - Identify and use double *o* (oo) spelling patterns.
> - Identify and use the short double *o* sound.
> - Identify and use the long double *o* sound.
> - Identify individual sounds in words.
> - Identify long vowel sounds.
> - Identify the new word when one sound is changed in a word.

3. Demonstrate the following for students:

   ► Draw a card from the pile.
   ► Read the word aloud.
   ► Place the word in a pile and say the sound /o͝o/ or /o͞o/.

4. Have students continue the procedure with the remaining words:

   ► /o͝o/ **Words:** *book, brook, cook, hook, look, rook, shook, took, should, would, could, good, hood, wood, foot, soot*
   ► /o͞o/ **Words:** *droop, stoop, troop, loop, fool, stool, cool, spool, room, zoom, boom, noon, spoon, loot, root, tooth*

Word Chains

Have students build words by adding and changing letters to help them recognize and use individual sounds in words.

1. Place the following letter tiles at the top of students' whiteboard: *ai, ea, k, l, m, n, oa, oo, s,* and *t.*

2. **Say:** I am going to build the first word in a chain. The word is *lean.*

   ► I will pull down the letters for the sounds /l/, /ē/, and /n/ to spell the word *lean.*
   ► I will touch and say *lean.* To change *lean* to *loan,* I will think about what sound is changed from the word *lean* to *loan.* I will need to replace the letter tile *ea* with the letter tile *oa.*
   ► Touch and say the word *loan.* Now it's your turn to change *loan* to *moan.* You can spell *moan* by making only one change. Touch and say the new word.

3. Redirect students if they select the incorrect letter for any sound.

   Say: That letter is for the sound [incorrect sound]. We want the letter for the sound [target sound]. What letter makes that sound? Answers will vary.

4. Redirect students if they name the sound incorrectly.

   Say: To change the word [first word] to [target word], we need the letter for the sound [target sound].

   Show students how to make the change. Have them touch and say the new word after they move the letters.

5. Follow this procedure to make the following words: *main, mean, meal, seal, steal, steam, team, teak, took, look.*

6. For every new word, have students add, replace, or remove only one letter tile.

TIP If students struggle, review the sounds and letters that are confusing them.

Try It •

By Sight

Have students complete page PH 60 in *K¹² PhonicsWorks Advanced Activity Book* for more practice with reading sight words. Have students see how many sight words they can read correctly in one minute. They should read the words aloud, moving from left to right. Have them start over when they reach the bottom of the page.

Objectives

- Read aloud grade-level text with appropriate automaticity, prosody, accuracy, and rate.
- Read sight words.

[Online] ⑮ minutes

REVIEW: Long Vowels and Double *o* Sounds

Students will work online independently to

▸ Practice long vowels and sounds /o͝o/ and /o͞o/.
▸ Practice decoding text by reading a story.

Help students locate the online activities and provide support as needed.

Offline Alternative

No computer access? Say each long vowel word to students and have them tell you the spelling for the vowel sound in the word: *able, a; stair, ai; lay, ay; sleigh, eigh; rake, a-e; pint, i; tie, ie; shy, y; fight, igh; ripe, i-e; so, o; toad, oa; mow, ow; roe, oe; tone, o-e; he, e; see, ee; Steve, e-e; team, ea; shield, ie; sunny, y; unit, u; cue, ue; fewest, ew;* and *fuse, u-e.* Say each double *o* sound word to students and have them tell you the spelling for the vowel sound in the word: sound /o͞o/ words: *tuna, u; flue, ue; flew, ew; spook, oo; dude, u-e;* sound /o͝o/ words: *wood* and *hood.*

Objectives

- Identify individual sounds in words.
- Identify and use double *o* (oo) spelling patterns.
- Identify and use the short double *o* sound.
- Identify and use the long double *o* sound.
- Identify long vowel sounds.
- Read aloud grade-level text with appropriate automaticity, prosody, accuracy, and rate.
- Decode words by applying grade-level word analysis skills.

Review Long Vowels and Double *o* Sounds (D)

Lesson Overview

[Offline] FOCUS: Review Long Vowels and Double *o* Sounds	**15** minutes	

Sight Words	Sight Word Fun
Practice	Quick Word Review
	Review Long Vowel Sounds and Their Spellings
Try It	"Ray"

[Online] REVIEW: Long Vowels and Double *o* Sounds   **15** minutes

Materials

Supplied
- *K¹² PhonicsWorks Readers Advanced 11*, pp. 13–18
- whiteboard, student
- Tile Kit

Also Needed
- sight words box
- index cards (40)

Advance Preparation

For Quick Word Review, print each of the following words on index cards, using one card per word: *like, alike, use, amuse, try, cute, cue, rescue, due, spice, rice, twice, rise, arise, revise, bite, invite, quite, cry, why, shy, tune, tuna, tuba, student, cool, fool, moon, soon, spoon, book, cook, wood, took, foot, shook, stood, brook, broom,* and *room.*

[Offline] 🕐 15 minutes

FOCUS: Review Long Vowels and Double *o* Sounds

Work **together** with students to complete offline Sight Words, Practice, and Try It activities.

Sight Words ●

Sight Word Fun

Help students learn the sight words *please, follow,* and *saw,* and up to two additional sight words they have yet to master.

1. Gather the sight word cards *please, follow,* and *saw,* and up to two additional sight word cards.

2. Choose one sight word card to begin.

   Say: Look at this word and take a picture of it in your mind. When you think you can spell the word yourself, turn the card over and use your letter tiles to spell the word.

3. After students spell the word, have them check the card to see if they spelled the word correctly.

   Say: Read aloud the word you spelled with the letter tiles.

4. Repeat the activity with the remaining sight words.

TIP Sight words can be very difficult for some students. Let them work at their own pace and really master these words.

> **Objectives**
> - Read sight words.
> - Spell sight words.

Practice ●

Quick Word Review

Have students practice reading words quickly to build fluency.

1. Gather the index cards you prepared.

2. Give students the stack of cards, and have them read as many words as possible in one minute.

3. If students finish the stack in less than one minute, have them start over.

4. Have students read the stack of words three times.

> **Objectives**
> - Read aloud grade-level text with appropriate automaticity, prosody, accuracy, and rate.
> - Identify and use double *o* (oo) spelling patterns.
> - Identify and use the short double *o* sound.
> - Identify and use the long double *o* sound.
> - Identify long vowel sounds.
> - Given the letter, identify the most common sound.
> - Given the sound, identify the most common letter or letters.

Review Long Vowel Sounds and Their Spellings

Help students review the long vowel sounds and their spellings.

1. Place the following letter tiles in random order on students' whiteboard: *a, a-e, ai, ay, e, ea, ee, e-e, eigh, ew, i, ie, i-e, igh, o, oa, oe, o-e, ow, u, ue, u-e,* and *y.*

2. **Say:** I am going to point to each letter tile. Tell me the long vowel sound for the letter or letters.

   ▸ *a, ai, ay, eigh, a-e /ā/*
   ▸ *e, ea, ee, ie, y, e-e /ē/*
   ▸ *i, ie, igh, y, i-e /ī/*
   ▸ *o, oa, oe, ow, o-e /ō/*
   ▸ *u, ue, ew, u-e /ū/*

3. **Say:** I am going to say a long vowel sound. Repeat the sound and touch at least two of the spellings for that sound.

   ▸ /ā/ Possible spellings: *a, ai, ay, eigh, a-e*
   ▸ /ē/ Possible spellings: *e, ea, ee, ie, y, e-e*
   ▸ /ī/ Possible spellings: *i, ie, igh, y, i-e*
   ▸ /ō/ Possible spellings: *o, oa, oe, ow, o-e*
   ▸ /ū/ Possible spellings: *u, ue, ew, u-e*

4. Redirect students if they name the sound incorrectly.

   Say: That is the sound of another long vowel.

5. Provide additional guidance if students touch the wrong letter tile during the review.

   Say: That spelling is for the sound [sound for incorrect letter tile]. We are looking for spelling for the long vowel sound [target sound].

6. If students touch the wrong letter tile again, point to the correct one.

   Say: This is the spelling for the sound [target sound]. Touch this letter tile and say its sound.

Try It

"Ray"

Have students read "Ray" on page 13 of *K¹² PhonicsWorks Readers Advanced 11.*

Students should read the story silently once or twice before reading the story aloud. When students miss a word that can be sounded out, point to it and give them three to six seconds to try the word again. If students still miss the word, tell them the word so the flow of the story isn't interrupted.

After reading the story, make a list of all the words students missed, and go over those words with them. You may use letter tiles to show students how to read the words.

Objectives
- Read aloud grade-level text with appropriate automaticity, prosody, accuracy, and rate.
- Decode words by applying grade-level word analysis skills.

REVIEW: Long Vowels and Double *o* Sounds

Students will work online independently to

► Practice long vowels and sounds /ŏŏ/ and /ōō/.

Help students locate the online activities and provide support as needed.

Offline Alternative

No computer access? Say each long vowel word to students and have them tell you the spelling for the vowel sound in the word: *ankle, a; tail, ai; May, ay; weigh, eigh; lace, a-e; kind, i; lie, ie; try, y; sight, igh; rice, i-e; Mo, o; load, oa; bow, ow; doe, oe; zone, o-e; she, e; Lee, ee; Steve, e-e; seam, ea; yield, ie; runny, y; unite, u; Sue, ue; newest, ew;* and *ruse, u-e.* Say each double *o* sound word to students and have them tell you the spelling for the word: sound /ōō/ words: *truth, u; true, ue; threw, ew; school, oo; dude, u-e;* sound /ŏŏ/ words: *foot* and *took.*

Unit Checkpoint

Lesson Overview

🖥	**《Online 》** REVIEW: Long Vowels and Double *o* Sounds	**15** minutes
📄	**《Offline 》** UNIT CHECKPOINT: Review Long Vowels and Double *o* Sounds	**15** minutes

Materials

Supplied

- *K¹² PhonicsWorks Advanced Assessments,* pp. PH 175–180

Objectives

- Identify individual sounds in words.
- Identify and use double *o* (oo) spelling patterns.
- Identify long vowel sounds.
- Identify and use the long double *o* sound.
- Identify and use the short double *o* sound.
- Read instructional-level text with 90% accuracy.
- Read aloud grade-level text with appropriate automaticity, prosody, accuracy, and rate.
- Write words by applying grade-level phonics knowledge.
- Write sight words.
- Read sight words.

《Online 》 **15** minutes

REVIEW: **Long Vowels and Double *o* Sounds**

Students will review long vowels and sounds /o͝o/ and /o͞o/ to prepare for the Unit Checkpoint. Help students locate the online activities and provide support as needed.

UNIT CHECKPOINT: Review Long Vowels and Double *o* Sounds

Explain that students are going to show what they have learned about sounds, letters, and words.

1. Give students the Unit Checkpoint pages for the Review Long Vowels and Double *o* Sounds unit and print the Unit Checkpoint Answer Key, if you'd like.

2. Use the instructions below to help administer the Checkpoint to students. On the Answer Key or another sheet of paper, note student answers to oral response questions to help with scoring the Checkpoint later.

3. Use the Answer Key to score the Checkpoint, and then enter the results online.

Part 1. Circle Words with the Short Double *o* Sound Have students circle the words with the sound /o͝o/.

Part 2. Circle Words with the Long Double *o* Sound Have students circle the words with the sound /o͞o/.

Part 3. Circle Words with Long Vowel Sounds Have students circle the words with long vowel sounds.

Part 4. Writing Read each sentence to students. Have them repeat and write the sentence.

21. *I hope Sue was not rude to her new roommate.*

22. *Can I glue a few of these stars to the edge of the card?*

23. *The bikes will zoom past us on June Street.*

Part 5. Read Aloud Listen to students read the sentences aloud. Count and note the number of words they read correctly.

Part 6. Read Words Have students read each word aloud. Note any words they read incorrectly.

Part 7. Read Sight Words Have students read each sight word aloud. Note any words they read incorrectly.

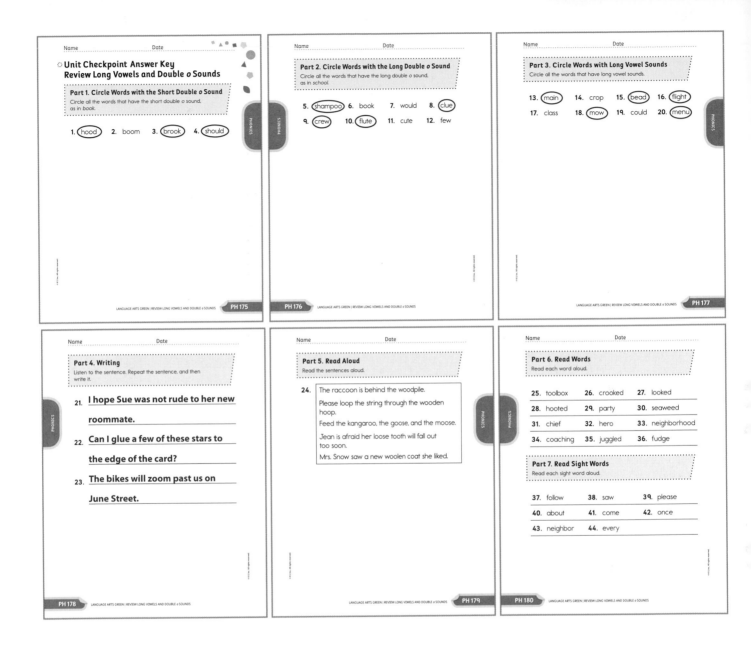

Name _____ Date _____

○ **Unit Checkpoint Answer Key**
Review Long Vowels and Double *o* Sounds

Part 1. Circle Words with the Short Double *o* Sound
Circle all the words that have the short double *o* sound,
as in *book.*

1. (hood)   2. boom   3. (brook)   4. (should)

PHONICS

Name _____ Date _____

Part 2. Circle Words with the Long Double *o* Sound
Circle all the words that have the long double *o* sound,
as in *school.*

5. (shampoo)   6. book   7. would   8. (clue)
9. (crew)   10. (flute)   11. cute   12. few

PHONICS

Name _____ Date _____

Part 3. Circle Words with Long Vowel Sounds
Circle all the words that have long vowel sounds.

13. (main)   14. crop   15. (bead)   16. (flight)
17. class   18. (mow)   19. could   20. (menu)

PHONICS

Name _____ Date _____

Part 4. Writing
Listen to the sentence. Repeat the sentence, and then
write it.

21. **I hope Sue was not rude to her new
    roommate.**

22. **Can I glue a few of these stars to
    the edge of the card?**

23. **The bikes will zoom past us on
    June Street.**

PHONICS

Name _____ Date _____

Part 5. Read Aloud
Read the sentences aloud.

24. | The raccoon is behind the woodpile.
    Please loop the string through the wooden hoop.
    Feed the kangaroo, the goose, and the moose.
    Jean is afraid her loose tooth will fall out too soon.
    Mrs. Snow saw a new woolen coat she liked.

PHONICS

Name _____ Date _____

Part 6. Read Words
Read each word aloud.

25. toolbox   26. crooked   27. looked
28. hooted   29. party   30. seaweed
31. chief   32. hero   33. neighborhood
34. coaching   35. juggled   36. fudge

Part 7. Read Sight Words
Read each sight word aloud.

37. follow   38. saw   39. please
40. about   41. come   42. once
43. neighbor   44. every

PHONICS

Introduce Sound /er/ Spelled –er, –ir, –ur, and –ear

Unit Overview

In this unit, students will
- Review sight words.
- Learn the spellings –er, –ir, –ur, and –ear for the sound /er/.
- Read and write sentences.
- Read stories silently and aloud.

Materials

Supplied
- *K¹² PhonicsWorks Advanced Activity Book*, p. PH 61
- *K¹² PhonicsWorks Readers Advanced*, any volume
- whiteboard, Learning Coach
- whiteboard, student
- Tile Kit

Also Needed
- sight words box
- dictation notebook

Lesson Overview

	Offline FOCUS: Introduce Sound /er/ Spelled –er, –ir, –ur, and –ear	15 minutes
Sight Words	Review Sight Words	
Learn	Introduce Spellings for Sound /er/	
	Review Spellings for Sound /er/	
Try It	Many Spellings for One Sound	
	Online REVIEW: Sound /er/ Spelled –er, –ir, –ur, and –ear	15 minutes
Review	Sound /er/ Spelled –er, –ir, –ur, and –ear	
Practice	Fluency	

[Offline] 15 minutes

FOCUS: Introduce Sound /er/ Spelled –er, –ir, –ur, and –ear

Work **together** with students to complete offline Sight Words, Learn, and Try It activities.

Sight Words

Review Sight Words

Help students learn to recognize sight words.

1. Gather all the sight word cards students have yet to master from their sight words box. Stack the cards on the table face down.

2. Have students pick a word and read it to you.

3. If they read it quickly and correctly, put the card in one stack. If they hesitate or do not read the word correctly, put it in another stack. The second stack should have words that they will review again.

4. Take the stack of words that students read correctly and dictate each word to them. They may choose to either write the word or spell it aloud.

5. If students spell the word correctly, put the card in the first stack because they have mastered the word. If they misspell the word, add it to the stack of cards to review again.

6. Chart students' progress on the back of each card.

    ▸ Divide the back of the card into two columns.
    ▸ Label the first column "Read" and the second column "Spell."
    ▸ Record the dates that students read or spell the word correctly. When students can read and spell the word correctly three times in a row, they have mastered the word. You may want to put a star or sticker on their card when they have mastered that word.

TIP Even if students can read and spell all the words correctly, it is still beneficial for them to review sight words. Choose as many additional words as you would like for each subsequent activity.

Objectives

- Read sight words.
- Spell sight words.
- Write sight words.

Learn

Introduce Spellings for Sound /er/

Help students learn the spellings *–er*, *–ir*, *–ur*, and *–ear* for the sound /er/.

1. Place the following letter tiles on students' whiteboard: *b, d, ear, er, h, ir, l, n, t,* and *ur*.

2. Make the word *her* in the middle of students' whiteboard and point to it.

   Say: Today we are going to learn the four spellings for the sound /er/. Sometimes the letters *er* make the sound /er/. Let's touch and say the word *her*.

   ▸ Where is the sound /er/ in this word? end
   ▸ Which letters make this sound? *er*

3. Make the word *bird* and point to it.

   Say: Now let's look at the next word. This is the word *bird*. In the word *bird*, the sound /er/ is made by the letters *ir*.

   ▸ Touch and say *bird*.
   ▸ Where is the sound /er/ in this word? middle
   ▸ Which letters make this sound? *ir*

4. Make the word *turn* and point to it.

   Say: This word is *turn*. In the word *turn*, the sound /er/ is made by the letters *ur*.

   ▸ Touch and say *turn*.
   ▸ Where is the sound /er/ in this word? middle
   ▸ Which letters make this sound? *ur*

5. Make the word *learn* and point to it.

   Say: This last word is *learn*. In the word *learn*, the sound /er/ is made by the letters *ear*.

   ▸ Touch and say *learn*.
   ▸ Where is the sound /er/ in this word? middle
   ▸ Which letters make this sound? *ear*

TIP Refer to the *K¹² PhonicsWorks* video for a demonstration of how to teach the different spellings for the sound /er/.

Objectives

- Identify individual sounds in words.
- Identify and use *–er*.
- Identify and use *–ir*.
- Identify and use *–ur*.
- Identify and use *–ear*.
- Write words by applying grade-level phonics knowledge.

Review Spellings for Sound /er/

Help students review the spellings *–er*, *–ir*, *–ur*, and *–ear* for the sound /er/.

1. Gather the dictation notebook and pencil.

2. Place the following letter tiles at the top of students' whiteboard: *er, ir, ur,* and *ear*.

3. Write the following words on your whiteboard: *her, bird, turn,* and *learn*.

4. **Say:** Count the number of ways there are to spell the sound /er/.

   ▸ Touch and say the spellings for the sound /er/. *er, ir, ur, ear*
   ▸ Look at the words on the board and read them.
   ▸ Say how the sound /er/ is spelled in each word *er* in *her, ir* in *bird, ur* in *turn, ear* in *learn*
   ▸ Take a picture in your mind of the four ways of spelling the sound /er/.

5. **Say:** I am going to hide the words and the spellings on the board. Your job is to remember each way of spelling the sound /er/ and write the spellings in your notebook.

6. After students have finished writing the spellings in their notebook, have them check their answers against the spellings on the board.

TIP If students cannot remember one or more of the spellings for the sound /er/, tell them the guide word for that spelling (*er,* as in *her; ir,* as in *bird; ur,* as in *turn; ear,* as in *learn*).

Try It

Many Spellings for One Sound

Have students complete page PH 61 in *K¹² PhonicsWorks Advanced Activity Book* for more practice with spellings for the sound /er/. Have students read each word aloud going down each column, and then write the correct spelling after the word.

> **Try It**
>
> Introduce Sound /er/ Spelled –er, –ir, –ur, and –ear
>
> **Many Spellings for One Sound**
>
> Look for the spelling pattern in the word that spells the sound /er/. Write er, ir, ur, or ear after the word.
>
> 1. fern **er**
> 2. earth **ear**
> 3. turn **ur**
> 4. burp **ur**
> 5. third **ir**
> 6. her **er**
> 7. sir **ir**
> 8. fir **ir**
> 9. fur **ur**
> 10. learn **ear**
> 11. shirt **ir**
> 12. hurt **ur**
> 13. curl **ur**
> 14. jerk **er**
> 15. earn **ear**
> 16. skirt **ir**
> 17. surf **ur**
> 18. germ **er**
>
> LANGUAGE ARTS GREEN **PH 61**

Objectives

- Identify and use –er.
- Identify and use –ir.
- Identify and use –ur.
- Identify and use –ear.

[Online] ⏱ 15 minutes

REVIEW: Sound /er/ Spelled –*er*, –*ir*, –*ur*, and –*ear*

Students will work online independently to complete activities with the spellings –*er*, –*ir*, –*ur*, and –*ear* for the sound /er/ and develop fluency skills. Help students locate the online activities and provide support as needed.

Review ⋯⋯⋯⋯⋯⋯⋯⋯⋯⋯⋯⋯⋯⋯⋯⋯⋯⋯⋯⋯⋯

Sound /er/ Spelled –*er*, –*ir*, –*ur*, and –*ear*
Students will

▶ Practice the spellings –*er*, –*ir*, –*ur*, and –*ear* for the sound /er/.
▶ Practice decoding text by reading a story.

Offline Alternative

No computer access? Have students spell words that have the spellings –*er*, –*ir*, –*ur*, and –*ear* for the sound /er/, such as *perk*, *girl*, *curb*, and *earn*.

Objectives
- Identify and use –*er*.
- Identify and use –*ir*.
- Identify and use –*ur*.
- Identify and use –*ear*.
- Read aloud grade-level text with appropriate automaticity, prosody, accuracy, and rate.
- Decode words by applying grade-level word analysis skills.

Practice ⋯⋯⋯⋯⋯⋯⋯⋯⋯⋯⋯⋯⋯⋯⋯⋯⋯⋯⋯⋯⋯

Fluency
Good readers read often and reread texts. Students will practice their fluency skills by rereading a *K¹² PhonicsWorks Readers Advanced* story aloud as they are recorded.

Have students gather their favorite *K¹² PhonicsWorks Readers Advanced* story that they have already read. Follow the instructions online to record students as they read.

Offline Alternative

No computer access? Have students gather their favorite *K¹² PhonicsWorks Readers Advanced* story. Have them read the story aloud, and record the amount of time it takes them to read the story. Have them read the story again to beat their original time.

Objectives
- Increase reading fluency rate.
- Demonstrate automaticity.
- Demonstrate prosody.

Practice Sound /er/ Spelled –er, –ir, –ur, and –ear (A)

Lesson Overview

📋	**[Offline]**	**FOCUS:** Practice Sound /er/ Spelled –er, –ir, –ur, and –ear	**15** minutes

Sight Words	Use Words in Sentences
Practice	Search Sentences for Words with the Sound /er/
	Build Words
Try It	"Jill's First Pet"

🖥️	**[Online]**	**REVIEW:** Sound /er/ Spelled –er, –ir, –ur, and –ear	**15** minutes

Review	Sound /er/ Spelled –er, –ir, –ur, and –ear
Practice	Fluency

[Materials]

Supplied

- *K¹² PhonicsWorks Readers Advanced 11*, pp. 19–25
- *K¹² PhonicsWorks Readers Advanced,* any volume
- whiteboard, student
- Tile Kit

Also Needed

- sight words box

⟦ Offline ⟧ 🕐 15 minutes

FOCUS: Practice Sound /er/ Spelled –er, –ir, –ur, and –ear

Work **together** with students to complete offline Sight Words, Practice, and Try It activities.

Sight Words ••

Use Words in Sentences

Help students use sight words in sentences.

1. Gather all the sight word cards students have yet to master from their sight words box. Spread the sight word cards on the table.

2. **Say:** Let's use sight words in sentences.

3. Have students

   ▸ Touch each card and read the word on it.
   ▸ Make up a sentence using the word.
   ▸ Put the card in a pile after using the word in a sentence.
   ▸ Go through the pile of cards and read each sight word again.
   ▸ Spell each word.

TIP If students have difficulty with any of the sight words, place those cards in a pile to review again.

> **Objectives**
> • Read sight words.
> • Spell sight words.

Practice ••

Search Sentences for Words with the Sound /er/

Have students identify words with the sound /er/ spelled –er, –ir, –ur, and –ear.

1. Write the following sentence on students' whiteboard and point to it: *What did Mom tell her?*

   Say: I will read a sentence to you. You will repeat the sentence and tell me the word that has the sound /er/. The first sentence is, *What did Mom tell her?* Which word in the sentence has the sound /er/? *her*

2. Have students do the following steps:

   ▸ Repeat the sentence.
   ▸ Find the word in the sentence with the sound /er/ and underline it.
   ▸ Circle the letters for the spelling of the sound /er/.
   ▸ Read the sentence aloud again.

> **Objectives**
> • Identify individual sounds in words.
> • Identify and use –er.
> • Identify and use –ir.
> • Identify and use –ur.
> • Identify and use –ear.
> • Blend sounds to create words.
> • Identify individual sounds in words.
> • Write words by applying grade-level phonics knowledge.

3. Use the same procedure for the following sentences:

- ▸ *Jake plays first base.* first
- ▸ *The race car drove by in a blur.* blur
- ▸ *What did you learn today?* learn
- ▸ *Let's wash the germs off our hands.* germs

TIP If students have difficulty choosing from among the words in the sentence, say two words and have them choose the correct word with the target sound.

TIP If students cannot remember one or more of the spellings for the sound /er/, tell them the guide word for that spelling (*er,* as in *her*; *ir,* as in *bird*; *ur,* as in *turn*; *ear,* as in *learn*).

Build Words

Help students use letters and sounds to build words.

1. Place the following letter tiles at the top of students' whiteboard: *b, d, ear, er, g, h, ir, m, n, t,* and *ur.*

2. Draw three horizontal lines across the middle of students' whiteboard to represent the sounds in a word.

3. **Say:** Let's use letters and sounds to build the word *bird.*

4. Have students finger stretch the sounds in *bird.*

5. Have students

- ▸ Identify the first, next, and last sounds in *bird.*
- ▸ Choose the corresponding letter tile for each of the sounds.
- ▸ Move the letters to the correct lines on their whiteboard.

6. Guide students with these questions:

- ▸ What is the first sound in *bird*? /b/
  Which line does the letter for that sound go on? the first one
- ▸ What is the next sound in *bird*? /er/
  Which line do the letters for that sound go on? the second one
- ▸ What's the last sound in *bird*? /d/
  Which line does the letter for that sound go on? the last one

7. Redirect students if they select the incorrect letter.

   Say: That sound is in the word [word], and it is the [first, second, third] sound. We want the sound [target sound].

   Continue until students select the correct letter.

8. Have students touch and say the word.

9. Have them say the word as they use a dry-erase marker to write the word on the whiteboard.

10. Repeat the activity to build the following words:

- ▸ *dirt* /d/ /er/ /t/
- ▸ *germ* /j/ /er/ /m/
- ▸ *turn* /t/ /er/ /n/
- ▸ *heard* /h/ /er/ /d/

Try It

"Jill's First Pet"

Have students read "Jill's First Pet" on page 19 of *K¹² PhonicsWorks Readers Advanced 11.*

Students should read the story silently once or twice before reading the story aloud. When students miss a word that can be sounded out, point to it and give them three to six seconds to try the word again. If students still miss the word, tell them the word so the flow of the story isn't interrupted.

After reading the story, make a list of all the words students missed, and go over those words with them. You may use letter tiles to show students how to read the words.

> **Objectives**
> - Read aloud grade-level text with appropriate automaticity, prosody, accuracy, and rate.
> - Decode words by applying grade-level word analysis skills.

 **[Online]** ⏱ **15 minutes**

REVIEW: Sound /er/ Spelled *–er, –ir, –ur,* and *–ear*

Students will work online independently to complete activities with the spellings *–er, –ir, –ur,* and *–ear* for the sound /er/ and develop fluency skills. Help students locate the online activities and provide support as needed.

Review

Sound /er/ Spelled *–er, –ir, –ur,* and *–ear*
Students will

  ▸ Practice the spellings *–er, –ir, –ur,* and *–ear* for the sound /er/.

> **Objectives**
> - Identify and use *–er.*
> - Identify and use *–ir.*
> - Identify and use *–ur.*
> - Identify and use *–ear.*

Offline Alternative

No computer access? Have students spell words that have the spellings *–er, –ir, –ur,* and *–ear* for the sound /er/, such as *perch, stir, fur,* and *yearn.*

Practice

Fluency
Good readers read often and reread texts. Students will practice their fluency skills by rereading a *K¹² PhonicsWorks Readers Advanced* story aloud as they are recorded.

Have students gather their favorite *K¹² PhonicsWorks Readers Advanced* story that they have already read. Follow the instructions online to record students as they read.

> **Objectives**
> - Increase reading fluency rate.
> - Demonstrate automaticity.
> - Demonstrate prosody.

Offline Alternative

No computer access? Have students gather their favorite *K¹² PhonicsWorks Readers Advanced* story. Have them read the story aloud, and record the amount of time it takes them to read the story. Have them read the story again to beat their original time.

Practice Sound /er/ Spelled –er, –ir, –ur, and –ear (B)

Lesson Overview

[Offline]	**FOCUS:** Practice Sound /er/ Spelled –er, –ir, –ur, and –ear	**15** minutes	
Sight Words	Sight Word Concentration		
Practice	Word Play		
Try It	Identification, Please		
[Online]	**REVIEW:** Sound /er/ Spelled –er, –ir, –ur, and –ear	**15** minutes	
Review	Sound /er/ Spelled –er, –ir, –ur, and –ear		
Practice	Fluency		

[Materials]

Supplied

- *K¹² PhonicsWorks Advanced Activity Book*, p. PH 62
- *K¹² PhonicsWorks Readers Advanced*, any volume

Also Needed

- sight words box
- dictation notebook
- index cards (15)
- crayons

Advance Preparation

Gather two sets of the sight word cards students have yet to master.

For Word Play, print each of the following words on index cards, using one card per word: *butter, platter, checkers, letter, paper, finger, teacher, farmer, skirt, shirt, girl, sunburn, fur, birthday,* and *fir*.

[Offline] ⏱ minutes

FOCUS: Practice Sound /er/ Spelled –er, –ir, –ur, and –ear

Work **together** with students to complete offline Sight Words, Practice, and Try It activities.

Sight Words

Sight Word Concentration

Help students review sight words.

1. Gather the two sets of sight word cards.

2. Scramble both sets of sight word cards and place them face down on the table or floor.

3. Turn over two cards at a time; take turns with students. If the cards match, the person turning over the matching cards reads the word and uses it in a sentence. If the cards don't match, the person turns them back over.

4. Remove and save the matching cards.

5. Continue the activity until all the cards are paired.

6. Have students read all the words.

7. Take the stack of words that students read correctly and dictate each word to them.

8. Have students write each word or spell it aloud.

TIP If students have difficulty with any sight words, let them work at their own pace to really master these words.

> **Objectives**
> - Read sight words.
> - Spell sight words.
> - Write sight words.

Practice

Word Play

Have students practice reading and writing sentences with words that have the sound /er/.

1. Gather the index cards you prepared, a pencil, and the dictation notebook.

2. Give students the stack of words and have them read all the words.

3. Have students select one –er, one –ir, one –ur, and one –ear word.

4. Have students write a sentence for each word they chose.

5. Help students use proper capitalization and punctuation in their written sentences.

> **Objectives**
> - Identify and use –er.
> - Identify and use –ir.
> - Identify and use –ur.
> - Identify and use –ear.

Try It

Identification, Please

Have students complete page PH 62 in *K¹² PhonicsWorks Advanced Activity Book* for more practice with the spellings for the sound /er/. Have students read aloud moving across the rows, find words with the sound /er/, and color those boxes yellow.

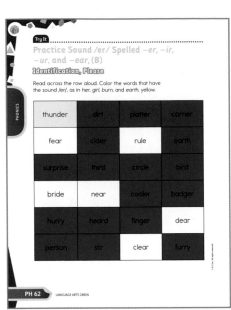

⟦Online⟧ ⏱ 15 minutes

REVIEW: **Sound /er/ Spelled *–er*, *–ir*, *–ur*, and *–ear***

Students will work online independently to complete activities with the spellings *–er*, *–ir*, *–ur*, and *–ear* for the sound /er/ and develop fluency skills. Help students locate the online activities and provide support as needed.

�no Review ···

Sound /er/ Spelled *–er*, *–ir*, *–ur*, and *–ear*
Students will

- ▸ Practice the spellings *–er*, *–ir*, *–ur*, and *–ear* for the sound /er/.
- ▸ Practice decoding text by reading a story.

Offline Alternative

No computer access? Have students spell words that have the spellings *–er*, *–ir*, *–ur*, and *–ear* for the sound /er/, such as *perk*, *girl*, *curb*, and *earn*.

> **Objectives**
> - Identify and use *–er*.
> - Identify and use *–ir*.
> - Identify and use *–ur*.
> - Identify and use *–ear*.
> - Identify individual sounds in words.
> - Read aloud grade-level text with appropriate automaticity, prosody, accuracy, and rate.
> - Decode words by applying grade-level word analysis skills.

Practice ···

Fluency
Good readers read often and reread texts. Students will practice their fluency skills by rereading a *K¹² PhonicsWorks Readers Advanced* story aloud as they are recorded.

Have students gather their favorite *K¹² PhonicsWorks Readers Advanced* story that they have already read. Follow the instructions online to record students as they read.

Offline Alternative

No computer access? Have students gather their favorite *K¹² PhonicsWorks Readers Advanced* story. Have them read the story aloud, and record the amount of time it takes them to read the story. Have them read the story again to beat their original time.

> **Objectives**
> - Increase reading fluency rate.
> - Demonstrate automaticity.
> - Demonstrate prosody.

Practice Sound /er/ Spelled –*er*, –*ir*, –*ur*, and –*ear* (C)

Lesson Overview

[Offline] FOCUS: Practice Sound /er/ Spelled –*er*, –*ir*, –*ur*, and –*ear* — **15** minutes

Sight Words	Pick a Pair
Practice	Sort Spellings for Sound /er/
Try It	"Meg's Big Change"

[Online] REVIEW: Sound /er/ Spelled –*er*, –*ir*, –*ur*, and –*ear* — **15** minutes

Review	Sound /er/ Spelled –*er*, –*ir*, –*ur*, and –*ear*
Practice	Fluency

[Materials]

Supplied

- *K¹² PhonicsWorks Readers Advanced 11*, pp. 26–32
- *K¹² PhonicsWorks Readers Advanced*, any volume

Also Needed

- sight words box
- dictation notebook
- index cards (32)

Advance Preparation

For Sort Spellings for Sound /er/, print each of the following words on index cards, using one card per word: *jerk, verb, finger, hammer, ladder, letter, zipper, after, over, under, winter, sister, river, teacher, chirp, dirt, firm, first, shirt, sir, third, skirt, blur, burst, church, curb, curl, hurt, learn, heard, earn,* and *earth.*

〖 Offline 〗 ⏱ 15 minutes

FOCUS: Practice Sound /er/ Spelled –er, –ir, –ur, and –ear

Work **together** with students to complete offline Sight Words, Practice, and Try It activities.

Sight Words

Pick a Pair

Play a card game with students for more practice with sight words.

1. Gather the sight word cards that students are reviewing. Choose two words and place the cards on the table.

2. Ask questions to help students identify each word. For example, if the words are *or* and *one*, you could ask, "Which word names a number?" If the words are *on* and *but*, you could ask, "Which word is the opposite of *off*?"

3. Continue the activity until students identify all the words.

4. Take the stack of words that students read correctly and dictate each word to them.

5. Have students write each word or spell it aloud.

> **Objectives**
> - Read sight words.
> - Spell sight words.
> - Write sight words.

Practice

Sort Spellings for Sound /er/

Help students practice identifying words that have the spellings –er, –ir, –ur, and –ear for the sound /er/.

1. Gather the index cards you prepared. Mix the cards well and place them in a stack face down on the table.

2. Gather the dictation notebook. Draw four columns and label them *er, ir, ur,* and *ear* to represent the four different ways to spell the sound /er/.

3. **Say:** You are going to sort words by the four spellings for the sound /er/. You will take a card from the pile and read it to me. Then you will think about the spelling for the sound /er/ in the word and write that word in the correct column. I'll do the first one for you.

> **Objectives**
> - Identify individual sounds in words.
> - Identify and use –er.
> - Identify and use –ir.
> - Identify and use –ur.
> - Identify and use –ear.

4. Demonstrate the following for students:

  ▸ Draw a card from the pile.
  ▸ Read the word aloud.
  ▸ Write the word in the correct column for the spelling for the sound /er/.

5. Have students continue the procedure with the remaining words:

  ▸ **Spelling *er* Words**: *jerk, verb, finger, hammer, ladder, letter, zipper, after, over, under, winter, sister, river, teacher*
  ▸ **Spelling *ir* Words:** *chirp, dirt, firm, first, shirt, sir, third, skirt*
  ▸ **Spelling *ur* Words:** *blur, burst, church, curb, curl, hurt*
  ▸ **Spelling *ear* Words:** *learn, heard, earn, earth*

"Meg's Big Change"

Have students read "Meg's Big Change" on page 26 of *K¹² PhonicsWorks Readers Advanced 11*.

  Students should read the story silently once or twice before reading the story aloud. When students miss a word that can be sounded out, point to it and give them three to six seconds to try the word again. If students still miss the word, tell them the word so the flow of the story isn't interrupted.

  After reading the story, make a list of all the words students missed, and go over those words with them. You may use letter tiles to show students how to read the words.

Objectives
- Read aloud grade-level text with appropriate automaticity, prosody, accuracy, and rate.
- Decode words by applying grade-level word analysis skills.

[Online] 🕒 minutes

REVIEW: Sound /er/ Spelled *–er, –ir, –ur,* and *–ear*

Students will work online independently to complete activities with the spellings *–er, –ir, –ur,* and *–ear* for the sound /er/ and develop fluency skills. Help students locate the online activities and provide support as needed.

Review

Sound /er/ Spelled *–er, –ir, –ur,* and *–ear*
Students will

  ▸ Practice the spellings *–er, –ir, –ur,* and *–ear* for the sound /er/.

Offline Alternative

No computer access? Have students spell words that have the spellings *–er, –ir, –ur,* and *–ear* for the sound /er/, such as *herd, squirm, disturb,* and *learn*.

Objectives
- Identify and use *–er*.
- Identify and use *–ir*.
- Identify and use *–ur*.
- Identify and use *–ear*.
- Identify individual sounds in words.

Fluency

Good readers read often and reread texts. Students will practice their fluency skills by rereading a *K¹² PhonicsWorks Readers Advanced* story aloud as they are recorded.

Have students gather their favorite *K¹² PhonicsWorks Readers Advanced* story that they have already read. Follow the instructions online to record students as they read.

Offline Alternative

No computer access? Have students gather their favorite *K¹² PhonicsWorks Readers Advanced* story. Have them read the story aloud, and record the amount of time it takes them to read the story. Have them read the story again to beat their original time.

Objectives

- Increase reading fluency rate.
- Demonstrate automaticity.
- Demonstrate prosody.

Unit Checkpoint

Lesson Overview

🖥	**[Online]** **REVIEW:** Sound /er/ Spelled –*er*, –*ir*, –*ur*, and –*ear*	**15** minutes
📄	**[Offline]** **UNIT CHECKPOINT:** Sound /er/ Spelled –*er*, –*ir*, –*ur*, and –*ear*	**15** minutes

Objectives

- Identify individual sounds in words.
- Identify and use –*er*.
- Identify and use –*ir*.
- Identify and use –*ur*.
- Identify and use –*ear*.
- Read instructional-level text with 90% accuracy.
- Read aloud grade-level text with appropriate automaticity, prosody, accuracy, and rate.
- Write words by applying grade-level phonics knowledge.
- Write sight words.
- Read sight words.

[Materials]

Supplied

- *K¹² PhonicsWorks Advanced Assessments*, pp. PH 181–186

[Online] **15** minutes

REVIEW: **Sound /er/ Spelled –*er*, –*ir*, –*ur*, and –*ear***

Students will review spellings for the sound /er/ to prepare for the Unit Checkpoint. Help students locate the online activities and provide support as needed.

UNIT CHECKPOINT: Sound /er/ Spelled –er, –ir, –ur, and –ear

Explain that students are going to show what they have learned about sounds, letters, and words.

1. Give students the Unit Checkpoint pages for the Sound /er/ Spelled –er, –ir, –ur, and –ear unit and print the Unit Checkpoint Answer Key, if you'd like.

2. Use the instructions below to help administer the Checkpoint to students. On the Answer Key or another sheet of paper, note student answers to oral response questions to help with scoring the Checkpoint later.

3. Use the Answer Key to score the Checkpoint, and then enter the results online.

Part 1. Circle Words with Sound /er/ Have students circle the words with the sound /er/.

Part 2. Many Spellings, One Sound Have students circle the four ways to spell the sound /er/.

Part 3. Read Sight Words Have students read each sight word aloud. Note any words they read incorrectly.

Part 4. Writing Read each sentence to students. Have them repeat and write the sentence.

23. *Where did you learn that?*

24. *Let's burn the new candle.*

25. *I like the blue shirt.*

Part 5. Read Aloud Listen to students read the sentences aloud. Count and note the number of words they read correctly.

Part 6. Read Nonsense Words Have students read each nonsense word aloud. Note any words they read incorrectly.

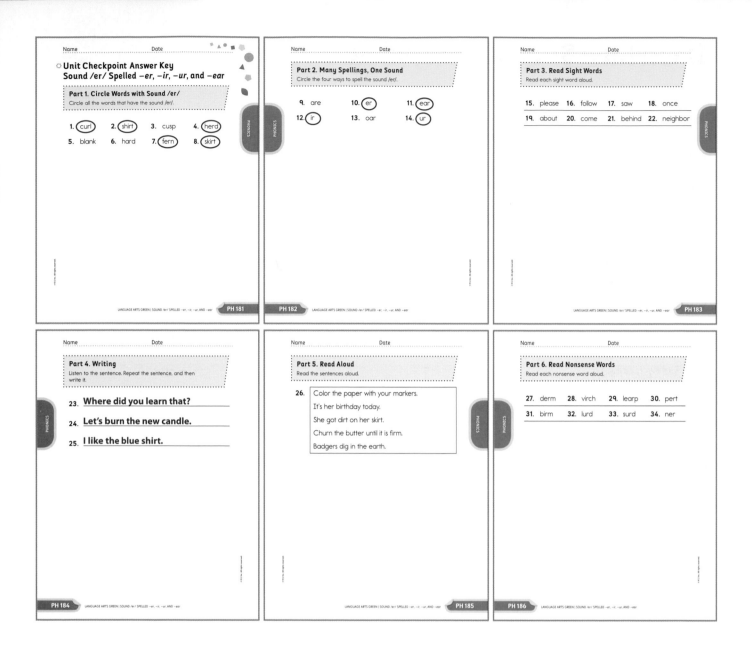

Name _____ Date _____

○ Unit Checkpoint Answer Key
Sound /er/ Spelled –er, –ir, –ur, and –ear

Part 1. Circle Words with Sound /er/
Circle all the words that have the sound /er/.

1. (curl)   2. (shirt)   3. cusp   4. (herd)
5. blank   6. hard   7. (fern)   8. (skirt)

PH 181

Name _____ Date _____

Part 2. Many Spellings, One Sound
Circle the four ways to spell the sound /er/.

9. are   10. (er)   11. (ear)
12. (ir)   13. oar   14. (ur)

PH 182   LANGUAGE ARTS GREEN | SOUND /er/ SPELLED –er, –ir, –ur, AND –ear

---

Name _____ Date _____

Part 3. Read Sight Words
Read each sight word aloud.

15. please   16. follow   17. saw   18. once
19. about   20. come   21. behind   22. neighbor

PH 183

Name _____ Date _____

Part 4. Writing
Listen to the sentence. Repeat the sentence, and then write it.

23. **Where did you learn that?**
24. **Let's burn the new candle.**
25. **I like the blue shirt.**

PH 184

Name _____ Date _____

Part 5. Read Aloud
Read the sentences aloud.

26. | Color the paper with your markers.
It's her birthday today.
She got dirt on her skirt.
Churn the butter until it is firm.
Badgers dig in the earth.

PH 185

Name _____ Date _____

Part 6. Read Nonsense Words
Read each nonsense word aloud.

27. derm   28. virch   29. learp   30. pert
31. birm   32. lurd   33. surd   34. ner

PH 186   LANGUAGE ARTS GREEN | SOUND /er/ SPELLED –er, –ir, –ur, AND –ear

Introduce Sound /ĕ/ Spelled *ea*

Unit Overview

In this unit, students will
- ► Learn the sight words *everything*, *under*, and *whether*.
- ► Learn the spelling *ea* for the sound /ē/ and /ĕ/.
- ► Read and write sentences.
- ► Read stories silently and aloud.

Lesson Overview

【Offline】 FOCUS: Introduce Sound /ĕ/ Spelled *ea*		**15** minutes
Sight Words	Introduce Sight Words	
Learn	Introduce Sound /ĕ/ Spelled *ea*	
	Review Sounds /ē/ and /ĕ/ Spelled *ea*	
Try It	Pick the Word	

【Online】 REVIEW: Sound /ĕ/ Spelled *ea*		**15** minutes
Review	Sound /ĕ/ Spelled *ea*	
Practice	Fluency	

[Offline] ⏱ 15 minutes

FOCUS: Introduce Sound /ĕ/ Spelled *ea*

Work **together** with students to complete offline Sight Words, Learn, and Try It activities.

Sight Words •

Introduce Sight Words

Help students learn the sight words *everything*, *under*, and *whether*.

1. Gather the sight word cards *everything*, *under*, and *whether*.

2. Show students the *everything* card.

3. **Say:** This is the word *everything*. We see this word so often that we want to be able to read and spell it quickly without thinking about it. Look closely at the word *everything*. Spell the word *everything* aloud. Take a picture of the word *everything* in your mind. When you think you can spell *everything* yourself, turn the card over and use your letter tiles to spell the word *everything*. Check the card to see if you spelled the word *everything* correctly. Read aloud the word you spelled with the letter tiles.

4. Repeat the activity with the remaining sight words.

5. Chart students' progress on the back of each card.

   ▸ Divide the back of the card into two columns.
   ▸ Label the first column "Read" and the second column "Spell."
   ▸ Record the dates that students read or spell the word correctly. When students can read and spell the word correctly three times in a row, they have mastered the word. You may want to put a star or sticker on the card when they have mastered that word.

6. Add the cards to students' sight words box.

TIP Sight words can be very difficult for some students. Let students work at their own pace and really master these words, as they occur frequently in reading and writing.

Objectives
- Read sight words.
- Spell sight words.

Introduce Sound /ĕ/ Spelled *ea*

Help students learn the spelling *ea* for the sound /ĕ/.

1. Place the following letter tiles on students' whiteboard: *b, d, e, ea, g, h, r,* and *t*.

2. Make the word *get* in the middle of students' whiteboard and point to it.

    Say: Today we are going to learn another spelling for the sound /ĕ/. You already know one of them. In the word *get*, the sound /ĕ/ is made by the letter *e* all by itself.

    ► Touch and say *get*.
    ► Where is the sound /ĕ/ in this word? middle
    ► Which letter or letters make this sound? *e*

3. Make the word *head* and point to it.

    Say: This word is *head*. In the word *head*, the sound /ĕ/ is made by the letters *ea*.

    ► Touch and say *head*.
    ► Where is the sound /ĕ/ in this word? middle
    ► Which letters make this sound? *ea*

4. Make the word *bread* and point to it.

    Say: This word is *bread*. In the word *bread*, the sound /ĕ/ is also made by the letters *ea*.

    ► Touch and say *bread*.
    ► Where is the sound /ĕ/ in this word? middle
    ► Which letter or letters make this sound? *ea*

Review Sounds /ĕ/ and /ē/ Spelled *ea*

Help students review the spelling *ea* for the sounds /ĕ/ and /ē/.

1. Write the following words on your whiteboard: *head* and *mean*.

2. **Say:** The letters *ea* can make the sound /ĕ/, as in *head*.

    ► Touch and say the sounds in *head*. /h/ /ĕ/ /d/

3. **Say:** The letters *ea* can also make the sound /ē/, as in *mean*.

    ► Touch and say the sounds in *mean*. /m/ /ē/ /n/

4. **Say:** If you see a word with the letters *ea* in it, do the following:

    ► If it's a word you don't already know, first try saying the word with the sound /ē/, because the sound /ē/ is the most common way to say *ea*.
    ► If the sound /ē/ doesn't work, then try the sound /ĕ/. You may have to try both sounds before you find the one that makes sense.

Objectives

- Identify individual sounds in words.
- Identify and use the sound /ĕ/.
- Identify the letter, given the sound /ĕ/.
- Identify and use the sound /ē/.
- Identify and use *ea* spelling patterns.
- Write words by applying grade-level phonics knowledge.

5. Write the following words on your whiteboard: *lead* and *read*.

   Say: Some words spelled with the letters *ea* can be said with the sound /ĕ/ or the sound /ē/.

6. Point to the word *lead*.

   Say: This word can be read as /lĕd/ or /lēd/. Let's look at how the word can be used in sentences. We can say /lĕd/, as in *The lead in my pencil keeps breaking off*, or we can say /lēd/, as in *He can lead the band*.

7. Have students make up one sentence using the word *read* as in /rĕd/ and another sentence using *read* as in /rēd/.

Try It

Pick the Word

Have students complete page PH 63 in *K¹² PhonicsWorks Advanced Activity Book* for more practice with the spelling *ea* for the sound /ĕ/. Have students read each sentence aloud and find the word in the sentence that has the sound /ĕ/. Have them write the word next to the sentence.

Objectives
- Identify and use the sound /ĕ/.
- Identify and use *ea* spelling patterns.

Try It

Introduce Sound /ĕ/ Spelled *ea*

Pick the Word

Read the sentence. Find the word that has the sound /ĕ/ as in *bread*. Write the word.

1. We ate too much bread. — **bread**
2. This thread is perfect for my skirt. — **thread**
3. Will you be my partner instead? — **instead**
4. I have a blue feather. — **feather**
5. I ate after I read my book. — **read**
6. She dealt five cards to each player. — **dealt**
7. I don't know if she is ready. — **ready**

LANGUAGE ARTS GREEN   PH 63

[Online] ⓯ minutes

REVIEW: Sound /ĕ/ Spelled *ea*

Students will work online independently to complete activities with the *ea* spelling for the sounds /ĕ/ and /ē/ and develop fluency skills. Help students locate the online activities and provide support as needed.

Review ....

Sound /ĕ/ Spelled *ea*

Students will

- ▸ Practice the *ea* spelling for the sounds /ĕ/ and /ē/.
- ▸ Practice decoding text by reading a story.

Offline Alternative

No computer access? Have students spell words that have the spelling *ea* for the sounds /ĕ/ and /ē/, such as *bread, lead, meant, lean, mean,* and *bean*. You might also ask them to write the words in their dictation notebook.

Objectives

- Identify individual sounds in words.
- Identify and use *ea* spelling patterns.
- Identify and use the sound /ĕ/.
- Identify the letter, given the sound /ĕ/.
- Identify the letter, given the sound /ē/.
- Read aloud grade-level text with appropriate automaticity, prosody, accuracy, and rate.
- Decode words by applying grade-level word analysis skills.

Practice ....

Fluency

Good readers read often and reread texts. Students will practice their fluency skills by rereading a *K¹² PhonicsWorks Readers Advanced* story aloud as they are recorded.

Have students gather their favorite *K¹² PhonicsWorks Readers Advanced* story that they have already read. Follow the instructions online to record students as they read.

Offline Alternative

No computer access? Have students gather their favorite *K¹² PhonicsWorks Readers Advanced* story. Have them read the story aloud, and record the amount of time it takes them to read the story. Have them read the story again to beat their original time.

Objectives

- Increase reading fluency rate.
- Demonstrate automaticity.
- Demonstrate prosody.

Practice Sound /ĕ/ Spelled *ea* (A)

Lesson Overview

[Offline] **FOCUS:** Practice Sound /ĕ/ Spelled *ea*   **15** minutes

Sight Words	Sight Word Fun
Practice	Pairs of Sounds
	Spell One-Syllable Words
	Spell Two-Syllable Words
Try It	"Heather's Picnic"

[Online] **REVIEW:** Sound /ĕ/ Spelled *ea*   **15** minutes

Review	Sound /ĕ/ Spelled *ea*
Practice	Fluency

[Materials]

Supplied
- *K¹² PhonicsWorks Readers Advanced 11*, pp. 33–38
- *K¹² PhonicsWorks Readers Advanced,* any volume
- whiteboard, Learning Coach
- whiteboard, student
- small whiteboards (2)
- Tile Kit

Also Needed
- sight words box
- dictation notebook

[Offline] ⏱ 15 minutes

FOCUS: Practice Sound /ĕ/ Spelled *ea*

Work **together** with students to complete offline Sight Words, Practice, and Try It activities.

Sight Words •

Sight Word Fun

Help students learn the sight words *everything, under,* and *whether,* and up to two additional sight words they have yet to master.

1. Gather the sight word cards *everything, under,* and *whether,* and up to two additional sight word cards.

2. Choose one sight word card to begin.

   Say: Look at this word and take a picture of it in your mind. When you think you can spell the word yourself, turn the card over and use your letter tiles to spell the word.

3. After students spell the word, have them check the card to see if they spelled the word correctly.

   Say: Read aloud the word you spelled with the letter tiles.

4. Repeat the activity with the remaining sight words.

(TIP) Sight words can be very difficult for some students. Let them work at their own pace and really master these words.

> **Objectives**
> * Read sight words.
> * Spell sight words.

Practice •

Pairs of Sounds

Help students recognize the sound /ĕ/ or sound /ē/ for the spelling *ea*. Grab your whiteboard and dry-erase marker.

1. Write the following words on your whiteboard: *dead* and *pea*.

2. **Say:** I am going to write a pair of words. I will read the pair of words and you will repeat the words I say. Your job is to listen for the vowel sound in the word for the spelling *ea* and tell me if the vowel sound is the sound /ĕ/ or sound /ē/.

   ▸ For example, if I say *dead* and *pea*, you will repeat both words, and tell me the word *dead* has the sound /ĕ/ and the word *pea* has the sound /ē/ for the spelling *ea*.

3. Write the following words on your whiteboard: *squeak* and *thread*.

> **Objectives**
> * Identify and use *ea* spelling patterns.
> * Identify and use the sound /ĕ/.
> * Identify the letters, given the sound /ĕ/.
> * Identify and use the sound /ē/.
> * Identify the letters, given the sound /ē/.
> * Identify individual sounds in words.
> * Identify syllables in words.

4. **Say:** Now it's your turn. The first pair of words is *squeak* and *thread*. Students should repeat the words *squeak* and *thread,* and say *squeak* has the sound /ē/ and *thread* has the sound /ĕ/.

5. Follow the procedure with the following pairs of words:

   ▸ *weather* and *year* weather has the sound /ĕ/ and *year* has the sound /ē/
   ▸ *please* and *breath* please has the sound /ē/ and *breath* has the sound /ĕ/

Spell One-Syllable Words

Help students use letters and sounds to build one-syllable words that have the sound /ĕ/ spelled *ea*.

1. Place the following letter tiles at the top of students' whiteboard: *b, d, d, ea, h, r,* and *th.*

2. **Say:** You are going to place letters around the letters *ea* to make one-syllable words that have the sound /ĕ/. The first word is *breath.*

3. Have students

   ▸ Repeat the word.
   ▸ Find the vowel sound for /ĕ/. *ea*
   ▸ Find the letters that make the beginning sounds and place them before the vowel sound. *b, r*
   ▸ Find the letters that make the ending sound and place them after the vowel sound to make the word *breath. th*
   ▸ Touch and say the word.

4. Follow the procedure with the following words: *bread, dead, dread, head, thread.*

Spell Two-Syllable Words

Help students write two-syllable words that have the sound /ĕ/ spelled *ea*. Grab two small whiteboards and the dry-erase marker.

1. **Say:** You are going to write two-syllable words that have the sound /ĕ/ spelled *ea*. The first word is *heather.*

2. Have students

   ▸ Repeat the word.
   ▸ Fist tap the syllables. *heath / er*
   ▸ Write the first syllable on one board. *heath*
   ▸ Write the second syllable on the other board. *er*
   ▸ Touch and say the word.

3. Follow the procedure with the following words: *feather, weather.*

Try It ●

"Heather's Picnic"
Have students read "Heather's Picnic" on page 33 of *K¹² PhonicsWorks Readers Advanced 11.*

Students should read the story silently once or twice before reading the story aloud. When students miss a word that can be sounded out, point to it and give them three to six seconds to try the word again. If students still miss the word, tell them the word so the flow of the story isn't interrupted.

After reading the story, make a list of all the words students missed, and go over those words with them. You may use letter tiles to show students how to read the words.

Objectives
- Read aloud grade-level text with appropriate automaticity, prosody, accuracy, and rate.
- Decode words by applying grade-level word analysis skills.

**[Online]** **15** minutes

REVIEW: Sound /ĕ/ Spelled *ea*
Students will work online independently to complete activities with the *ea* spelling for the sound /ĕ/ and develop fluency skills. Help students locate the online activities and provide support as needed.

Review ●

Sound /ĕ/ Spelled *ea*
Students will

▶ Practice the *ea* spelling for the sound /ĕ/.

Offline Alternative

No computer access? Have students spell words that have the spelling *ea* for the sound /ĕ/, such as *dead, instead,* and *tread.* You might also ask them to write the words in their dictation notebook.

Objectives
- Identify individual sounds in words.
- Identify and use *ea* spelling patterns.
- Identify and use the sound /ĕ/.
- Identify the letters, given the sound /ĕ/.

Practice ●

Fluency
Good readers read often and reread texts. Students will practice their fluency skills by rereading a *K¹² PhonicsWorks Readers Advanced* story aloud as they are recorded.

Have students gather their favorite *K¹² PhonicsWorks Readers Advanced* story that they have already read. Follow the instructions online to record students as they read.

Objectives
- Increase reading fluency rate.
- Demonstrate automaticity.
- Demonstrate prosody.

Offline Alternative

No computer access? Have students gather their favorite *K¹² PhonicsWorks Readers Advanced* story. Have them read the story aloud, and record the amount of time it takes them to read the story. Have them read the story again to beat their original time.

Practice Sound /ĕ/ Spelled *ea* (B)

Lesson Overview

【 Offline 】 FOCUS: Practice Sound /ĕ/ Spelled *ea*

15 minutes

Sight Words	Sight Word Fun
Practice	Build Words
Try It	Hunt for Information

【 Online 】 REVIEW: Sound /ĕ/ Spelled *ea*

15 minutes

Review	Sound /ĕ/ Spelled *ea*
Practice	Fluency

【 Materials 】

Supplied
- *K¹² PhonicsWorks Advanced Activity Book,* p. PH 64
- *K¹² PhonicsWorks Readers Advanced,* any volume
- whiteboard, student
- Tile Kit

Also Needed
- sight words box
- dictation notebook

〔 Offline 〕 ⑮ minutes

FOCUS: Practice Sound /ĕ/ Spelled *ea*

Work **together** with students to complete offline Sight Words, Practice, and Try It activities.

Sight Words ···

Sight Word Fun

Help students learn the sight words *everything, under,* and *whether,* and up to two additional sight words they have yet to master.

1. Gather the sight word cards *everything, under,* and *whether,* and up to two additional sight word cards.

2. Choose one sight word card to begin.

   Say: Look at this word and take a picture of it in your mind. When you think you can spell the word yourself, turn the card over and use your letter tiles to spell the word.

3. After students spell the word, have them check the card to see if they spelled the word correctly.

   Say: Read aloud the word you spelled with the letter tiles.

4. Repeat the activity with the remaining sight words.

   TIP Sight words can be very difficult for some students. Let them work at their own pace and really master these words.

Objectives
- Read sight words.
- Spell sight words.

Practice ···

Build Words

Help students use letters and sounds to build words.

1. Place the following letter tiles at the top of students' whiteboard: *a, b, d, ea, l, m, n, p, r, s, t, th,* and *w.*

2. Draw four horizontal lines across the middle of students' whiteboard to represent the sounds in a word.

3. **Say:** Let's use letters and sounds to build the word *meant.*

4. Have students finger stretch the sounds in *meant.*

5. Have students
   ▸ Identify the first, next, and last sounds in *meant.*
   ▸ Choose the corresponding letter tile for each of the sounds.
   ▸ Move the letters to the correct lines on their whiteboard.

Objectives
- Blend sounds to create words.
- Identify individual sounds in words.
- Write words by applying grade-level phonics knowledge.
- Identify and use the sound /ĕ/.
- Identify the letters, given the sound /ĕ/.
- Identify and use *ea* spelling patterns.

6. Guide students with these questions:

   ▸ What is the first sound in *meant*? /m/
     Which line does the letter for that sound go on? the first one
   ▸ What is the next sound in *meant*? /ĕ/
     Which line do the letters for that sound go on? the second one
   ▸ What is the next sound in *meant*? /n/
     Which line does the letter for that sound go on? the third one
   ▸ What's the last sound in *meant*? /t/
     Which line does the letter for that sound go on? the last one

7. Redirect students if they select the incorrect letter.

   Say: That sound is in the word [word], and it is the [first, second, third, fourth] sound. We want the sound [target sound].

   Continue until students select the correct letter.

8. Have students touch and say the word.

9. Have them say the word as they use a dry-erase marker to write the word on the whiteboard.

10. Draw horizontal lines across the middle of students' whiteboard that represent the number of sounds in each word. Repeat the activity to build the following words:

    ▸ *weather* /w/ /ĕ/ /th/ /er/
    ▸ *bread* /b/ /r/ /ĕ/ /d/
    ▸ *pleasant* /p/ /l/ /ĕ/ /z/ /ă/ /n/ /t/

Try It

Hunt for Information

Have students complete page PH 64 in *K¹² PhonicsWorks Advanced Activity Book* for more practice with the spelling *ea* for the sound /ĕ/. Have them read the story aloud and highlight the words in the story that have the sound /ĕ/ spelled *ea*. Have students choose words from the story to best complete each sentence and write those words.

Try It

Practice Sound /ĕ/ Spelled *ea* (B)

Hunt for Information

Highlight words that have the sound /ĕ/ spelled *ea* as in bread. Choose a word from the story that completes the sentence. Write the word.

> The Golden Pheasant is kept on many bird farms. It is easy to raise these birds. They stay healthy for a long time. The male has a bright golden breast and feathers. The female has a dull brown breast and feathers. Pheasants like to eat corn, grain, chopped apples, peanuts, crickets, and earthworms.

1. A pheasant is a kind of __**bird**__.

2. The Golden __**Pheasant**__ is kept on many farms.

3. The pheasant stays __**healthy**__ for a long time.

4. The male has a golden __**breast**__ and feathers.

5. The female has a brown breast and __**feathers**__.

PH 64 — LANGUAGE ARTS GREEN

Objectives

- Identify and use the sound /ĕ/.
- Identify the letters, given the sound /ĕ/.
- Identify and use *ea* spelling patterns.
- Read aloud grade-level text with appropriate automaticity, prosody, accuracy, and rate.
- Decode words by applying grade-level word analysis skills.
- Write words by applying grade-level phonics knowledge.

REVIEW: Sound /ĕ/ Spelled *ea*

Students will work online independently to complete activities with the *ea* spelling for the sound /ĕ/ and develop fluency skills. Help students locate the online activities and provide support as needed.

Review

· ·

Sound /ĕ/ Spelled *ea*

Students will

▸ Practice the sound /ĕ/ spelled *ea*.
▸ Practice decoding text by reading a story.

Offline Alternative

No computer access? Have students spell words that have the spelling *ea* for the sound /ĕ/, such as *head*, *breath*, and *heather*. You might also ask them to write the words in their dictation notebook.

Objectives
- Identify individual sounds in words.
- Identify and use *ea* spelling patterns.
- Identify and use the sound /ĕ/.
- Identify the letters, given the sound /ĕ/.
- Read aloud grade-level text with appropriate automaticity, prosody, accuracy, and rate.
- Decode words by applying grade-level word analysis skills.

Practice

· ·

Fluency

Good readers read often and reread texts. Students will practice their fluency skills by rereading a *K¹² PhonicsWorks Readers Advanced* story aloud as they are recorded.

Have students gather their favorite *K¹² PhonicsWorks Readers Advanced* story that they have already read. Follow the instructions online to record students as they read.

Objectives
- Increase reading fluency rate.
- Demonstrate automaticity.
- Demonstrate prosody.

Offline Alternative

No computer access? Have students gather their favorite *K¹² PhonicsWorks Readers Advanced* story. Have them read the story aloud, and record the amount of time it takes them to read the story. Have them read the story again to beat their original time.

Practice Sound /ĕ/ Spelled *ea* (C)

Lesson Overview

📄 **〖 Offline 〗 FOCUS:** Practice Sound /ĕ/ Spelled *ea*	⏱ **15** minutes

Sight Words	Sight Word Fun
Practice	Draw a Picture
Try It	"Andy"

🖥 **〖 Online 〗 REVIEW:** Sound /ĕ/ Spelled *ea*	⏱ **15** minutes

Review	Sound /ĕ/ Spelled *ea*
Practice	Fluency

〖 Materials 〗

Supplied
- *K¹² PhonicsWorks Readers Advanced 12*, pp. 1–6
- *K¹² PhonicsWorks Readers Advanced*, any volume

Also Needed
- sight words box
- dictation notebook
- index cards (5)
- crayons

Advance Preparation

For Draw a Picture, print each of the following words on index cards, using one card per word: *thread, feather, breadbox, headband,* and *weatherman.*

〖 Offline 〗 ⑮ minutes

FOCUS: Practice Sound /ĕ/ Spelled *ea*

Work **together** with students to complete offline Sight Words, Practice, and Try It activities.

Sight Words ....

Sight Word Fun

Help students learn the sight words *everything, under,* and *whether,* and up to two additional sight words they have yet to master.

1. Gather the sight word cards *everything, under,* and *whether,* and up to two additional sight word cards.

2. Choose one sight word card to begin.

   Say: Look at this word and take a picture of it in your mind. When you think you can spell the word yourself, turn the card over and use your letter tiles to spell the word.

3. After students spell the word, have them check the card to see if they spelled the word correctly.

   Say: Read aloud the word you spelled with the letter tiles.

4. Repeat the activity with the remaining sight words.

TIP Sight words can be very difficult for some students. Let them work at their own pace and really master these words.

> **Objectives**
> - Read sight words.
> - Spell sight words.

Practice ....

Draw a Picture

Help students practice /ĕ/ spelled *ea* words by having them draw pictures to match the word.

1. Gather the index cards you prepared and the crayons.

2. **Say:** Let's read some words that have the sound /ĕ/ spelled *ea.*
   - ▸ If you read the word correctly the first time, put it in one stack.
   - ▸ If a word takes you more than one try, put it in another stack.

3. Have students read each of the words on the cards.

4. Help students read the words from the stack that took them more than one try.

5. Have them select two words and use crayons to draw a picture of each word on the back of the card.

TIP If students have trouble reading the words, have them break them into syllables. Then help students finger stretch the sounds in each syllable.

> **Objectives**
> - Identify individual sounds in words.
> - Identify and use *ea* spelling patterns.
> - Identify and use the sound /ĕ/.
> - Identify the letter, given the sound /ĕ/.

Try It •••

"Andy"

Have students read "Andy" on page 1 of *K¹² PhonicsWorks Readers Advanced 12*.

Students should read the story silently once or twice before reading the story aloud. When students miss a word that can be sounded out, point to it and give them three to six seconds to try the word again. If students still miss the word, tell them the word so the flow of the story isn't interrupted.

After reading the story, make a list of all the words students missed, and go over those words with them. You may use letter tiles to show students how to read the words.

> **Objectives**
> * Read aloud grade-level text with appropriate automaticity, prosody, accuracy, and rate.
> * Decode words by applying grade-level word analysis skills.

 **15** minutes

REVIEW: Sound /ĕ/ Spelled *ea*

Students will work online independently to complete activities with the *ea* spelling for the sound /ĕ/ and develop fluency skills. Help students locate the online activities and provide support as needed.

Review ••

Sound /ĕ/ Spelled *ea*

Students will

▸ Practice the sound /ĕ/ spelled *ea*.

_____

Offline Alternative

No computer access? Have students spell words that have the spelling *ea* for the sound /ĕ/, such as *death*, *read*, and *leather*. You might also ask them to write the words in their dictation notebook

> **Objectives**
> * Identify individual sounds in words.
> * Identify and use *ea* spelling patterns.
> * Identify and use the sound /ĕ/.
> * Identify the letters, given the sound /ĕ/.

Practice •••

Fluency

Good readers read often and reread texts. Students will practice their fluency skills by rereading a *K¹² PhonicsWorks Readers Advanced* story aloud as they are recorded.

Have students gather their favorite *K¹² PhonicsWorks Readers Advanced* story that they have already read. Follow the instructions online to record students as they read.

_____

Offline Alternative

No computer access? Have students gather their favorite *K¹² PhonicsWorks Readers Advanced* story. Have them read the story aloud, and record the amount of time it takes them to read the story. Have them read the story again to beat their original time.

> **Objectives**
> * Increase reading fluency rate.
> * Demonstrate automaticity.
> * Demonstrate prosody.

Unit Checkpoint

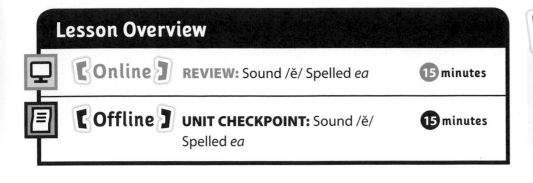

Lesson Overview

Online REVIEW: Sound /ĕ/ Spelled *ea* **15** minutes

Offline UNIT CHECKPOINT: Sound /ĕ/ Spelled *ea* **15** minutes

Materials

Supplied
- *K¹² PhonicsWorks Advanced Assessments*, pp. PH 187–192

Objectives
- Identify individual sounds in words.
- Identify and use *ea* spelling patterns.
- Identify and use the sound /ĕ/.
- Read aloud grade-level text with appropriate automaticity, prosody, accuracy, and rate.
- Read instructional-level text with 90% accuracy.
- Write words by applying grade-level phonics knowledge.
- Write sight words.
- Read sight words.

Online **15** minutes

REVIEW: **Sound /ĕ/ Spelled *ea***

Students will review the spelling *ea* for the sound /ĕ/ to prepare for the Unit Checkpoint. Help students locate the online activities and provide support as needed.

【 Offline 】 ⏱ 15 minutes

UNIT CHECKPOINT: Sound /ĕ/ Spelled *ea*

Explain that students are going to show what they have learned about sounds, letters, and words.

1. Give students the Unit Checkpoint pages for the Sound /ĕ/ Spelled *ea* unit and print the Unit Checkpoint Answer Key, if you'd like.

2. Use the instructions below to help administer the Checkpoint to students. On the Answer Key or another sheet of paper, note student answers to oral response questions to help with scoring the Checkpoint later.

3. Use the Answer Key to score the Checkpoint, and then enter the results online.

Part 1. Circle Words with Sound /ĕ/ Have students circle the words with the sound /ĕ/.

Part 2. Count Sounds. Have students read each word aloud, count the number of sounds in each word, and write that number.

Part 3. Read Sight Words Have students read each sight word aloud. Note any words they read incorrectly.

Part 4. Writing Read each sentence to students. Have them repeat and write the sentence.

23. *Heather read that book last week.*

24. *I need a new leather belt.*

25. *Mom made me a sweater.*

Part 5. Read Aloud Listen to students read the sentences aloud. Count and note the number of words they read correctly.

Part 6. Read Nonsense Words Have students read each nonsense word aloud. Note any words they read incorrectly.

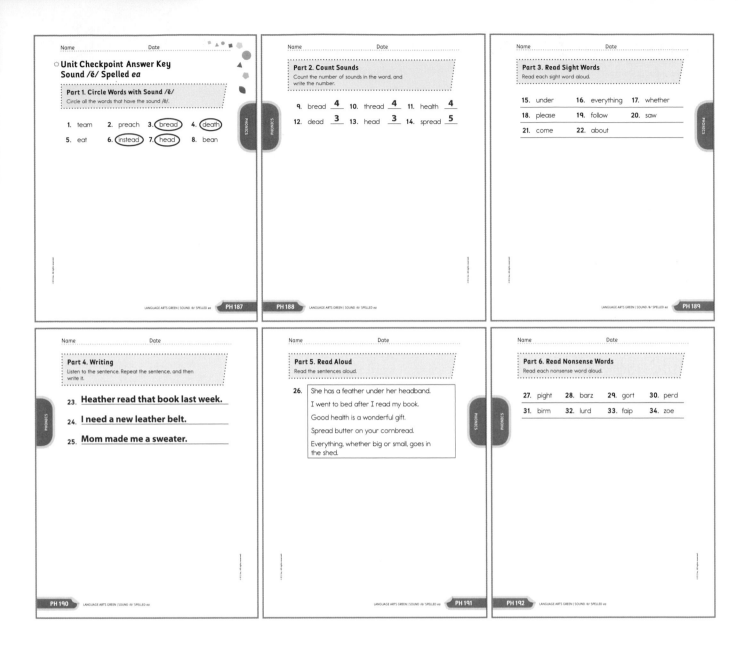

Name _____ **Date** _____

☼ Unit Checkpoint Answer Key
Sound /ĕ/ Spelled *ea*

Part 1. Circle Words with Sound /ĕ/
Circle all the words that have the sound /ĕ/.

1. team   2. preach   3. (bread)   4. (death)

5. eat   6. (instead)   7. (head)   8. bean

Name _____ **Date** _____

Part 2. Count Sounds
Count the number of sounds in the word, and write the number.

9. bread __4__   10. thread __4__   11. health __4__

12. dead __3__   13. head __3__   14. spread __5__

Name _____ **Date** _____

Part 3. Read Sight Words
Read each sight word aloud.

15. under   16. everything   17. whether

18. please   19. follow   20. saw

21. come   22. about

Name _____ **Date** _____

Part 4. Writing
Listen to the sentence. Repeat the sentence, and then write it.

23. **Heather read that book last week.**

24. **I need a new leather belt.**

25. **Mom made me a sweater.**

Name _____ **Date** _____

Part 5. Read Aloud
Read the sentences aloud.

26.
> She has a feather under her headband.
> I went to bed after I read my book.
> Good health is a wonderful gift.
> Spread butter on your cornbread.
> Everything, whether big or small, goes in the shed.

Name _____ **Date** _____

Part 6. Read Nonsense Words
Read each nonsense word aloud.

27. pight   28. barz   29. gort   30. perd

31. birm   32. lurd   33. faip   34. zoe

Introduce Sound /oi/ Spelled *oi* and *oy*

Unit Overview

In this unit, students will

- ► Learn the sight words *nothing*, *almost*, and *over*.
- ► Learn the spellings *oi* and *oy* for the sound /oi/.
- ► Read and write sentences.
- ► Read stories silently and aloud.

[Materials]

Supplied

- *K¹² PhonicsWorks Advanced Activity Book,* p. PH 65
- *K¹² PhonicsWorks Readers Advanced,* any volume
- whiteboard, student
- Tile Kit

Also Needed

- sight words box
- dictation notebook

Lesson Overview

	[Offline] FOCUS: Introduce Sound /oi/ Spelled *oi* and *oy*	15 minutes
Sight Words	Introduce Sight Words	
Learn	Introduce Sound /oi/ Spelled *oi*	
	Introduce Sound /oi/ Spelled *oy*	
Try It	Investigator	
	[Online] REVIEW: Sound /oi/ Spelled *oi* and *oy*	15 minutes
Review	Sound /oi/ Spelled *oi* and *oy*	
Practice	Fluency	

〔Offline〕 ⏱ 15 minutes

FOCUS: Introduce Sound /oi/ Spelled *oi* and *oy*

Work **together** with students to complete offline Sight Words, Learn, and Try It activities.

Sight Words ·

Introduce Sight Words

Help students learn the sight words *nothing, almost,* and *over.*

1. Gather the sight word cards *nothing, almost,* and *over.*

2. Show students the *nothing* card.

3. **Say:** This is the word *nothing.* We see this word so often that we want to be able to read and spell it quickly without thinking about it. Look closely at the word *nothing.* Spell the word *nothing* aloud. Take a picture of the word *nothing* in your mind. When you think you can spell *nothing* yourself, turn the card over and use your letter tiles to spell the word *nothing.* Check the card to see if you spelled the word *nothing* correctly. Read aloud the word you spelled with the letter tiles.

4. Repeat the activity with the remaining sight words.

5. Chart students' progress on the back of each card.

   ▸ Divide the back of the card into two columns.
   ▸ Label the first column "Read" and the second column "Spell."
   ▸ Record the dates that students read or spell the word correctly. When students can read and spell the word correctly three times in a row, they have mastered the word. You may want to put a star or sticker on the card when they have mastered that word.

6. Add the cards to students' sight words box.

TIP Sight words can be very difficult for some students. Let students work at their own pace and really master these words, as they occur frequently in reading and writing.

> ### Objectives
> - Read sight words.
> - Spell sight words.

Learn

Introduce Sound /oi/ Spelled *oi*

Help students learn the spelling *oi* for the sound /oi/.

1. Place the following letter tiles on students' whiteboard: *c, l, n, oi,* and *s.*

2. Make the word *coin* in the middle of students' whiteboard and point to it.

   Say: Today we are going to learn a spelling for the sound /oi/. In the word *coin,* the sound /oi/ is made by the letters *oi.*

   ▸ Touch and say *coin.*
   ▸ Say and write the word on your whiteboard.
   ▸ What is the vowel sound in this word? /oi/
   ▸ Which letters make this sound? *oi*

3. Make the word *soil* and point to it.

   Say: This word is *soil.* In the word *soil,* the sound /oi/ is made by the letters *oi.*

   ▸ Touch and say *soil.*
   ▸ Say and write the word on your whiteboard.
   ▸ What is the vowel sound in this word? /oi/
   ▸ Which letters make this sound? *oi*

Introduce Sound /oi/ Spelled *oy*

Help students learn the spelling *oy* for the sound /oi/.

1. Place the following letter tiles on students' whiteboard: *b, c, j, l, n, oi,* and *oy.*

2. Make the word *join* in the middle of students' whiteboard and point to it.

   Say: This word is *join.* The letters *oi* make the sound /oi/.

   ▸ Touch and say *join.*
   ▸ Say and write the word on your whiteboard.
   ▸ What is the vowel sound in this word? /oi/
   ▸ Is the sound /oi/ at the beginning, middle, or end of the word? middle

3. Make the word *joy* and point to it.

   Say: Let's look at another way to spell the sound /oi/. This is the word *joy.*

   ▸ Touch and say *joy.*
   ▸ Say and write the word on your whiteboard.
   ▸ What is the vowel sound in this word? /oi/
   ▸ Is the sound /oi/ at the beginning, middle, or end of the word? end

Objectives

- Identify individual sounds in words.
- Identify and use the sound /oi/.
- Identify and use *oi* and *oy* spelling patterns.
- Write words by applying grade-level phonics knowledge.

4. Write the words *join* and *joy* on students' whiteboard and point to them.

Say: The sound /oi/ can be made by the letters *oi* or by the letters *oy*.

▸ When the sound /oi/ is in the middle of a word, what letters make the sound /oi/? *oi*
▸ When the sound /oi/ is at the end of a word, what letters make the sound /oi/? *oy*

5. Repeat the procedure with the following words: *boil, boy, coin, coil.*

Try It

Investigator

Have students complete page PH 65 in *K¹² PhonicsWorks Advanced Activity Book* for more practice with the spellings *oi* and *oy* for the sound /oi/. Have students read each word aloud and write word in the correct column.

Try It

Introduce Sound /oi/ Spelled *oi* and *oy*

Investigator

Read each word aloud. Write the word in the correct column.

joy	coin	boy	noise
point	join	toy	joint
boil	ahoy	Roy	Troy

oy	oi
joy	coin
boy	noise
toy	point
ahoy	join
Roy	joint
Troy	boil

LANGUAGE ARTS GREEN   PH 65

PHONICS

Objectives

• Identify individual sounds in words.
• Identify and use the sound /oi/.
• Identify and use *oi* and *oy* spelling patterns.

[Online] ⏱ minutes

REVIEW: Sound /oi/ Spelled *oi* and *oy*

Students will work online to complete activities with the sound /oi/ spelled *oi* and *oy* and develop fluency skills. Help students locate the online activities and provide support as needed.

Review ••

Sound /oi/ Spelled *oi* and *oy*

Students will

▸ Practice the *oi* and *oy* spellings for the sound /oi/.

▸ Practice decoding text by reading a story.

Offline Alternative

No computer access? Have students spell words that have the spellings *oi* and *oy* for the sound /oi/, such as *boil* and *toy*. You might also ask them to write the words in their dictation notebook.

Objectives

- Identify individual sounds in words.
- Identify and use the sound /oi/.
- Identify and use *oi* and *oy* spelling patterns.
- Read aloud grade-level text with appropriate automaticity, prosody, accuracy, and rate.
- Decode words by applying grade-level word analysis skills.

Practice •••

Fluency

Good readers read often and reread texts. Students will practice their fluency skills by rereading a *K¹² PhonicsWorks Readers Advanced* story aloud as they are recorded.

Have students gather their favorite *K¹² PhonicsWorks Readers Advanced* story that they have already read. Follow the instructions online to record students as they read.

Offline Alternative

No computer access? Have students gather their favorite *K¹² PhonicsWorks Readers Advanced* story. Have them read the story aloud, and record the amount of time it takes them to read the story. Have them read the story again to beat their original time.

Objectives

- Increase reading fluency rate.
- Demonstrate automaticity.
- Demonstrate prosody.

Practice Sound /oi/ Spelled *oi* and *oy* (A)

Lesson Overview

[Offline] **FOCUS:** Practice Sound /oi/ Spelled *oi* and *oy*　　**15** minutes

Sight Words	Sight Word Fun
Practice	Word Chains
Try It	"Will Roy Find the Toy?"

[Online] **REVIEW:** Sound /oi/ Spelled *oi* and *oy*　　**15** minutes

Review	Sound /oi/ Spelled *oi* and *oy*
Practice	Fluency

Materials

Supplied
- *K¹² PhonicsWorks Readers Advanced 12,* pp. 7–12
- *K¹² PhonicsWorks Readers Advanced,* any volume
- whiteboard, student
- Tile Kit

Also Needed
- sight words box
- dictation notebook

【 Offline 】 ⑮ minutes

FOCUS: Practice Sound /oi/ Spelled *oi* and *oy*

Work **together** with students to complete offline Sight Words, Practice, and Try It activities.

Sight Words

Sight Word Fun

Help students learn the sight words *nothing, almost,* and *over,* and up to two additional sight words they have yet to master.

1. Gather the sight word cards *nothing, almost,* and *over,* and up to two additional sight word cards.

2. Choose one sight word card to begin.

   Say: Look at this word and take a picture of it in your mind. When you think you can spell the word yourself, turn the card over and use your letter tiles to spell the word.

3. After students spell the word, have them check the card to see if they spelled the word correctly.

   Say: Read aloud the word you spelled with the letter tiles.

4. Repeat the activity with the remaining sight words.

   TIP Sight words can be very difficult for some students. Let them work at their own pace and really master these words.

> **Objectives**
> - Read sight words.
> - Spell sight words.

Practice

Word Chains

Have students build words by adding and changing letters to help them recognize and use the spellings *oi* and *oy* for the sound /oi/.

1. Place the following letter tiles at the top of students' whiteboard: *b, c, f, j, l, n, oi, oy, s,* and *t.*

2. **Say:** You will spell words in short word chains today. There will be one chain for each of the spellings of the sound /oi/ that we know. How many spellings do you know for the sound /oi/? two

3. **Say:** I'll do the first word. The word is *foil.*

   ▸ I will pull down the letters for the sounds /f/, /oi/, and /l/ to spell the word *foil.*

   ▸ I will touch and say *foil.* To change *foil* to *boil,* I will think about which sound is changed from the word *foil* to *boil.* I will need to replace the letter *f* with the letter *b.*

   ▸ Touch and say the word *boil.* Now it's your turn to change *boil* to *soil.* You can spell *soil* by making only one change. Touch and say the new word.

> **Objectives**
> - Identify the new word when one sound is changed in a word.
> - Identify individual sounds in words.
> - Identify and use the sound /oi/.
> - Identify and use *oi* and *oy* spelling patterns.

4. Redirect students if they select the incorrect letter for any sound.

   Say: That letter is for the sound [incorrect sound]. We want the letter for the sound [target sound]. What letter makes that sound? Answers will vary.

5. Redirect students if they name the sound incorrectly.

   Say: To change the word [first word] to [target word], we need the letter for the sound [target sound].

   Show students how to make the change. Have them touch and say the new word after they move the letters.

6. Follow this procedure to make the following groups of word chains:

   ▸ *oil, coil, coin, join*
   ▸ *joy, boy, soy, toy*

7. For every new word, have students add, replace, or remove only one letter tile. Remind students that in these word chains only one sound—and only one letter tile—will change when the word changes.

Try It

"Will Roy Find the Toy?"
Have students read "Will Roy Find the Toy?" on page 7 of *K¹² PhonicsWorks Readers Advanced 12.*

   Students should read the story silently once or twice before reading the story aloud. When students miss a word that can be sounded out, point to it and give them three to six seconds to try the word again. If students still miss the word, tell them the word so the flow of the story isn't interrupted.

   After reading the story, make a list of all the words students missed, and go over those words with them. You may use letter tiles to show students how to read the words.

Objectives
- Read aloud grade-level text with appropriate automaticity, prosody, accuracy, and rate.
- Decode words by applying grade-level word analysis skills.

[Online] ⑮ minutes

REVIEW: Sound /oi/ Spelled *oi* and *oy*

Students will work online to complete activities with the sound /oi/ spelled *oi* and *oy* and develop fluency skills. Help students locate the online activities and provide support as needed.

Review ··

Sound /oi/ Spelled *oi* and *oy*

Students will

▸ Practice the *oi* and *oy* spellings for the sound /oi/.

___

Offline Alternative

No computer access? Have students spell words that have the spellings *oi* and *oy* for the sound /oi/, such as *join* and *joy*. You might also ask them to write the words in their dictation notebook.

> **Objectives**
> - Identify individual sounds in words.
> - Identify and use the sound /oi/.
> - Identify and use *oi* and *oy* spelling patterns.

Practice ···

Fluency

Good readers read often and reread texts. Students will practice their fluency skills by rereading a *K¹² PhonicsWorks Readers Advanced* story aloud as they are recorded.

Have students gather their favorite *K¹² PhonicsWorks Readers Advanced* story that they have already read. Follow the instructions online to record students as they read.

___

Offline Alternative

No computer access? Have students gather their favorite *K¹² PhonicsWorks Readers Advanced* story. Have them read the story aloud, and record the amount of time it takes them to read the story. Have them read the story again to beat their original time.

> **Objectives**
> - Increase reading fluency rate.
> - Demonstrate automaticity.
> - Demonstrate prosody.

Practice Sound /oi/ Spelled *oi* and *oy* (B)

Lesson Overview

[Offline] **FOCUS:** Practice Sound /oi/ Spelled *oi* and *oy* **15** minutes

Sight Words	Sight Word Fun
Practice	Spell One-Syllable Words
Try It	Sentence Spree

[Online] **REVIEW:** Sound /oi/ Spelled *oi* and *oy* **15** minutes

Review	Sound /oi/ Spelled *oi* and *oy*
Practice	Fluency

Materials

Supplied

- *K¹² PhonicsWorks Advanced Activity Book,* p. PH 66
- *K¹² PhonicsWorks Readers Advanced,* any volume
- whiteboard, student
- Tile Kit

Also Needed

- sight words box
- dictation notebook

[Offline] ⏱ minutes

FOCUS: Practice Sound /oi/ Spelled *oi* and *oy*

Work **together** with students to complete offline Sight Words, Practice, and Try It activities.

Sight Words ....

Sight Word Fun

Help students learn the sight words *nothing, almost,* and *over,* and up to two additional sight words they have yet to master.

1. Gather the sight word cards *nothing, almost,* and *over,* and up to two additional sight word cards.

2. Choose one sight word card to begin.

   Say: Look at this word and take a picture of it in your mind. When you think you can spell the word yourself, turn the card over and use your letter tiles to spell the word.

3. After students spell the word, have them check the card to see if they spelled the word correctly.

   Say: Read aloud the word you spelled with the letter tiles.

4. Repeat the activity with the remaining sight words.

   TIP Sight words can be very difficult for some students. Let them work at their own pace and really master these words.

> **Objectives**
> - Read sight words.
> - Spell sight words.

Practice ....

Spell One-Syllable Words

Help students use letters and sounds to build one-syllable words that have the sound /oi/ spelled *oi* and *oy*.

1. Gather the dictation notebook and a pencil.

2. Place the following letter tiles at the top of students' whiteboard: *b, c, ch, e, j, l, n, oi, oy, p, s,* and *t.*

3. Make the word *soy* and point to it.

   Say: This word is *soy.*

   Have students

   - ▶ Touch and say *soy.*
   - ▶ Say where the sound /oi/ is in the word. end
   - ▶ Say the letters that make the sound. *oy*

> **Objectives**
> - Identify individual sounds in words.
> - Identify syllables in words.
> - Identify and use the sound /oi/.
> - Identify and use *oi* and *oy* spelling patterns.

4. Make the word *join* and point to it.

   Say: This word is *join*.

   Have students

   ▸ Touch and say *join*.
   ▸ Say where the sound /oi/ is in the word. middle
   ▸ Say the letters that make the sound. *oi*

5. **Say:** Now I will say some words. The first word is *boil*.

   ▸ Finger stretch the sounds in the word.
   ▸ Say where the sound /oi/ is in the word. end
   ▸ Spell the word with the letter tiles.
   ▸ Write the word in your notebook.

6. Have students repeat Step 7 with the following words: *point, oil, coy, choice*.

Try It

Sentence Spree

Have students complete page PH 66 in *K¹² PhonicsWorks Advanced Activity Book* for more practice with the spellings *oi* and *oy* for the sound /oi/. Have students read the sentences aloud and highlight each word that has the sound /oi/ spelled *oi* or *oy*.

Try It
Practice Sound /oi/ Spelled *oi* and *oy* (B)
Sentence Spree

Read the sentence aloud. Highlight each word that has the sound /oi/, as in boy or coin.

1. Roy is such a pleasant little boy.
2. They enjoyed their new toys so much.
3. I know that noise will annoy Father.
4. They will join us after the show.
5. After the water boils, we will put in the eggs.
6. Do you think the bread will spoil?
7. I have only one coin in my pocket.
8. Only one pencil has a sharp point.

PH 66   LANGUAGE ARTS GREEN

Objectives

- Identify individual sounds in words.
- Identify and use the sound /oi/.
- Identify and use *oi* and *oy* spelling patterns.
- Read aloud grade-level text with appropriate automaticity, prosody, accuracy, and rate.

[Online] ⏱ **15** minutes

REVIEW: Sound /oi/ Spelled *oi* and *oy*

Students will work online to complete activities with the sound /oi/ spelled *oi* and *oy* and develop fluency skills. Help students locate the online activities and provide support as needed.

Review ••

Sound /oi/ Spelled *oi* and *oy*

Students will

- ▸ Practice the *oi* and *oy* spellings for the sound /oi/.
- ▸ Practice decoding text by reading a story.

Offline Alternative

No computer access? Have students spell words that have the spellings *oi* and *oy* for the sound /oi/, such as *voice* and *enjoy*. You might also ask them to write the words in their dictation notebook.

> **Objectives**
> - Identify individual sounds in words.
> - Identify and use the sound /oi/.
> - Identify and use *oi* and *oy* spelling patterns.
> - Read aloud grade-level text with appropriate automaticity, prosody, accuracy, and rate.
> - Decode words by applying grade-level word analysis skills.

Practice ••

Fluency

Good readers read often and reread texts. Students will practice their fluency skills by rereading a *K¹² PhonicsWorks Readers Advanced* story aloud as they are recorded.

Have students gather their favorite *K¹² PhonicsWorks Readers Advanced* story that they have already read. Follow the instructions online to record students as they read.

Offline Alternative

No computer access? Have students gather their favorite *K¹² PhonicsWorks Readers Advanced* story. Have them read the story aloud, and record the amount of time it takes them to read the story. Have them read the story again to beat their original time.

> **Objectives**
> - Increase reading fluency rate.
> - Demonstrate automaticity.
> - Demonstrate prosody.

Practice Sound /oi/ Spelled *oi* and *oy* (C)

Lesson Overview

[Offline] FOCUS: Practice Sound /oi/ Spelled *oi* and *oy*   **15** minutes

Sight Words	Sight Word Fun
Practice	Sentence Scramble
Try It	"Deb and Her Friends"

[Online] REVIEW: Sound /oi/ Spelled *oi* and *oy*   **15** minutes

Review	Sound /oi/ Spelled *oi* and *oy*
Practice	Fluency

[Materials]

Supplied
- *K¹² PhonicsWorks Readers Advanced 12*, pp. 13–18
- *K¹² PhonicsWorks Readers Advanced*, any volume
- whiteboard, student
- Tile Kit

Also Needed
- sight words box
- dictation notebook
- index cards (19)

Advance Preparation

For Sentence Scramble, print each of the following words on index cards, using one card per word: *Roy, can, spoil, annoy, the, noisy, boy, toy, join, dog, to, with, and, Beth, plays, point, coin, them,* and *she.*

〖 Offline 〗 ⓫ minutes

FOCUS: Practice Sound /oi/ Spelled *oi* and *oy*

Work **together** with students to complete offline Sight Words, Practice, and Try It activities.

Sight Words

Sight Word Fun

Help students learn the sight words *nothing*, *almost*, and *over*, and up to two additional sight words they have yet to master.

1. Gather the sight word cards *nothing*, *almost*, and *over*, and up to two additional sight word cards.

2. Choose one sight word card to begin.

   Say: Look at this word and take a picture of it in your mind. When you think you can spell the word yourself, turn the card over and use your letter tiles to spell the word.

3. After students spell the word, have them check the card to see if they spelled the word correctly.

   Say: Read aloud the word you spelled with the letter tiles.

4. Repeat the activity with the remaining sight words.

TIP Sight words can be very difficult for some students. Let them work at their own pace and really master these words.

> ### Objectives
> • Read sight words.
> • Spell sight words.

Practice

Sentence Scramble

Have students build sentences by rearranging words to help them learn the meaning of words and phrases.

1. Gather the index cards you prepared, a pencil, and the dictation notebook.

2. Place the index cards in front of students.

3. Point to each word and have students read it aloud with you.

4. Arrange four of the cards as follows: *can she join them*.

5. Have students say if the words make sense. Tell them that the words make an asking sentence.

6. Write the words as a sentence on students' whiteboard. Be sure to capitalize the first letter in *can* and insert the proper punctuation at the end of the sentence.

7. Point out the capital letter and the question mark in the sentence.

8. Read the sentence with students.

9. **Say:** I am going to put these words back with the others. Choose some word cards and put them together to make a different sentence. Read the words in the order you put them.

   ▸ Does your sentence make sense? Is it an asking or a telling sentence?
   ▸ Now write the sentence. Be sure to start with a capital letter. Remember to put a period or a question mark at the end.

10. Return the words to the original group and repeat the steps so that students can create and write two to three sentences.

11. Help students if they have difficulty arranging the words correctly to make a sentence.

    Say: Read the sentence aloud. Does it make sense?

12. Point to any word that seems out of place and state the following:

    ▸ What is this word?
    ▸ Find a word that would make better sense.
    ▸ Switch the words. Now read the sentence.
    ▸ Does it make sense now?

Objectives

- Identify complete sentences.
- Capitalize the first word in a sentence.
- Use question marks to end asking sentences.
- Use periods to end telling sentences.
- Identify individual sounds in words.
- Identify and use the sound /oi/.
- Identify and use *oi* and *oy* spelling patterns.
- Read aloud grade-level text with appropriate automaticity, prosody, accuracy, and rate.
- Write words by applying grade-level phonics knowledge.

Try It

"Deb and Her Friends"

Have students read "Deb and Her Friends" on page 13 of *K¹² PhonicsWorks Readers Advanced 12*.

Students should read the story silently once or twice before reading the story aloud. When students miss a word that can be sounded out, point to it and give them three to six seconds to try the word again. If students still miss the word, tell them the word so the flow of the story isn't interrupted.

After reading the story, make a list of all the words students missed, and go over those words with them. You may use letter tiles to show students how to read the words.

[Online] 15 minutes

REVIEW: Sound /oi/ Spelled *oi* and *oy*

Students will work online to complete activities with the sound /oi/ spelled *oi* and *oy* and develop fluency skills. Help students locate the online activities and provide support as needed.

Review

Sound /oi/ Spelled *oi* and *oy*

Students will

▸ Practice the *oi* and *oy* spellings for the sound /oi/.

Offline Alternative

No computer access? Have students spell words that have the spellings *oi* and *oy* for the sound /oi/, such as *voice* and *decoy*. You might also ask them to write the words in their dictation notebook.

Practice

Fluency

Good readers read often and reread texts. Students will practice their fluency skills by rereading a *K¹² PhonicsWorks Readers Advanced* story aloud as they are recorded.

Have students gather their favorite *K¹² PhonicsWorks Readers Advanced* story that they have already read. Follow the instructions online to record students as they read.

Offline Alternative

No computer access? Have students gather their favorite *K¹² PhonicsWorks Readers Advanced* story. Have them read the story aloud, and record the amount of time it takes them to read the story. Have them read the story again to beat their original time.

Unit Checkpoint

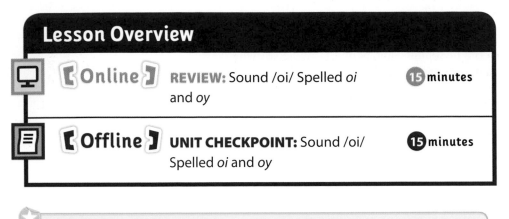

Lesson Overview

🖥	**[Online]** **REVIEW:** Sound /oi/ Spelled *oi* and *oy*	**15** minutes
📄	**[Offline]** **UNIT CHECKPOINT:** Sound /oi/ Spelled *oi* and *oy*	**15** minutes

[Materials]

Supplied
- *K¹² PhonicsWorks Advanced Assessments,* pp. PH 193–198

Objectives
- Identify individual sounds in words.
- Identify and use the sound /oi/.
- Identify and use *oi* and *oy* spelling patterns.
- Read aloud grade-level text with appropriate automaticity, prosody, accuracy, and rate.
- Read instructional-level text with 90% accuracy.
- Write words by applying grade-level phonics knowledge.
- Write sight words.
- Read sight words.

[Online] **20** minutes

REVIEW: Sound /oi/ Spelled *oi* and *oy*

Students will review the sound /oi/ spelled *oi* and *oy* to prepare for the Unit Checkpoint. Help students locate the online activities and provide support as needed.

【 Offline 】 ⑮ minutes

UNIT CHECKPOINT: Sound /oi/ Spelled *oi* and *oy*

Explain that students are going to show what they have learned about sounds, letters, and words.

1. Give students the Unit Checkpoint pages for the Sound /oi/ Spelled *oi* and *oy* unit and print the Unit Checkpoint Answer Key, if you'd like.

2. Use the instructions below to help administer the Checkpoint to students. On the Answer Key or another sheet of paper, note student answers to oral response questions to help with scoring the Checkpoint later.

3. Use the Answer Key to score the Checkpoint, and then enter the results online.

Part 1. Circle Words with Sound /oi/ Have students circle the words with the sound /oi/.

Part 2. Count Sounds. Have students read each word aloud, count the number of sounds in each word, and write that number.

Part 3. Read Sight Words Have students read each sight word aloud. Note any words they read incorrectly.

Part 4. Writing Read each sentence to students. Have them repeat and write the sentence.

23. *Roy will broil the steaks.*

24. *Hoist the boy up on the rope.*

25. *Joy has to make a choice.*

Part 5. Read Aloud Listen to students read the sentences aloud. Count and note the number of words they read correctly.

Part 6. Read Nonsense Words Have students read each nonsense word aloud. Note any words they read incorrectly.

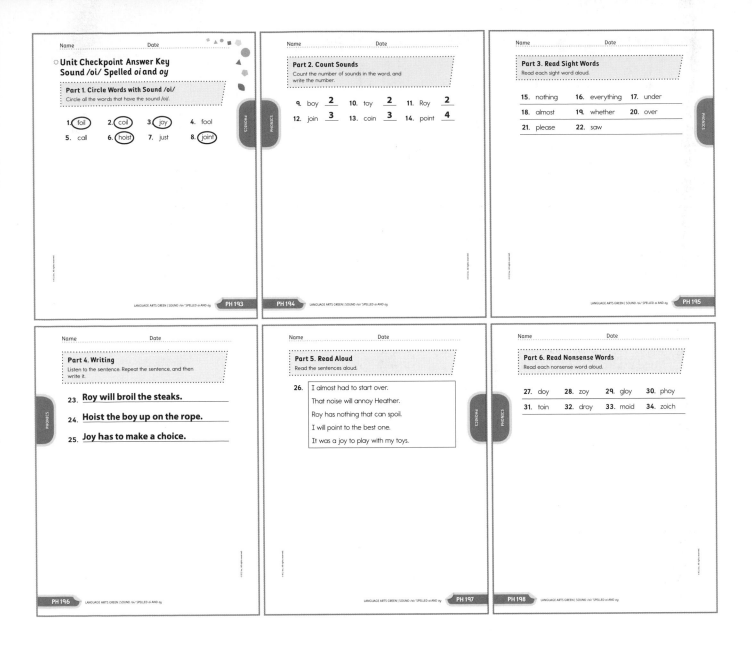

Name _____ Date _____

Unit Checkpoint Answer Key
Sound /oi/ Spelled *oi* and *oy*

Part 1. Circle Words with Sound /oi/
Circle all the words that have the sound /oi/.

1. (foil) 2. (coil) 3. (joy) 4. fool
5. call 6. (hoist) 7. just 8. (joint)

Name _____ Date _____

Part 2. Count Sounds
Count the number of sounds in the word, and write the number.

9. boy **2** 10. toy **2** 11. Roy **2**
12. join **3** 13. coin **3** 14. point **4**

Name _____ Date _____

Part 3. Read Sight Words
Read each sight word aloud.

15. nothing 16. everything 17. under
18. almost 19. whether 20. over
21. please 22. saw

Name _____ Date _____

Part 4. Writing
Listen to the sentence. Repeat the sentence, and then write it.

23. **Roy will broil the steaks.**
24. **Hoist the boy up on the rope.**
25. **Joy has to make a choice.**

Name _____ Date _____

Part 5. Read Aloud
Read the sentences aloud.

26.
I almost had to start over.
That noise will annoy Heather.
Roy has nothing that can spoil.
I will point to the best one.
It was a joy to play with my toys.

Name _____ Date _____

Part 6. Read Nonsense Words
Read each nonsense word aloud.

27. doy 28. zoy 29. gloy 30. phoy
31. toin 32. droy 33. moid 34. zoich

PH 193 PH 194 PH 195 PH 196 PH 197 PH 198

Introduce Sound /aw/ Spelled *au* and *aw*

Unit Overview

In this unit, students will

- Review sight words.
- Learn the spellings *au* and *aw* for the sound /aw/.
- Read and write sentences.
- Read stories silently and aloud.

Materials

Supplied

- *K¹² PhonicsWorks Advanced Activity Book*, p. PH 67
- *K¹² PhonicsWorks Readers Advanced*, any volume
- whiteboard, student
- Tile Kit

Also Needed

- sight words box
- dictation notebook

Lesson Overview

	Offline	FOCUS: Introduce Sound /aw/ Spelled *au* and *aw*	15 minutes
Sight Words		Review Sight Words	
Learn		Introduce Sound /aw/ Spelled *au*	
		Introduce Sound /aw/ Spelled *aw*	
Try It		Investigator	

	Online	REVIEW: Sound /aw/ Spelled *au* and *aw*	15 minutes
Review		Sound /aw/ Spelled *au* and *aw*	
Practice		Fluency	

Offline 15 minutes

FOCUS: Introduce Sound /aw/ Spelled *au* and *aw*

Work **together** with students to complete offline Sight Words, Learn, and
Try It activities.

Sight Words

Review Sight Words

Help students learn to recognize sight words.

1. Gather all the sight word cards students have yet to master from their sight
   words box. Stack the cards on the table face down.

2. Have students pick a word and read it to you.

3. If they read it quickly and correctly, put the card in one stack. If they hesitate or
   do not read the word correctly, put it in another stack. The second stack should
   have words that they will review again.

4. Take the stack of words that students read correctly and dictate each word to
   them. They may choose to either write the word or spell it aloud.

5. If students spell the word correctly, put the card in the first stack because they
   have mastered the word. If they misspell the word, add it to the stack of cards
   to review again.

6. Chart students' progress on the back of each card.

   ▸ Divide the back of the card into two columns.
   ▸ Label the first column "Read" and the second column "Spell."
   ▸ Record the dates that students read or spell the word correctly. When
     students can read and spell the word correctly three times in a row, they
     have mastered the word. You may want to put a star or sticker on their card
     when they have mastered that word.

TIP Even if students can read and spell all the words correctly, it is still beneficial for
them to review sight words. Choose as many additional words as you would like for
each subsequent activity.

> **Objectives**
> - Read sight words.
> - Spell sight words.
> - Write sight words.

Introduce Sound /aw/ Spelled *au*

Help students learn the spelling *au* for the sound /aw/.

1. Place the following letter tiles on students' whiteboard: *au, d, f, h, l, or, P, r, t, th,* and *v*.

2. Make the word *haul* in the middle of students' whiteboard and point to it.

   Say: Today we are going to learn a spelling for the sound /aw/. In the word *haul*, the sound /aw/ is made by the letters *au*.

   ▶ Touch and say *haul*.
   ▶ Say and write the word on your whiteboard.
   ▶ What is the vowel sound in this word? /aw/
   ▶ Which letters make this sound? *au*

3. Make the word *Paul* and point to it.

   Say: This word is *Paul*. In the word *Paul*, the sound /aw/ is made by the letters *au*.

   ▶ Touch and say *Paul*.
   ▶ Say and write the word on your whiteboard.
   ▶ What is the vowel sound in this word? /aw/
   ▶ Which letters make this sound? *au*

4. Repeat the procedure with the following words: *fraud, vault, author*.

Introduce Sound /aw/ Spelled *aw*

Help students learn the spelling *aw* for the sound /aw/.

1. Place the following letter tiles on students' whiteboard: *au, aw, b, c, h, k, l, r, s,* and *S*.

2. Make the word *Saul* in the middle of students' whiteboard and point to it.

   Say: This word is *Saul*. The letters *au* make the sound /aw/ in *Saul*.

   ▶ Touch and say the word. *Saul*
   ▶ Say and write the word on your whiteboard.
   ▶ What is the vowel sound in this word? /aw/
   ▶ Which letters make this sound? *au*

3. Make the word *saw* in the middle of students' whiteboard and point to it.

   Say: Let's look at another way to spell the sound /aw/. This is the word *saw*. The letters *aw* make the sound /aw/ in *saw*.

   ▶ Touch and say *saw*.
   ▶ Say and write the word on your whiteboard.
   ▶ What is the vowel sound in this word? /aw/
   ▶ Which letters make this sound? *aw*
   ▶ What are the two ways to spell the sound /aw/? *au, aw*

4. Repeat the procedure with the following words: *raw, hawk, crawl, brawl*.

Objectives

- Identify individual sounds in words.
- Identify and use the sound /aw/.
- Identify and use *au* and *aw* spelling patterns.
- Write words by applying grade-level phonics knowledge.

Investigator

Have students complete page PH 67 in *K¹² PhonicsWorks Advanced Activity Book* for more practice with the spellings for the sound /aw/. Have students read each word aloud and write the word in the correct column for that spelling.

Try It

Introduce Sound /aw/ Spelled *au* and *aw*

Investigator

Read each word aloud. Write the word in the correct column.

paw	pause	lawn	Paul
draw	straw	laundry	August
fawn	faucet		

aw	*au*
paw	pause
lawn	Paul
fawn	laundry
draw	August
straw	faucet

LANGUAGE ARTS GREEN   **PH 67**

Objectives

- Identify and use the sound /aw/.

- Identify and use *au* and *aw* spelling patterns.

- Read aloud grade-level text with appropriate automaticity, prosody, accuracy, and rate.

- Write words by applying grade-level phonics knowledge.

[Online] 15 minutes

REVIEW: Sound /aw/ Spelled *au* and *aw*

Students will work online to complete activities with the sound /aw/ spelled *au* and *aw* and develop fluency skills. Help students locate the online activities and provide support as needed.

Review

Sound /aw/ Spelled *au* and *aw*

Students will

- ▸ Practice the spellings *au* and *aw* for the sound /aw/.
- ▸ Practice decoding text by reading a story.

Offline Alternative

No computer access? Have students spell words that have the spellings *au* and *aw* for the sound /aw/, such as *haul* and *crawl*. You might also ask them to write the words in their dictation notebook.

Objectives
- Identify and use the sound /aw/.
- Identify and use *au* and *aw* spelling patterns.
- Identify individual sounds in words.
- Read aloud grade-level text with appropriate automaticity, prosody, accuracy, and rate.
- Decode words by applying grade-level word analysis skills.

Practice

Fluency

Good readers read often and reread texts. Students will practice their fluency skills by rereading a *K¹² PhonicsWorks Readers Advanced* story aloud as they are recorded.

Have students gather their favorite *K¹² PhonicsWorks Readers Advanced* story that they have already read. Follow the instructions online to record students as they read.

Offline Alternative

No computer access? Have students gather their favorite *K¹² PhonicsWorks Readers Advanced* story. Have them read the story aloud, and record the amount of time it takes them to read the story. Have them read the story again to beat their original time.

Objectives
- Increase reading fluency rate.
- Demonstrate automaticity.
- Demonstrate prosody.

Practice Sound /aw/ Spelled *au* and *aw* (A)

Lesson Overview

[Offline] FOCUS: Practice Sound /aw/ Spelled *au* and *aw*   **15** minutes

Sight Words	Use Words in Sentences
Practice	Make and Read Rhyming Words
Try It	"Baby Paul"
	Dictation: Write Sentences

[Online] REVIEW: Sound /aw/ Spelled *au* and *aw*   **15** minutes

Review	Sound /aw/ Spelled *au* and *aw*
Practice	Fluency

[Materials]

Supplied
- *K¹² PhonicsWorks Readers Advanced 12*, pp. 19–24
- *K¹² PhonicsWorks Readers Advanced*, any volume
- whiteboard, Learning Coach
- whiteboard, student

Also Needed
- sight words box
- dictation notebook

[Offline] 15 minutes

FOCUS: Practice Sound /aw/ Spelled *au* and *aw*

Work **together** with students to complete offline Sight Words, Practice, and Try It activities.

Sight Words

Use Words in Sentences

Help students use sight words in sentences.

1. Gather all the sight word cards students have yet to master from their sight words box. Spread the sight word cards on the table.

2. **Say:** Let's use sight words in sentences.

3. Have students

   ▸ Touch each card and read the word on it.
   ▸ Make up a sentence using the word.
   ▸ Put the card in a pile after using the word in a sentence.
   ▸ Go through the pile of cards and read each sight word again.
   ▸ Spell each word.

TIP If students have difficulty with any of the sight words, place those cards in a pile to review again.

> **Objectives**
> - Read sight words.
> - Spell sight words.

Practice

Make and Read Rhyming Words

Have students make and read words that rhyme. Grab students' whiteboard and dry-erase marker.

1. Write the following words on students' whiteboard: *claw* and *draw*.

2. Have students read each word aloud.

   Say: How are these two words alike? The words have the same last sound, /aw/, and they rhyme.

3. Have students' write pairs of words that rhyme and have the sound /aw/. The words may have the spelling *au* or *aw* for the sound /aw/. Possible rhyming words: *straw, paw, jaw, raw, daunt, gaunt, haunt, jaunt*

> **Objectives**
> - Identify individual sounds in words.
> - Produce rhyming words.
> - Identify and use the sound /aw/.
> - Identify and use *au* and *aw* spelling patterns.
> - Write words by applying grade-level phonics knowledge.

Try It

"Baby Paul"

Have students read "Baby Paul" on page 19 of *K¹² PhonicsWorks Readers Advanced 12.*

Students should read the story silently once or twice before reading the story aloud. When students miss a word that can be sounded out, point to it and give them three to six seconds to try the word again. If students still miss the word, tell them the word so the flow of the story isn't interrupted.

After reading the story, make a list of all the words students missed, and go over those words with them. You may use letter tiles to show students how to read the words.

Dictation: Write Sentences

Use sentences to help students identify individual sounds in words.

1. Gather a pencil and the dictation notebook. Say the sentence, *This August we will join my aunts at the beach.* Then give these directions to students:

   ▸ Repeat the sentence.
   ▸ Write the sentence in your notebook.
   ▸ Read the sentence aloud.

2. When students have finished, write the following sentence on your whiteboard: *This August we will join my aunts at the beach.*

3. Have them compare their answer to your correct version.

4. Repeat this procedure with the following sentence: *Laura said the mess is not her fault.*

   ▸ If students make an error and don't see it, help them correct their mistake by having them finger stretch the sounds in the word they missed.
   ▸ If students are having difficulty selecting the correct letters or sounds, review those letters or sounds that are confusing them.
   ▸ If students have difficulty with first, middle, and last sounds, have them finger stretch the sounds in words.

Objectives

- Read aloud grade-level text with appropriate automaticity, prosody, accuracy, and rate.
- Decode words by applying grade-level word analysis skills.
- Follow three-step directions.
- Write words by applying grade-level phonics knowledge.

REVIEW: Sound /aw/ Spelled *au* and *aw*

Students will work online to complete activities with the sound /aw/ spelled *au* and *aw* and develop fluency skills. Help students locate the online activities and provide support as needed.

Review ·

Sound /aw/ Spelled *au* and *aw*

Students will

▸ Practice the spellings *au* and *aw* for the sound /aw/.

Offline Alternative

No computer access? Have students spell words that have the spellings *au* and *aw* for the sound /aw/, such as *fault* and *straw*. You might also ask them to write the words in their dictation notebook.

Objectives
- Identify individual sounds in words.
- Identify and use the sound /aw/.
- Identify and use *au* and *aw* spelling patterns.

Practice ·

Fluency

Good readers read often and reread texts. Students will practice their fluency skills by rereading a *K¹² PhonicsWorks Readers Advanced* story aloud as they are recorded.

Have students gather their favorite *K¹² PhonicsWorks Readers Advanced* story that they have already read. Follow the instructions online to record students as they read.

Offline Alternative

No computer access? Have students gather their favorite *K¹² PhonicsWorks Readers Advanced* story. Have them read the story aloud, and record the amount of time it takes them to read the story. Have them read the story again to beat their original time.

Objectives
- Increase reading fluency rate.
- Demonstrate automaticity.
- Demonstrate prosody.

Practice Sound /aw/ Spelled *au* and *aw* (B)

Lesson Overview

[Offline] FOCUS: Practice Sound /aw/ Spelled *au* and *aw*   15 minutes

Sight Words	Sight Word Concentration
Practice	Sort Spellings for Sound /aw/
Try It	Alphabet Addition

[Online] REVIEW: Sound /aw/ Spelled *au* and *aw*   15 minutes

Review	Sound /aw/ Spelled *au* and *aw*
Practice	Fluency

Materials

Supplied

- *K¹² PhonicsWorks Advanced Activity Book*, p. PH 68
- *K¹² PhonicsWorks Readers Advanced,* any volume

Also Needed

- sight words box
- dictation notebook
- index cards (14)

Advance Preparation

Gather two sets of the sight word cards students have yet to master.

For Sort Spellings for Sound /aw/, print each of the following words on index cards, using one card per word: *Paul, August, fraud, astronaut, author, vault, sauce, coleslaw, crawfish, hacksaw, hawk, jigsaw, sawdust,* and *shawl*.

〔 Offline 〕 ⏱ 15 minutes

FOCUS: Practice Sound /aw/ Spelled *au* and *aw*

Work **together** with students to complete offline Sight Words, Practice, and Try It activities.

Sight Words ●

Sight Word Concentration

Help students review sight words.

1. Gather the two sets of sight word cards.

2. Scramble both sets of sight word cards and place them face down on the table or floor.

3. Turn over two cards at a time; take turns with students. If the cards match, the person turning over the matching cards reads the word and uses it in a sentence. If the cards don't match, the person turns them back over.

4. Remove and save the matching cards.

5. Continue the activity until all the cards are paired.

6. Have students read all the words.

7. Take the stack of words that students read correctly and dictate each word to them.

8. Have students write each word or spell it aloud.

TIP If students have difficulty with any sight words, let them work at their own pace to really master these words.

> **Objectives**
> * Read sight words.
> * Spell sight words.
> * Write sight words.

Practice ●

Sort Spellings for Sound /aw/

Help students practice identifying words that have the spellings *au* and *aw* for the sound /aw/.

1. Gather the index cards you prepared. Mix the cards well and place them in a stack face down on the table.

2. Gather the dictation notebook. Draw two columns and label them *au* and *aw* to represent two different ways to spell the sound /aw/.

> **Objectives**
> * Identify individual sounds in words.
> * Identify and use the sound /aw/.
> * Identify and use *au* and *aw* spelling patterns.

3. **Say:** You are going to sort words by the two spellings for the sound /aw/. You will take a card from the pile and read it to me. Then you will think about the spelling for the sound /aw/ in the word and write that word in the correct column. I'll do the first one for you.

4. Demonstrate the following for students:

   ▸ Draw a card from the pile.
   ▸ Read the word aloud.
   ▸ Write the word in the correct column for the spelling for sound /aw/.

5. Have students continue the procedure with the remaining words:

   ▸ **Spelling *au* Words:** *Paul, August, fraud, astronaut, author, vault, sauce*
   ▸ **Spelling *aw* Words:** *coleslaw, crawfish, hacksaw, hawk, jigsaw, sawdust, shawl*

Try It

Alphabet Addition

Have students complete page PH 68 in *K¹² PhonicsWorks Advanced Activity Book* for more practice with the spellings for the sound /aw/. Have students add the letters together to make a word, write the word, and then read it aloud.

Try It
Practice Sound /aw/ Spelled *au* and *aw* (B)
Alphabet Addition

Add the letters to make a word. Write the word, and then read it aloud.

1.	jaw	+	bone	=	**jawbone**
2.	cole	+	slaw	=	**coleslaw**
3.	be	+	cause	=	**because**
4.	aw	+	ful	=	**awful**
5.	law	+	yer	=	**lawyer**
6.	squawk	+	ing	=	**squawking**
7.	draw	+	ing	=	**drawing**

PH 68   LANGUAGE ARTS GREEN

Objectives

- Identify individual sounds in words.
- Identify and use the sound /aw/.
- Identify and use *au* and *aw* spelling patterns.
- Write words by applying grade-level phonics knowledge.

[Online] (15) minutes

REVIEW: Sound /aw/ Spelled *au* and *aw*

Students will work online to complete activities with the sound /aw/ spelled *au* and *aw* and develop fluency skills. Help students locate the online activities and provide support as needed.

Review ·

Sound /aw/ Spelled *au* and *aw*

Students will

▸ Practice the spellings *au* and *aw* for the sound /aw/.
▸ Practice decoding text by reading a story.

___

Offline Alternative

No computer access? Have students spell words that have the spellings *au* and *aw* for the sound /aw/, such as *launch* and *drawn*. You might also ask them to write the words in their dictation notebook.

⭐ **Objectives**
- Identify individual sounds in words.
- Identify and use the sound /aw/.
- Identify and use *au* and *aw* spelling patterns.
- Read aloud grade-level text with appropriate automaticity, prosody, accuracy, and rate.
- Decode words by applying grade-level word analysis skills.

Practice ·

Fluency

Good readers read often and reread texts. Students will practice their fluency skills by rereading a *K¹² PhonicsWorks Readers Advanced* story aloud as they are recorded.

Have students gather their favorite *K¹² PhonicsWorks Readers Advanced* story that they have already read. Follow the instructions online to record students as they read.

___

Offline Alternative

No computer access? Have students gather their favorite *K¹² PhonicsWorks Readers Advanced* story. Have them read the story aloud, and record the amount of time it takes them to read the story. Have them read the story again to beat their original time.

⭐ **Objectives**
- Increase reading fluency rate.
- Demonstrate automaticity.
- Demonstrate prosody.

Practice Sound /aw/ Spelled *au* and *aw* (C)

Lesson Overview

[Offline] FOCUS: Practice Sound /aw/ Spelled *au* and *aw* — 15 minutes

Sight Words	Pick a Pair
Practice	Word Chains
Try It	"Dawn's Animals"

[Online] REVIEW: Sound /aw/ Spelled *au* and *aw* — 15 minutes

Review	Sound /aw/ Spelled *au* and *aw*
Practice	Fluency

[Materials]

Supplied
- *K¹² PhonicsWorks Readers Advanced 12*, pp. 25–30
- *K¹² PhonicsWorks Readers Advanced*, any volume
- whiteboard, student

Also Needed
- sight words box
- dictation notebook

[Offline] ⑮ minutes

FOCUS: Practice Sound /aw/ Spelled *au* and *aw*

Work **together** with students to complete offline Sight Words, Practice, and Try It activities.

Sight Words ···

Pick a Pair

Play a card game with students for more practice with sight words.

1. Gather the sight word cards that students are reviewing. Choose two words and place the cards on the table.

2. Ask questions to help students identify each word. For example, if the words are *or* and *one*, you could ask, "Which word names a number?" If the words are *on* and *but*, you could ask, "Which word is the opposite of *off*?"

3. Continue the activity until students identify all the words.

4. Take the stack of words that students read correctly and dictate each word to them.

5. Have students write each word or spell it aloud.

> **Objectives**
> * Read sight words.
> * Spell sight words.
> * Write sight words.

Practice ···

Word Chains

Have students build words by adding and changing letters to help them recognize and use the spellings *au* and *aw* for the sound /aw/.

1. Place the following letter tiles at the top of students' whiteboard: *au, aw, b, c, f, h, j, l, n, r, s, t,* and *t*.

2. **Say:** You will spell words in short word chains today. There will be one chain for each of the spellings of the sound /aw/ that we know. How many spellings do you know for the sound /aw/? two

3. **Say:** I'll do the first word. The word is *claw*.

   ▸ I will pull down the letters for the sounds /k/, /l/, and /aw/ to spell the word *claw*.

   ▸ I will touch and say *claw*. To change *claw* to *flaw*, I will think about which sound is changed from the word *claw* to *flaw*. I will need to replace the letter *c* with the letter *f*.

   ▸ Touch and say the word *flaw*. Now it's your turn to change *flaw* to *law*. You can spell *law* by making only one change. Touch and say the new word.

4. Redirect students if they select the incorrect letter for any sound.

   Say: That letter is for the sound [incorrect sound]. We want the letter for the sound [target sound]. What letter makes that sound? Answers will vary.

> **Objectives**
> * Identify the new word when one sound is changed in a word.
> * Identify individual sounds in words.
> * Identify and use the sound /aw/.
> * Identify and use *au* and *aw* spelling patterns.

5. Redirect students if they name the sound incorrectly.

   Say: To change the word [first word] to[target word], we need the letter for the sound [target sound].

   Show students how to make the change. Have them touch and say the new word after they move the letters.

6. Follow this procedure to make the following groups of word chains:

   ▸ *raw, craw, crawl, brawl, bawl, awl*
   ▸ *jaunts, jaunt, aunt, haunt, taunt, taunts, aunts*

7. For every new word, have students add, replace, or remove only one letter tile. Remind students that in these word chains only one sound—and only one letter tile—will change when the word changes.

Try It

"Dawn's Animals"
Have students read "Dawn's Animals" on page 25 of *K¹² PhonicsWorks Readers Advanced 12.*

   Students should read the story silently once or twice before reading the story aloud. When students miss a word that can be sounded out, point to it and give them three to six seconds to try the word again. If students still miss the word, tell them the word so the flow of the story isn't interrupted.

   After reading the story, make a list of all the words students missed, and go over those words with them. You may use letter tiles to show students how to read the words.

> **Objectives**
> - Read aloud grade-level text with appropriate automaticity, prosody, accuracy, and rate.
> - Decode words by applying grade-level word analysis skills.

⟦ Online ⟧ 15 minutes

REVIEW: Sound /aw/ Spelled *au* and *aw*

Students will work online to complete activities with the sound /aw/ spelled *au* and *aw* and develop fluency skills. Help students locate the online activities and provide support as needed.

Review

Sound /aw/ Spelled *au* and *aw*
Students will

▸ Practice the spellings *au* and *aw* for the sound /aw/.

> **Objectives**
> - Identify and use the sound /aw/.
> - Identify and use *au* and *aw* spelling patterns.
> - Identify individual sounds in words.

Offline Alternative

No computer access? Have students spell words that have the spellings *au* and *aw* for the sound /aw/, such as *aunt* and *brawn.* You might also ask them to write the words in their dictation notebook.

Fluency

Good readers read often and reread texts. Students will practice their fluency skills by rereading a *K¹² PhonicsWorks Readers Advanced* story aloud as they are recorded.

Have students gather their favorite *K¹² PhonicsWorks Readers Advanced* story that they have already read. Follow the instructions online to record students as they read.

Offline Alternative

No computer access? Have students gather their favorite *K¹² PhonicsWorks Readers Advanced* story. Have them read the story aloud, and record the amount of time it takes them to read the story. Have them read the story again to beat their original time.

Objectives
- Increase reading fluency rate.
- Demonstrate automaticity.
- Demonstrate prosody.

Unit Checkpoint

Lesson Overview

Online REVIEW: Sound /aw/ Spelled *au* and *aw* — **15** minutes

Offline UNIT CHECKPOINT: Sound /aw/ Spelled *au* and *aw* — **15** minutes

Materials

Supplied
- *K¹² PhonicsWorks Advanced Assessments*, pp. PH 199–204

Objectives
- Identify individual sounds in words.
- Identify and use the sound /aw/.
- Identify and use *au* and *aw* spelling patterns.
- Read aloud grade-level text with appropriate automaticity, prosody, accuracy, and rate.
- Read instructional-level text with 90% accuracy.
- Write words by applying grade-level phonics knowledge.
- Write sight words.
- Read sight words.

Online 15 minutes

REVIEW: Sound /aw/ Spelled *au* and *aw*

Students will review spellings for the sound /aw/ to prepare for the Unit Checkpoint. Help students locate the online activities and provide support as needed.

[Offline] ⏱ **minutes**

UNIT CHECKPOINT: Sound /aw/ Spelled *au* and *aw*

Explain that students are going to show what they have learned about sounds, letters, and words.

1. Give students the Unit Checkpoint pages for the Sound /aw/ Spelled *au* and *aw* unit and print the Unit Checkpoint Answer Key, if you'd like.

2. Use the instructions below to help administer the Checkpoint to students. On the Answer Key or another sheet of paper, note student answers to oral response questions to help with scoring the Checkpoint later.

3. Use the Answer Key to score the Checkpoint, and then enter the results online.

Part 1. Circle Words with Sound /aw/ Have students circle the words with the sound /aw/.

Part 2. Count Sounds. Have students read each word aloud, count the number of sounds in each word, and write that number.

Part 3. Read Sight Words Have students read each sight word aloud. Note any words they read incorrectly.

Part 4. Writing Read each sentence to students. Have them repeat and write the sentence.

23. *We had coleslaw at the picnic.*

24. *Saul has a jigsaw puzzle of a fawn.*

25. *The astronaut locked the vault.*

Part 5. Read Aloud Listen to students read the sentences aloud. Count and note the number of words they read correctly.

Part 6. Read Nonsense Words Have students read each nonsense word aloud. Note any words they read incorrectly.

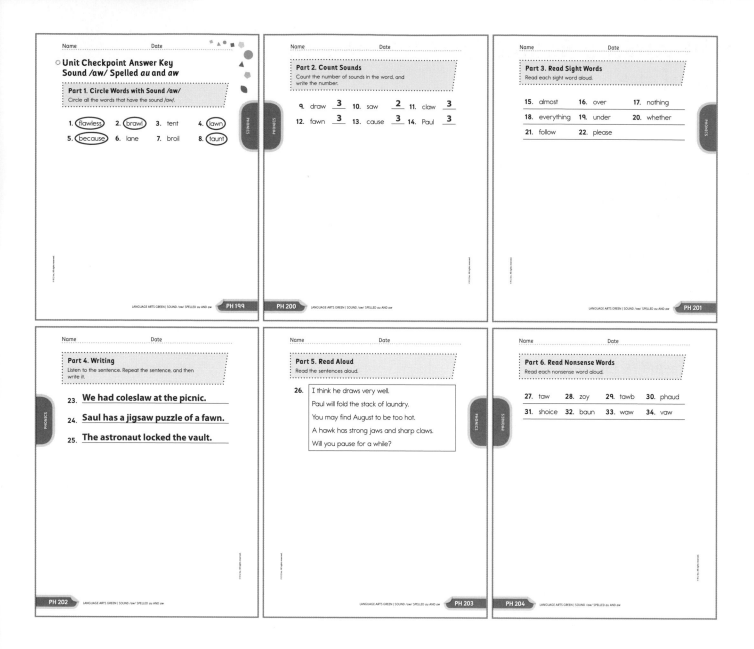

Name .... **Date** ....

○ Unit Checkpoint Answer Key
Sound /aw/ Spelled *au* and *aw*

Part 1. Circle Words with Sound /aw/
Circle all the words that have the sound /aw/.

1. (flawless) 2. (brawl) 3. tent 4. (lawn)
5. (because) 6. lane 7. broil 8. (taunt)

Name .... **Date** ....

Part 2. Count Sounds
Count the number of sounds in the word, and write the number.

9. draw __3__ 10. saw __2__ 11. claw __3__
12. fawn __3__ 13. cause __3__ 14. Paul __3__

Name .... **Date** ....

Part 3. Read Sight Words
Read each sight word aloud.

15. almost 16. over 17. nothing
18. everything 19. under 20. whether
21. follow 22. please

Name .... **Date** ....

Part 4. Writing
Listen to the sentence. Repeat the sentence, and then write it.

23. **We had coleslaw at the picnic.**
24. **Saul has a jigsaw puzzle of a fawn.**
25. **The astronaut locked the vault.**

Name .... **Date** ....

Part 5. Read Aloud
Read the sentences aloud.

26.

| I think he draws very well. |
| Paul will fold the stack of laundry. |
| You may find August to be too hot. |
| A hawk has strong jaws and sharp claws. |
| Will you pause for a while? |

Name .... **Date** ....

Part 6. Read Nonsense Words
Read each nonsense word aloud.

27. taw 28. zoy 29. tawb 30. phaud
31. shoice 32. baun 33. waw 34. vaw

Introduce Sound /ow/ Spelled *ou* and *ow*

Unit Overview

In this unit, students will

- ▸ Learn the sight words *children*, *number*, and *right*.
- ▸ Learn the spellings *ou* and *ow* for the sound /ow/.
- ▸ Read and write sentences.
- ▸ Read stories silently and aloud.

Materials

Supplied

- K[12] PhonicsWorks Advanced Activity Book, p. PH 69
- K[12] PhonicsWorks Readers Advanced, any volume
- whiteboard, student
- Tile Kit

Also Needed

- sight words box

Lesson Overview

Offline FOCUS: Introduce Sound /ow/ Spelled *ou* and *ow*	**15** minutes
Sight Words	Introduce Sight Words
Learn	Introduce Sound /ow/ Spelled *ou*
	Introduce Sound /ow/ Spelled *ow*
	Build Words
Try It	Investigator

Online REVIEW: Sound /ow/ Spelled *ou* and *ow*	**15** minutes
Review	Sound /ow/ Spelled *ou* and *ow*
Practice	Fluency

[Offline] 15 minutes

FOCUS: Introduce Sound /ow/ Spelled *ou* and *ow*

Work **together** with students to complete offline Sight Words, Learn, and Try It activities.

Sight Words ....

Introduce Sight Words

Help students learn the sight words *children*, *number*, and *right*.

1. Gather the sight word cards *children*, *number*, and *right*.

2. Show students the *children* card.

3. **Say:** This is the word *children*. We see this word so often that we want to be able to read and spell it quickly without thinking about it. Look closely at the word *children*. Spell the word *children* aloud. Take a picture of the word *children* in your mind. When you think you can spell *children* yourself, turn the card over and use your letter tiles to spell the word *children*. Check the card to see if you spelled the word *children* correctly. Read aloud the word you spelled with the letter tiles.

4. Repeat the activity with the remaining sight words.

5. Chart students' progress on the back of each card.

   ▸ Divide the back of the card into two columns.
   ▸ Label the first column "Read" and the second column "Spell."
   ▸ Record the dates that students read or spell the word correctly. When students can read and spell the word correctly three times in a row, they have mastered the word. You may want to put a star or sticker on the card when they have mastered that word.

6. Add the cards to students' sight words box.

TIP Sight words can be very difficult for some students. Let students work at their own pace and really master these words, as they occur frequently in reading and writing.

Objectives
- Read sight words.
- Spell sight words.

Learn

Introduce Sound /ow/ Spelled *ou*

Help students learn the spelling *ou* for the sound /ow/.

1. Place the following letter tiles on students' whiteboard: *c, d, l,* and *ou.*

2. Make the word *loud* in the middle of students' whiteboard and point to it.

   Say: Today we are going to learn a spelling for the sound /ow/. In the word *loud,* the sound /ow/ is made by the letters *ou.*

   ▸ Touch and say *loud.*
   ▸ Say and write the word on your whiteboard.
   ▸ What is the vowel sound in this word? /ow/
   ▸ Which letters make this sound? *ou*

3. Make the word *cloud* and point to it.

   Say: This word is *cloud.* In the word *cloud,* the sound /ow/ is made by the letters *ou.*

   ▸ Touch and say *cloud.*
   ▸ Say and write the word on your whiteboard.
   ▸ What is the vowel sound in this word? /ow/
   ▸ Which letters make this sound? *ou*

Introduce Sound /ow/ Spelled *ow*

Help students learn the spelling *ow* for the sound /ow/.

1. Place the following letter tiles on students' whiteboard: *g, n, ow,* and *t.*

2. Make the word *town* in the middle of students' whiteboard and point to it.

   Say: In the word *town,* the sound /ow/ is made by the letters *ow.*

   ▸ Touch and say *town.*
   ▸ Say and write the word on your whiteboard.
   ▸ What is the vowel sound in this word? /ow/
   ▸ Which letters make this sound? *ow*

3. Make the word *gown* and point to it.

   Say: This word is *gown.* In the word *gown,* the sound /ow/ is made by the letters *ow.*

   ▸ Touch and say *gown.*
   ▸ Say and write the word on your whiteboard.
   ▸ What is the vowel sound in this word? /ow/
   ▸ Which letters make this sound? *ow*

Objectives

- Identify individual sounds in words.
- Blend sounds to create words.
- Identify and use the sound /ow/.
- Identify and use *ou* and *ow* spelling patterns.
- Write words by applying grade-level phonics knowledge.

Build Words

Help students use letters and sounds to build words.

1. Place the following letter tiles at the top of students' whiteboard: *c, d, er, f, l, n, ou, ow, r, s, sh,* and *t.*

2. Draw four horizontal lines across the middle of students' whiteboard to represent the sounds in a word.

3. **Say:** Let's use letters and sounds to build the word *frown.*

4. Have students finger stretch the sounds in *frown.*

5. Have students

   ▸ Identify the first, next, and last sounds in *frown.*
   ▸ Choose the corresponding letter tile for each of the sounds.
   ▸ Move the letters to the correct lines on their whiteboard.

6. Guide students with these questions:

   ▸ What is the first sound in *frown*? /f/
   Which line does the letter for that sound go on? the first one
   ▸ What is the next sound in *frown*? /r/
   Which line does the letter for that sound go on? the second one
   ▸ What is the next sound in *frown*? /ow/
   Which line do the letters for that sound go on? the third one
   ▸ What's the last sound in *frown*? /n/
   Which line does the letter for that sound go on? the last one

7. Redirect students if they select the incorrect letter tile.

   Say: That sound is in the word [word], and it is the [first, second, third, fourth] sound. We want the sound [target sound].

   Continue until students select the correct letter tile.

8. Help students if they choose the wrong letter tile for the sound /ow/.

   Say: You have the sound right, but those letters don't spell the sound /ow/ in this word. When you're not sure whether to use *ou* or *ow* in a word, try building the word with the other tile for the sound /ow/.

9. Have students touch and say the word.

10. Have them say the word as they use a dry-erase marker to write the word on the whiteboard.

11. Draw horizontal lines across the middle of students' whiteboard that represent the number of sounds in each word. Repeat the activity to build the following words:

    ▸ *clown* /k/ /l/ /ow/ /n/
    ▸ *cow* /k/ /ow/
    ▸ *owl* /ow/ /l/
    ▸ *scout* /s/ /k/ /ow/ /t/
    ▸ *round* /r/ /ow/ /n/ /d/
    ▸ *shout* /sh/ /ow/ /t/
    ▸ *flounder* /f/ /l/ /ow/ /n/ /d/ /er/

Try It ••

Investigator

Have students complete page PH 69 in *K¹² PhonicsWorks Advanced Activity Book* for more practice with the spellings for the sound /ow/. Have students read each word aloud and write the word in the correct column for that spelling.

Try It ••••••••••••••••••••••••••••
Introduce Sound /ow/ Spelled *ou* and *ow*
Investigator

Read each word aloud. Write the word in the correct column.

trout	flower	around	shower
pound	frown	powder	cloud
cow	sour	found	down

ow	*ou*
flower	trout
shower	around
frown	pound
powder	cloud
cow	found
down	sour

LANGUAGE ARTS GREEN   **PH 69**

Objectives
- Identify and use the sound /ow/.
- Identify and use *ou* and *ow* spelling patterns.
- Read aloud grade-level text with appropriate automaticity, prosody, accuracy, and rate.
- Write words by applying grade-level phonics knowledge.

[Online] ⑮ minutes

REVIEW: Sound /ow/ Spelled *ou* and *ow*

Students will work online to complete activities with the sound /ow/ spelled *ou* and *ow* and develop fluency skills. Help students locate the online activities and provide support as needed.

Review ....

Sound /ow/ Spelled *ou* and *ow*

Students will

▸ Practice the spellings *ou* and *ow* for the sound /ow/.

▸ Practice decoding text by reading a story.

Offline Alternative

No computer access? Have students spell words that have the spellings *ou* and *ow* for the sound /ow/, such as *ouch* and *down*.

> **Objectives**
> - Identify and use the sound /ow/.
> - Identify and use *ou* and *ow* spelling patterns.
> - Identify individual sounds in words.
> - Read aloud grade-level text with appropriate automaticity, prosody, accuracy, and rate.
> - Decode words by applying grade-level word analysis skills.

Practice ....

Fluency

Good readers read often and reread texts. Students will practice their fluency skills by rereading a *K¹² PhonicsWorks Readers Advanced* story aloud as they are recorded.

Have students gather their favorite *K¹² PhonicsWorks Readers Advanced* story that they have already read. Follow the instructions online to record students as they read.

> **Objectives**
> - Increase reading fluency rate.
> - Demonstrate automaticity.
> - Demonstrate prosody.

Offline Alternative

No computer access? Have students gather their favorite *K¹² PhonicsWorks Readers Advanced* story. Have them reread the story aloud, and record the amount of time it takes them to read the story. Have them read the story again to beat their original time.

Practice Sound /ow/ Spelled *ou* and *ow* (A)

Lesson Overview

Offline **FOCUS:** Practice Sound /ow/ Spelled *ou* and *ow* — **15** minutes

Sight Words	Sight Word Fun
Practice	Search Sentences for Words with the Sound /ow/
Try It	"The Clowns Are in Town!"

Online **REVIEW:** Sound /ow/ Spelled *ou* and *ow* — **15** minutes

Review	Sound /ow/ Spelled *ou* and *ow*
Practice	Fluency

Materials

Supplied
- *K¹² PhonicsWorks Readers Advanced 13*, pp. 1–6
- *K¹² PhonicsWorks Readers Advanced*, any volume
- whiteboard, student
- Tile Kit

Also Needed
- sight words box

[Offline] ⏱ **15** minutes

FOCUS: Practice Sound /ow/ Spelled *ou* and *ow*

Work **together** with students to complete offline Sight Words, Practice, and Try It activities.

Sight Words ....

Sight Word Fun

Help students learn the sight words *children, number,* and *right,* and up to two additional sight words they have yet to master.

1. Gather the sight word cards *children, number,* and *right,* and up to two additional sight word cards.

2. Choose one sight word card to begin.

   Say: Look at this word and take a picture of it in your mind. When you think you can spell the word yourself, turn the card over and use your letter tiles to spell the word.

3. After students spell the word, have them check the card to see if they spelled the word correctly.

   Say: Read aloud the word you spelled with the letter tiles.

4. Repeat the activity with the remaining sight words.

TIP Sight words can be very difficult for some students. Let them work at their own pace and really master these words.

> **Objectives**
> - Read sight words.
> - Spell sight words.

Practice ....

Search Sentences for Words with the Sound /ow/

Have students identify words with the sound /ow/ spelled *ou* and *ow*.

1. Write the following sentence on students' whiteboard and point to it: *Set the crown on the new king's head.*

   Say: I will read a sentence to you. You will repeat the sentence and tell me the word that has the sound /ow/. The first sentence is, *Set the crown on the new king's head.* Which word in the sentence has the sound /ow/? *crown*

2. Have students do the following steps:

   ▸ Repeat the sentence.
   ▸ Find the word in the sentence with the sound /ow/ and underline it.
   ▸ Circle the letters for the spelling of the sound /ow/.
   ▸ Read the sentence aloud again.

> **Objectives**
> - Identify individual sounds in words.
> - Identify and use the sound /ow/.
> - Identify and use *ou* and *ow* spelling patterns.
> - Write words by applying grade-level phonics knowledge.

3. Use the same procedure for the following sentences:

 ► *Pam shouted when she saw the storm. shouted*
 ► *Head north, not south, on that road. south*
 ► *Jerry folded the towels for his mother. towels*
 ► *We saw owls, monkeys, and an elephant. owls*

(TIP) If students have difficulty choosing from among the words in the sentence, say two words and have them choose the correct word with the target sound.

(TIP) If students cannot remember the spellings for the sound /ow/, tell them the guide word for that spelling (*ou,* as in *loud; ow,* as in *town*).

Try It ....

"The Clowns Are in Town!"
Have students read "The Clowns Are in Town!" on page 1 of *K¹² PhonicsWorks Readers Advanced 13.*

   Students should read the story silently once or twice before reading the story aloud. When students miss a word that can be sounded out, point to it and give them three to six seconds to try the word again. If students still miss the word, tell them the word so the flow of the story isn't interrupted.

   After reading the story, make a list of all the words students missed, and go over those words with them. You may use letter tiles to show students how to read the words.

Objectives
- Read aloud grade-level text with appropriate automaticity, prosody, accuracy, and rate.
- Decode words by applying grade-level word analysis skills.

[Online] 🕐 minutes

REVIEW: Sound /ow/ Spelled *ou* and *ow*
Students will work online to complete activities with the sound /ow/ spelled *ou* and *ow* and develop fluency skills. Help students locate the online activities and provide support as needed.

Review ....

Sound /ow/ Spelled *ou* and *ow*
Students will

 ► Practice the spellings *ou* and *ow* for the sound /ow/.

Objectives
- Identify individual sounds in words.
- Identify and use the sound /ow/.
- Identify and use *ou* and *ow* spelling patterns.

Offline Alternative

No computer access? Have students spell words that have the spellings *ou* and *ow* for the sound /ow/, such as *pouch* and *frown.*

Practice

Fluency

Good readers read often and reread texts. Students will practice their fluency skills by rereading a *K¹² PhonicsWorks Readers Advanced* story aloud as they are recorded.

Have students gather their favorite *K¹² PhonicsWorks Readers Advanced* story that they have already read. Follow the instructions online to record students as they read.

Offline Alternative

No computer access? Have students gather their favorite *K¹² PhonicsWorks Readers Advanced* story. Have them read the story aloud, and record the amount of time it takes them to read the story. Have them read the story again to beat their original time.

Objectives
- Increase reading fluency rate.
- Demonstrate automaticity.
- Demonstrate prosody.

Practice Sound /ow/ Spelled *ou* and *ow* (B)

Lesson Overview

Offline	FOCUS: Practice Sound /ow/ Spelled *ou* and *ow*	15 minutes
Sight Words	Sight Word Fun	
Practice	Sort Spellings for Sound /ow/	
Try It	By Sight	

Online	REVIEW: Sound /ow/ Spelled *ou* and *ow*	15 minutes
Review	Sound /ow/ Spelled *ou* and *ow*	
Practice	Fluency	

[Materials]

Supplied
- *K¹² PhonicsWorks Advanced Activity Book*, p. PH 70
- *K¹² PhonicsWorks Readers Advanced,* any volume

Also Needed
- sight words box
- dictation notebook
- index cards (17)

Advance Preparation

For Sort Spellings for Sound /ow/, print each of the following words on index cards, using one card per word: *how, owl, cowl, fowl, now, chow, wow, gown, ouch, couch, foul, oust, out, scout, shout, loud,* and *cloud.*

[Offline] ⓫ minutes

FOCUS: Practice Sound /ow/ Spelled *ou* and *ow*

Work **together** with students to complete offline Sight Words, Practice, and Try It activities.

Sight Words ••

Sight Word Fun

Help students learn the sight words *children, number,* and *right,* and up to two additional sight words they have yet to master.

1. Gather the sight word cards *children, number,* and *right,* and up to two additional sight word cards.

2. Choose one sight word card to begin.

   Say: Look at this word and take a picture of it in your mind. When you think you can spell the word yourself, turn the card over and use your letter tiles to spell the word.

3. After students spell the word, have them check the card to see if they spelled the word correctly.

   Say: Read aloud the word you spelled with the letter tiles.

4. Repeat the activity with the remaining sight words.

   TIP Sight words can be very difficult for some students. Let them work at their own pace and really master these words.

> **Objectives**
> • Read sight words.
> • Spell sight words.

Practice ••

Sort Spellings for Sound /ow/

Help students practice identifying words that have the spellings *ou* and *ow* for the sound /ow/.

1. Gather the index cards you prepared. Mix the cards well and place them in a stack face down on the table.

2. Gather the dictation notebook. Draw two columns and label them *ou* and *ow* to represent the two different ways to spell the sound /ow/.

3. **Say:** You are going to sort words into two groups: one group for the spelling *ou* and one group for the spelling *ow* for sound /ow/. You will take a card from the pile and read it to me. Then you will say if the word has the spelling *ou* or *ow* for sound /ow/ and write that word in the correct column. You will place the card in the pile with the words that have the same sound. I'll do the first one for you.

> **Objectives**
> • Read aloud grade-level text with appropriate automaticity, prosody, accuracy, and rate.
> • Identify individual sounds in words.
> • Identify and use the sound /ow/.
> • Identify and use *ou* and *ow* spelling patterns.
> • Write words by applying grade-level phonics knowledge.

4. Demonstrate the following for students:

- ▸ Draw a card from the pile.
- ▸ Read the word aloud.
- ▸ Finger stretch the sounds in the word.
- ▸ Write the word in the correct column for the spelling for sound /ow/.

5. Have students continue the procedure with the remaining words:

- ▸ **Spelling *ou* Words:** *ouch, couch, foul, oust, out, scout, shout, loud, cloud*
- ▸ **Spelling *ow* Words:** *how, owl, cowl, fowl, now, chow, wow, gown*

TIP For the words *fowl* and *foul*, explain to students that the word has two spellings. The word *fowl* spelled with the letters *ow* describes a bird. The word *foul* spelled with the letters *ou* has two meanings: It is used to describe when something happens that goes against the rules of a sport, such as when a baseball goes out of the playing field, and it also means a bad odor.

Try It

By Sight

Have students complete page PH 70 in *K¹² PhonicsWorks Advanced Activity Book* for more practice with reading sight words. Have students read as many words as they can correctly in one minute.

Objectives
- Read sight words.

Try It
Practice Sound /ow/ Spelled *ou* and *ow* (B)
By Sight

Reading across the rows, see how many words you can read correctly in one minute. When you get to the bottom of the page, start over.

children	nothing	everything	please	once
every	these	against	now	behind
about	saw	whether	over	number
write	almost	under	follow	come
neighbor	children	number	now	write

PH 70 LANGUAGE ARTS GREEN

[Online] ⏱ minutes

REVIEW: Sound /ow/ Spelled *ou* and *ow*

Students will work online to complete activities with the sound /ow/ spelled *ou* and *ow* and develop fluency skills. Help students locate the online activities and provide support as needed.

Review ●●●

Sound /ow/ Spelled *ou* and *ow*

Students will

▶ Practice the spellings *ou* and *ow* for the sound /ow/.
▶ Practice decoding text by reading a story.

Offline Alternative

No computer access? Have students spell words that have the spellings *ou* and *ow* for the sound /ow/, such as *bounce* and *fowl*.

⭐ **Objectives**
- Identify individual sounds in words.
- Identify and use the sound /ow/.
- Identify and use *ou* and *ow* spelling patterns.
- Read aloud grade-level text with appropriate automaticity, prosody, accuracy, and rate.
- Decode words by applying grade-level word analysis skills.

Practice ●●●

Fluency

Good readers read often and reread texts. Students will practice their fluency skills by rereading a *K¹² PhonicsWorks Readers Advanced* story aloud as they are recorded.

Have students gather their favorite *K¹² PhonicsWorks Readers Advanced* story that they have already read. Follow the instructions online to record students as they read.

Offline Alternative

No computer access? Have students gather their favorite *K¹² PhonicsWorks Readers Advanced* story. Have them read the story aloud, and record the amount of time it takes them to read the story. Have them read the story again to beat their original time.

⭐ **Objectives**
- Increase reading fluency rate.
- Demonstrate automaticity.
- Demonstrate prosody.

Practice Sound /ow/ Spelled *ou* and *ow* (C)

Lesson Overview

[Offline]	**FOCUS:** Practice Sound /ow/ Spelled *ou* and *ow*	**15** minutes
Sight Words	Sight Word Fun	
Practice	Sound /ow/ Concentration	
Try It	"Shawn's Farm Friends"	
[Online]	**REVIEW:** Sound /ow/ Spelled *ou* and *ow*	**15** minutes
Review	Sound /ow/ Spelled *ou* and *ow*	
Practice	Fluency	

[Materials]

Supplied
- *K¹² PhonicsWorks Readers Advanced 13*, pp. 7–14
- *K¹² PhonicsWorks Readers Advanced*, any volume

Also Needed
- sight words box
- dictation notebook
- index cards (18)

Advance Preparation

For Sound /ow/ Concentration, print each of the following words on index cards, using one card per word: *how, owl, cowl, fowl, now, chow, wow, gown, ouch, couch, foul, oust, out, scout, shout, loud, cloud,* and *pouch.*

[Offline] ⏱ **15** minutes

FOCUS: Practice Sound /ow/ Spelled *ou* and *ow*

Work **together** with students to complete offline Sight Words, Practice, and Try It activities.

Sight Words ●●

Sight Word Fun

Help students learn the sight words *children*, *number*, and *right*, and up to two additional sight words they have yet to master.

1. Gather the sight word cards *children*, *number*, and *right*, and up to two additional sight word cards.

2. Choose one sight word card to begin.

    Say: Look at this word and take a picture of it in your mind. When you think you can spell the word yourself, turn the card over and use your letter tiles to spell the word.

3. After students spell the word, have them check the card to see if they spelled the word correctly.

    Say: Read aloud the word you spelled with the letter tiles.

4. Repeat the activity with the remaining sight words.

TIP Sight words can be very difficult for some students. Let them work at their own pace and really master these words.

> **Objectives**
> - Read sight words.
> - Spell sight words.

Practice ●●

Sound /ow/ Concentration

Help students review words with the sound /ow/.

1. Gather the index cards you prepared.

2. Mix up the index cards and place them face down on the table or floor.

3. Turn over two cards at a time; take turns with students. If the two words have the same spelling for the sound /ow/, it's a match. The person turning over the matching cards reads the words and uses them in a sentence. If the cards don't match, the person turns them back over.

4. Remove and save the matching cards.

5. Continue the activity until all the cards are paired.

6. Have students read all the words.

7. Take the stack of words that students read correctly and dictate each word to them.

8. Have students write each word or spell it aloud.

> **Objectives**
> - Identify individual sounds in words.
> - Identify and use the sound /ow/.
> - Identify and use *ou* and *ow* spelling patterns.
> - Write words by applying grade-level phonics knowledge.

Try It •••

"Shawn's Farm Friends"
Have students read "Shawn's Farm Friends" on page 7 of *K¹² PhonicsWorks Readers Advanced 13*.

Students should read the story silently once or twice before reading the story aloud. When students miss a word that can be sounded out, point to it and give them three to six seconds to try the word again. If students still miss the word, tell them the word so the flow of the story isn't interrupted.

After reading the story, make a list of all the words students missed, and go over those words with them. You may use letter tiles to show students how to read the words.

> **Objectives**
> • Read aloud grade-level text with appropriate automaticity, prosody, accuracy, and rate.
> • Decode words by applying grade-level word analysis skills.

 **15 minutes**

REVIEW: Sound /ow/ Spelled *ou* and *ow*

Students will work online to complete activities with the sound /ow/ spelled *ou* and *ow* and develop fluency skills. Help students locate the online activities and provide support as needed.

Review •••

Sound /ow/ Spelled *ou* and *ow*
Students will

▶ Practice the spellings *ou* and *ow* for the sound /ow/.

> **Objectives**
> • Identify and use the sound /ow/.
> • Identify and use *ou* and *ow* spelling patterns.
> • Identify individual sounds in words.

Offline Alternative

No computer access? Have students spell words that have the spellings *ou* and *ow* for the sound /ow/, such as *sour* and *growl*.

Practice •••

Fluency
Good readers read often and reread texts. Students will practice their fluency skills by rereading a *K¹² PhonicsWorks Readers Advanced* story aloud as they are recorded.

Have students gather their favorite *K¹² PhonicsWorks Readers Advanced* story that they have already read. Follow the instructions online to record students as they read.

> **Objectives**
> • Increase reading fluency rate.
> • Demonstrate automaticity.
> • Demonstrate prosody.

Offline Alternative

No computer access? Have students gather their favorite *K¹² PhonicsWorks Readers Advanced* story. Have them read the story aloud, and record the amount of time it takes them to read the story. Have them read the story again to beat their original time.

Unit Checkpoint

Lesson Overview

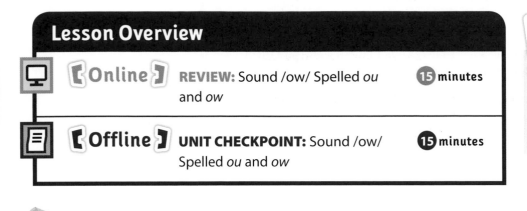

Online — **REVIEW:** Sound /ow/ Spelled *ou* and *ow* — **15** minutes

Offline — **UNIT CHECKPOINT:** Sound /ow/ Spelled *ou* and *ow* — **15** minutes

Materials

Supplied

- *K¹² PhonicsWorks Advanced Assessments*, pp. PH 205–210

Objectives

- Identify individual sounds in words.
- Identify and use the sound /ow/.
- Identify and use *ou* and *ow* spelling patterns.
- Read aloud grade-level text with appropriate automaticity, prosody, accuracy, and rate.
- Read instructional-level text with 90% accuracy.
- Write words by applying grade-level phonics knowledge.
- Write sight words.
- Read sight words.

Online **15** minutes

REVIEW: Sound /ow/ Spelled *ou* and *ow*

Students will review spellings for the sound /ow/ to prepare for the Unit Checkpoint. Help students locate the online activities and provide support as needed.

[Offline] ⏱ minutes

UNIT CHECKPOINT: Sound /ow/ Spelled *ou* and *ow*

Explain that students are going to show what they have learned about sounds, letters, and words.

1. Give students the Unit Checkpoint pages for the Sound /ow/ Spelled *ou* and *ow* unit and print the Unit Checkpoint Answer Key, if you'd like.

2. Use the instructions below to help administer the Checkpoint to students. On the Answer Key or another sheet of paper, note student answers to oral response questions to help with scoring the Checkpoint later.

3. Use the Answer Key to score the Checkpoint, and then enter the results online.

Part 1. Circle Words with Sound /ow/ Have students circle the words with the sound /ow/.

Part 2. Count Sounds. Have students read each word aloud, count the number of sounds in each word, and write that number.

Part 3. Read Sight Words Have students read each sight word aloud. Note any words they read incorrectly.

Part 4. Writing Read each sentence to students. Have them repeat and write the sentence.

23. *Paul can catch the foul ball.*

24. *How is the brown cow?*

25. *The scouts will learn about camping.*

Part 5. Read Aloud Listen to students read the sentences aloud. Count and note the number of words they read correctly.

Part 6. Read Words Have students read each word aloud. Note any words they read incorrectly.

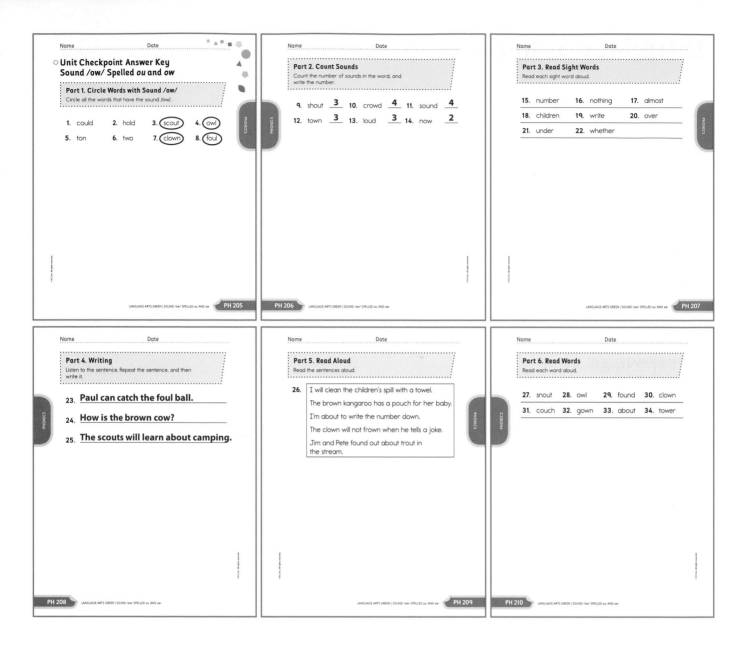

Name _____ Date _____

⚙ Unit Checkpoint Answer Key
Sound /ow/ Spelled *ou* and *ow*

Part 1. Circle Words with Sound /ow/
Circle all the words that have the sound /ow/.

1. could 2. hold 3. (scout) 4. (owl)

5. ton 6. two 7. (clown) 8. (foul)

Name _____ Date _____

Part 2. Count Sounds
Count the number of sounds in the word, and write the number.

9. shout __3__ 10. crowd __4__ 11. sound __4__

12. town __3__ 13. loud __3__ 14. now __2__

Name _____ Date _____

Part 3. Read Sight Words
Read each sight word aloud.

15. number 16. nothing 17. almost

18. children 19. write 20. over

21. under 22. whether

Name _____ Date _____

Part 4. Writing
Listen to the sentence. Repeat the sentence, and then write it.

23. **Paul can catch the foul ball.** _____

24. **How is the brown cow?** _____

25. **The scouts will learn about camping.**

Name _____ Date _____

Part 5. Read Aloud
Read the sentences aloud.

26.
> I will clean the children's spill with a towel.
> The brown kangaroo has a pouch for her baby.
> I'm about to write the number down.
> The clown will not frown when he tells a joke.
> Jim and Pete found out about trout in the stream.

Name _____ Date _____

Part 6. Read Words
Read each word aloud.

27. snout 28. owl 29. found 30. clown

31. couch 32. gown 33. about 34. tower

Introduce Sound /ō/ Spelled *ow*

Unit Overview

In this unit, students will

- ▸ Learn the sight words *because*, *its*, and *first*.
- ▸ Learn the spelling *ow* for the sound /ō/.
- ▸ Read and write sentences.
- ▸ Read stories silently and aloud.

Lesson Overview

📋 〔Offline〕 FOCUS: Introduce Sound /ō/ Spelled *ow* **15 minutes**

Sight Words	Introduce Sight Words
Get Ready	Review Sound /ow/ Spelled *ou* and *ow*
Learn	Introduce Sound /ō/ Spelled *ow*
	Sort Words with Sounds /ow/ or /ō/ for the Spelling *ow*
Try It	Investigator

💻 〔Online〕 REVIEW: Sound /ō/ Spelled *ow* **15 minutes**

Review	Sound /ō/ Spelled *ow*
Practice	Fluency

Advance Preparation

For Sort Words with Sounds /ow/ or /ō/ for the Spelling *ow*, print each of the following words on index cards, using one card per word: *show, window, snow, row, flow, blow, low, yellow, how, now, down, flower, brown, crowd, allow,* and *cow*.

[Offline] 15 minutes

FOCUS: Introduce Sound /ō/ Spelled *ow*

Work **together** with students to complete offline Sight Words, Get Ready, Learn, and Try It activities.

Sight Words

Introduce Sight Words

Help students learn the sight words *because, its,* and *first.*

1. Gather the sight word cards *because, its,* and *first.*

2. Show students the *because* card.

3. **Say:** This is the word *because.* We see this word so often that we want to be able to read and spell it quickly without thinking about it. Look closely at the word *because.* Spell the word *because* aloud. Take a picture of the word *because* in your mind. When you think you can spell *because* yourself, turn the card over and use your letter tiles to spell the word *because.* Check the card to see if you spelled the word *because* correctly. Read aloud the word you spelled with the letter tiles.

4. Repeat the activity with the remaining sight words.

5. Chart students' progress on the back of each card.
   - ► Divide the back of the card into two columns.
   - ► Label the first column "Read" and the second column "Spell."
   - ► Record the dates that students read or spell the word correctly. When students can read and spell the word correctly three times in a row, they have mastered the word. You may want to put a star or sticker on the card when they have mastered that word.

6. Add the cards to students' sight words box.

TIP Sight words can be very difficult for some students. Let students work at their own pace and really master these words, as they occur frequently in reading and writing.

Objectives
- Read sight words.
- Spell sight words.

Get Ready ···

Review Sound /ow/ Spelled *ou* and *ow*

Help students review the spelling *ou* for the sound /ow/.

1. Place the following letter tiles on students' whiteboard: *c, d, l, ou,* and *ow*.

2. Make the word *cow* in the middle of students' whiteboard and point to it.

   Say: Let's review the spellings for the sound /ow/. This is the word *cow*.

   ▸ Touch and say *cow*.
   ▸ Say and write the word on your whiteboard.
   ▸ What is the vowel sound in this word? /ow/
   ▸ Which letters make this sound? *ow*

3. Make the word *loud* and point to it.

   Say: This word is *loud*.

   ▸ Touch and say *loud*.
   ▸ Say and write the word on your whiteboard.
   ▸ What is the vowel sound in this word? /ow/
   ▸ Which letters make this sound? *ou*

Objectives

- Identify individual sounds in words.
- Identify and use the sound /ow/.
- Identify and use *ou* and *ow* spelling patterns.
- Write words by applying grade-level phonics knowledge.

Learn ···

Introduce Sound /ō/ Spelled *ow*

Help students learn the spelling *ow* for the sound /ō/.

1. Place the following letter tiles on students' whiteboard: *g, r, sh,* and *ow*.

2. Make the word *grow* in the middle of students' whiteboard and point to it.

   Say: Today we are going to learn a spelling for the sound /ō/. In the word *grow*, the sound /ō/ is made by the letters *ow*.

   ▸ Touch and say *grow*.
   ▸ Say and write the word on your whiteboard.
   ▸ What is the vowel sound in this word? /ō/
   ▸ Which letters make this sound? *ow*

3. Make the word *show* in the middle of students' whiteboard and point to it.

   Say: In the word *show*, the sound /ō/ is made by the letters *ow*.

   ▸ Touch and say *show*.
   ▸ Say and write the word on your whiteboard.
   ▸ What is the vowel sound in this word? /ō/
   ▸ Which letters make this sound? *ow*

Objectives

- Identify individual sounds in words.
- Identify and use *ow* for the sound /ō/.
- Identify and use the sound /ow/.
- Identify and use *ou* and *ow* spelling patterns.
- Write words by applying grade-level phonics knowledge.

Sort Words with Sounds /ow/ or /ō/ for the Spelling *ow*

Help students practice identifying words that have the sounds /ow/ and /ō/ for the spelling *ow*.

1. Gather the index cards you prepared. Mix the cards well and place them in a stack face down on the table.

2. Gather the dictation notebook. Draw two columns and label them sound /ō/ and sound /ow/ to represent the two different sounds for the spelling *ow*.

3. **Say:** You are going to sort words into two groups: one group for the sound /ō/ and one group for the sound /ow/ for the spelling *ow*. You will take a card from the pile and read it to me. Then you will say if the word has the sound /ō/ or the sound /ow/ and write that word in the correct column. You will place the card in the pile with the words that have the same sound. I'll do the first one for you.

4. Demonstrate the following for students:

   ▸ Draw a card from the pile.
   ▸ Read the word aloud.
   ▸ Finger stretch the sounds in the word.
   ▸ Write the word in the correct column for the sound.

5. Have students continue the procedure with the remaining words:

   ▸ **Sound /ō/ Words:** *show, window, snow, row, flow, blow, low, yellow*
   ▸ **Sound /ow/ Words:** *how, now, down, flower, brown, crowd, allow, cow*

Try It

Investigator

Have students complete page PH 71 in *K¹² PhonicsWorks Advanced Activity Book* for more practice with the spelling *ow*. Have students read each word aloud and write the word in the correct column for that spelling.

Objectives

- Identify and use *ow* for the sound /ō/.
- Identify and use the sound /ow/.
- Identify and use *ou* and *ow* spelling patterns.
- Read aloud grade-level text with appropriate automaticity, prosody, accuracy, and rate.
- Write words by applying grade-level phonics knowledge.

[Online] ⏱ **15** minutes

REVIEW: Sound /ō/ Spelled *ow*

Students will work online to complete activities with the sound /ō/ spelled *ow* and develop fluency skills. Help students locate the online activities and provide support as needed.

Review ●●

Sound /ō/ Spelled *ow*

Students will

- ► Practice the spelling *ow* for the sound /ō/.
- ► Practice decoding text by reading a story.

Offline Alternative

No computer access? Have students spell words that have the spelling *ow* for the sound /ō/, such as *grow* and *snow*.

> ### Objectives
> - Identify and use *ow* for the sound /ō/.
> - Identify individual sounds in words.
> - Read aloud grade-level text with appropriate automaticity, prosody, accuracy, and rate.
> - Decode words by applying grade-level word analysis skills.

Practice ●●●

Fluency

Good readers read often and reread texts. Students will practice their fluency skills by rereading a *K¹² PhonicsWorks Readers Advanced* story aloud as they are recorded.

Have students gather their favorite *K¹² PhonicsWorks Readers Advanced* story that they have already read. Follow the instructions online to record students as they read.

Offline Alternative

No computer access? Have students gather their favorite *K¹² PhonicsWorks Readers Advanced* story. Have them read the story aloud, and record the amount of time it takes them to read the story. Have them read the story again to beat their original time.

> ### Objectives
> - Increase reading fluency rate.
> - Demonstrate automaticity.
> - Demonstrate prosody.

Practice Sound /ō/ Spelled *ow* (A)

Lesson Overview

🗒 [Offline] FOCUS: Practice Sound /ō/ Spelled *ow*   **15** minutes

Sight Words	Sight Word Fun
Practice	Pairs of Sounds
Try It	"Mrs. Woods"

🖥 [Online] REVIEW: Sound /ō/ Spelled *ow*   **15** minutes

Review	Sound /ō/ Spelled *ow*
Practice	Fluency

[Materials]

Supplied
- *K¹² PhonicsWorks Readers Advanced 13,* pp. 15–22
- *K¹² PhonicsWorks Readers Advanced,* any volume
- whiteboard, Learning Coach
- whiteboard, student
- Tile Kit

Also Needed
- sight words box

[Offline] ⓯ minutes

FOCUS: Practice Sound /ō/ Spelled *ow*

Work **together** with students to complete offline Sight Words, Practice, and Try It activities.

Sight Words ··

Sight Word Fun
Help students learn the sight words *because, its,* and *first,* and up to two additional sight words they have yet to master.

1. Gather the sight word cards *because, its,* and *first,* and up to two additional sight word cards.

2. Choose one sight word card to begin.

   Say: Look at this word and take a picture of it in your mind. When you think you can spell the word yourself, turn the card over and use your letter tiles to spell the word.

3. After students spell the word, have them check the card to see if they spelled the word correctly.

   Say: Read aloud the word you spelled with the letter tiles.

4. Repeat the activity with the remaining sight words.

   TIP Sight words can be very difficult for some students. Let them work at their own pace and really master these words.

> **Objectives**
> * Read sight words.
> * Spell sight words.

Practice ··

Pairs of Sounds
Help students recognize the sound /ō/ or sound /ow/ for the spelling *ow*. Grab your whiteboard and dry-erase marker.

1. Write the following words on your whiteboard: *grow* and *cow*.

2. **Say:** I am going to write a pair of words. I will read the pair of words and you will repeat the words I say. Your job is to listen for the vowel sound in the word for the spelling *ow* and tell me if the vowel sound is the sound /ō/ or sound /ow/.

   ▶ For example, if I say *grow* and *cow*, you will repeat both words, and tell me the word *grow* has the sound /ō/ and the word *cow* has the sound /ow/ for the spelling *ow*.

> **Objectives**
> * Identify individual sounds in words.
> * Identify and use *ow* for the sound /ō/.
> * Identify and use the sound /ow/.
> * Identify and use *ou* and *ow* spelling patterns.

3. Write the following words on your whiteboard: *clown* and *glow*.

4. **Say:** Now it's your turn. The first pair of words is *clown* and *glow*. Students should repeat the words *clown* and *glow,* and say *clown* has the sound /ow/ and *glow* has the sound /ō/.

5. Follow the procedure with the following pairs of words:

   ▸ *brown* and *yellow brown* has the sound /ow/ and *yellow* has the sound /ō/
   ▸ *lower* and *crown lower* has the sound /ō/ and *crown* has the sound /ow/
   ▸ *flow* and *powder flow* has the sound /ō/ and *powder* has the sound /ow/
   ▸ *gown* and *snowman gown* has the sound /ow/ and *snowman* has the sound /ō/
   ▸ *pillow* and *owl pillow* has the sound /ō/ and *owl* has the sound /ow/
   ▸ *bowl* and *shower bowl* has the sound /ō/ and *shower* has the sound /ow/

Try It

"Mrs. Woods"

Have students read "Mrs. Woods" on page 15 of *K12 PhonicsWorks Readers Advanced 13.*

Students should read the story silently once or twice before reading the story aloud. When students miss a word that can be sounded out, point to it and give them three to six seconds to try the word again. If students still miss the word, tell them the word so the flow of the story isn't interrupted.

After reading the story, make a list of all the words students missed, and go over those words with them. You may use letter tiles to show students how to read the words.

> **Objectives**
> - Read aloud grade-level text with appropriate automaticity, prosody, accuracy, and rate.
> - Decode words by applying grade-level word analysis skills.

[Online] 15 minutes

REVIEW: Sound /ō/ Spelled *ow*

Students will work online to complete activities with the sound /ō/ spelled *ow* and develop fluency skills. Help students locate the online activities and provide support as needed.

Review

Sound /ō/ Spelled *ow*

Students will

▸ Practice the spelling *ow* for the sound /ō/.

> **Objectives**
> - Identify individual sounds in words.
> - Identify and use *ow* for the sound /ō/.

Offline Alternative

No computer access? Have students spell words that have the spelling *ow* for the sound /ō/, such as *tow* and *flown*.

Practice

Fluency

Good readers read often and reread texts. Students will practice their fluency skills by rereading a *K¹² PhonicsWorks Readers Advanced* story aloud as they are recorded.

Have students gather their favorite *K¹² PhonicsWorks Readers Advanced* story that they have already read. Follow the instructions online to record students as they read.

Offline Alternative

No computer access? Have students gather their favorite *K¹² PhonicsWorks Readers Advanced* story. Have them read the story aloud, and record the amount of time it takes them to read the story. Have them read the story again to beat their original time.

Objectives
- Increase reading fluency rate.
- Demonstrate automaticity.
- Demonstrate prosody.

Practice Sound /ō/ Spelled *ow* (B)

Lesson Overview

[Offline] FOCUS: Practice Sound /ō/ Spelled *ow*   **15** minutes

Sight Words	Sight Word Fun
Practice	Read for Fluency
	Sort Words with Sounds /ow/ or /ō/ for the Spelling *ow*
Try It	Finish the Job

[Online] REVIEW: Sound /ō/ Spelled *ow*   **15** minutes

Review	Sound /ō/ Spelled *ow*
Practice	Fluency

[Materials]

Supplied

- *K¹² PhonicsWorks Advanced Activity Book*, p. PH 72
- *K¹² PhonicsWorks Readers Advanced*, any volume
- whiteboard, student
- Tile Kit

Also Needed

- sight words box
- dictation notebook
- index cards (20)

Advance Preparation

For Read for Fluency and Sort Words with Sounds /ow/ or /ō/ for the Spelling *ow*, print each of the following words on index cards, using one card per word: *crown, brown, frown, how, cowboy, now, chowder, shower, downtown, lower, mow, show, tow, crow, bow, window, shadow, rowboat, blown,* and *crowbar.*

[Offline] ⓯ minutes

FOCUS: Practice Sound /ō/ Spelled *ow*

Work **together** with students to complete offline Sight Words, Practice, and Try It activities.

Sight Words ●

Sight Word Fun

Help students learn the sight words *because*, *its*, and *first*, and up to two additional sight words they have yet to master.

1. Gather the sight word cards *because*, *its*, and *first*, and up to two additional sight word cards.

2. Choose one sight word card to begin.

   Say: Look at this word and take a picture of it in your mind. When you think you can spell the word yourself, turn the card over and use your letter tiles to spell the word.

3. After students spell the word, have them check the card to see if they spelled the word correctly.

   Say: Read aloud the word you spelled with the letter tiles.

4. Repeat the activity with the remaining sight words.

   TIP Sight words can be very difficult for some students. Let them work at their own pace and really master these words.

> **Objectives**
> - Read sight words.
> - Spell sight words.

Practice ●

Read for Fluency

Have students practice reading words to become fluent.

1. Gather the index cards you prepared. Shuffle the cards and place them face down in a stack on the table.

2. Have students pick a word and read it to you.

3. If students read it quickly and correctly, put the card in one stack. If they hesitate or do not read the word correctly, put it in another stack. The second stack should have words that they will review again.

4. After students read all 20 words, have them read the difficult words again. Continue the procedure until they read all the words without hesitating.

> **Objectives**
> - Read aloud grade-level text with appropriate automaticity, prosody, accuracy, and rate.
> - Identify individual sounds in words.
> - Identify and use *ow* for the sound /ō/.
> - Write words by applying grade-level phonics knowledge.

Sort Words with Sounds /ow/ or /ō/ for the Spelling *ow*

Help students practice identifying words that have the sounds /ow/ and /ō/ for the spelling *ow*.

1. Gather the index cards you prepared. Mix the cards well and place them in a stack face down on the table.

2. Gather the dictation notebook. Draw two columns and label them sound /ō/ and sound /ow/ to represent the two different sounds for the spelling *ow*.

3. **Say:** You are going to sort words into two groups: one group for the sound /ō/ and one group for the sound /ow/ for the spelling *ow*. You will take a card from the pile and read it to me. Then you will say if the word has the sound /ō/ or the sound /ow/ and write that word in the correct column. You will place the card in the pile with the words that have the same sound. I'll do the first one for you.

4. Demonstrate the following for students:

   ▸ Draw a card from the pile.
   ▸ Read the word aloud.
   ▸ Finger stretch the sounds in the word.
   ▸ Write the word in the correct column for the sound.

5. Have students continue the procedure with the remaining words:

   ▸ **Sound /ō/ Words:** *lower, mow, show, tow, crow, bow, window, shadow, rowboat, blown, crowbar*
   ▸ **Sound /ow/ Words:** *crown, brown, frown, how, cowboy, now, chowder, shower, downtown*

Try It

Finish the Job

Have students complete page PH 72 in *K¹² PhonicsWorks Advanced Activity Book* for more practice with the sound /ō/ spelled *ow*. Have students choose a word from the box and write the word to complete the sentence.

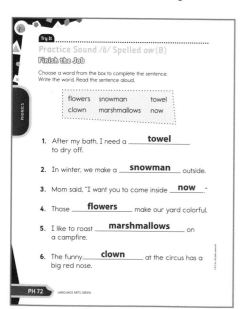

[Online] ⑮ minutes

REVIEW: Sound /ō/ Spelled *ow*

Students will work online to complete activities with the sound /ō/ spelled *ow* and develop fluency skills. Help students locate the online activities and provide support as needed.

Review

Sound /ō/ Spelled *ow*

Students will

▶ Practice the spelling *ow* for the sound /ō/.

▶ Practice decoding text by reading a story.

Offline Alternative

No computer access? Have students spell words that have the spelling *ow* for the sound /ō/, such as *show* and *shown*.

Objectives

- Identify individual sounds in words.
- Identify and use *ow* for the sound /ō/.
- Read aloud grade-level text with appropriate automaticity, prosody, accuracy, and rate.
- Decode words by applying grade-level word analysis skills.

Practice

Fluency

Good readers read often and reread texts. Students will practice their fluency skills by rereading a *K¹² PhonicsWorks Readers Advanced* story aloud as they are recorded.

Have students gather their favorite *K¹² PhonicsWorks Readers Advanced* story that they have already read. Follow the instructions online to record students as they read.

Offline Alternative

No computer access? Have students gather their favorite *K¹² PhonicsWorks Readers Advanced* story. Have them read the story aloud, and record the amount of time it takes them to read the story. Have them read the story again to beat their original time.

Objectives

- Increase reading fluency rate.
- Demonstrate automaticity.
- Demonstrate prosody.

Practice Sound /ō/ Spelled *ow* (C)

Lesson Overview

[Offline] **FOCUS:** Practice Sound /ō/ Spelled *ow* **15** minutes

Sight Words	Sight Word Fun
Practice	Build Words
Try It	"Nick's Snow Days"

[Online] **REVIEW:** Sound /ō/ Spelled *ow* **15** minutes

Review	Sound /ō/ Spelled *ow*
Practice	Fluency

Materials

Supplied
- *K¹² PhonicsWorks Readers Advanced 13*, pp. 23–30
- *K¹² PhonicsWorks Readers Advanced*, any volume
- whiteboard, student
- Tile Kit

Also Needed
- sight words box
- dictation notebook

[Offline] ⏱ 15 minutes

FOCUS: Practice Sound /ō/ Spelled *ow*

Work **together** with students to complete offline Sight Words, Practice, and Try It activities.

Sight Words

Sight Word Fun

Help students learn the sight words *because, its,* and *first,* and up to two additional sight words they have yet to master.

1. Gather the sight word cards *because, its,* and *first,* and up to two additional sight word cards.

2. Choose one sight word card to begin.

   Say: Look at this word and take a picture of it in your mind. When you think you can spell the word yourself, turn the card over and use your letter tiles to spell the word.

3. After students spell the word, have them check the card to see if they spelled the word correctly.

   Say: Read aloud the word you spelled with the letter tiles.

4. Repeat the activity with the remaining sight words.

TIP Sight words can be very difficult for some students. Let them work at their own pace and really master these words.

> **Objectives**
> - Read sight words.
> - Spell sight words.

Practice

Build Words

Help students use letters and sounds to build words.

1. Place the following letter tiles at the top of students' whiteboard: *a, ai, b, d, e, ea, f, l, ll, m, n, ow, r,* and *sh.*

2. Draw five horizontal lines across the middle of students' whiteboard to represent the sounds in a word.

3. **Say:** Let's use letters and sounds to build the word *rainbow.*

4. Have students fist tap the syllables in the word *rainbow.*

5. Have students finger stretch the sounds in *rainbow.*

6. Have students

   ▸ Identify the first, next, and last sounds in *rainbow.*
   ▸ Choose the corresponding letter tile for each of the sounds.
   ▸ Move the letters to the correct lines on their whiteboard.

> **Objectives**
> - Identify individual sounds in words.
> - Blend sounds to create words.
> - Identify and use *ow* for the sound /ō/.
> - Write words by applying grade-level phonics knowledge.

7. Guide students with these questions:

  ▸ What is the first sound in *rainbow*? /r/
    Which line does the letter for that sound go on? the first one
  ▸ What is the next sound in *rainbow*? /ā/
    Which line do the letters for that sound go on? the second one
  ▸ What is the next sound in *rainbow*? /n/
    Which line does the letter for that sound go on? the third one
  ▸ What is the next sound in *rainbow*? /b/
    Which line does the letter for that sound go on? the fourth one
  ▸ What is the next sound in *rainbow*? /ō/
    Which line do the letters for that sound go on? the last one

8. Redirect students if they select the incorrect letter.

   Say: That sound is in the word [word], and it is the [first, second, third, fourth, fifth] sound. We want the sound [target sound].

   Continue until students select the correct letter.

9. Have students touch and say the word.

10. Have them say the word as they use a dry-erase marker to write the word on the whiteboard.

11. Draw horizontal lines across the middle of students' whiteboard that represent the number of sounds in each word. Repeat the activity to build the following words:

  ▸ *fellow* /f/ /ĕ/ /l/ /ō/
  ▸ *below* /b/ /ē/ /l/ /ō/
  ▸ *shadow* /sh/ /ă/ /d/ /ō/
  ▸ *elbow* /ĕ/ /l/ /b/ /ō/
  ▸ *meadow* /m/ /ĕ/ /d/ /ō/

Try It

"Nick's Snow Days"
Have students read "Nick's Snow Days" on page 23 of *K¹² PhonicsWorks Readers Advanced 13*.

   Students should read the story silently once or twice before reading the story aloud. When students miss a word that can be sounded out, point to it and give them three to six seconds to try the word again. If students still miss the word, tell them the word so the flow of the story isn't interrupted.

   After reading the story, make a list of all the words students missed, and go over those words with them. You may use letter tiles to show students how to read the words.

Objectives
- Read aloud grade-level text with appropriate automaticity, prosody, accuracy, and rate.
- Decode words by applying grade-level word analysis skills.

 **⑮ minutes**

REVIEW: Sound /ō/ Spelled *ow*

Students will work online to complete activities with the sound /ō/ spelled *ow* and develop fluency skills. Help students locate the online activities and provide support as needed.

Review

Sound /ō/ Spelled *ow*

Students will

▸ Practice the spelling *ow* for the sound /ō/.

Objectives
- Identify and use *ow* for the sound /ō/.
- Identify individual sounds in words.

Offline Alternative

No computer access? Have students spell words that have the spelling *ow* for the sound /ō/, such as *sown* and *thrown*.

Practice

Fluency

Good readers read often and reread texts. Students will practice their fluency skills by rereading a *K¹² PhonicsWorks Readers Advanced* story aloud as they are recorded.

Have students gather their favorite *K¹² PhonicsWorks Readers Advanced* story that they have already read. Follow the instructions online to record students as they read.

Objectives
- Increase reading fluency rate.
- Demonstrate automaticity.
- Demonstrate prosody.

Offline Alternative

No computer access? Have students gather their favorite *K¹² PhonicsWorks Readers Advanced* story. Have them read the story aloud, and record the amount of time it takes them to read the story. Have them read the story again to beat their original time.

Unit Checkpoint

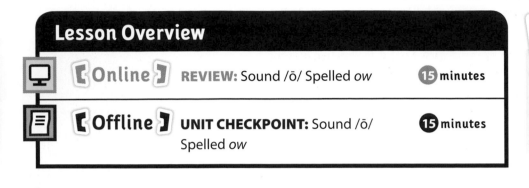

Lesson Overview

🖥 **〔Online〕** **REVIEW:** Sound /ō/ Spelled *ow* ⓯ minutes

📄 **〔Offline〕** **UNIT CHECKPOINT:** Sound /ō/ Spelled *ow* ⓯ minutes

⭐ Objectives

- Identify individual sounds in words.
- Identify and use /ō/ spelling patterns.
- Identify and use *ow* for the sound /ō/.
- Identify and use the sound /ow/.
- Identify and use *ou* and *ow* spelling patterns.
- Read instructional-level text with 90% accuracy.
- Read aloud grade-level text with appropriate automaticity, prosody, accuracy, and rate.
- Write words by applying grade-level phonics knowledge.
- Write sight words.
- Read sight words.

〔Materials〕

Supplied
- *K¹² PhonicsWorks Advanced Assessments,* pp. PH 211–216

〔Online〕 ⓯ minutes

REVIEW: Sound /ō/ Spelled *ow*

Students will review the sound /ō/ for the spelling *ow* to prepare for the Unit Checkpoint. Help students locate the online activities and provide support as needed.

〔 Offline 〕 ⑮ minutes

UNIT CHECKPOINT: Sound /ō/ Spelled *ow*

Explain that students are going to show what they have learned about sounds, letters, and words.

1. Give students the Unit Checkpoint pages for the Sound /ō/ Spelled *ow* unit and print the Unit Checkpoint Answer Key, if you'd like.

2. Use the instructions below to help administer the Checkpoint to students. On the Answer Key or another sheet of paper, note student answers to oral response questions to help with scoring the Checkpoint later.

3. Use the Answer Key to score the Checkpoint, and then enter the results online.

Part 1. Circle Words with Sound /ō/ Have students circle the words with the sound /ō/.

Part 2. Count Sounds Have students read each word aloud, count the number of sounds in each word, and write that number.

Part 3. Read Sight Words Have students read each sight word aloud. Note any words they read incorrectly.

Part 4. Writing Read each sentence to students. Have them repeat and write the sentence.

23. *Uncle Rob will show you how to use the crowbar.*

24. *Will you lower the window?*

25. *The rowboat was blown downstream.*

Part 5. Read Aloud Listen to students read the sentences aloud. Count and note the number of words they read correctly.

Part 6. Read Words Have students read each word aloud. Note any words they read incorrectly.

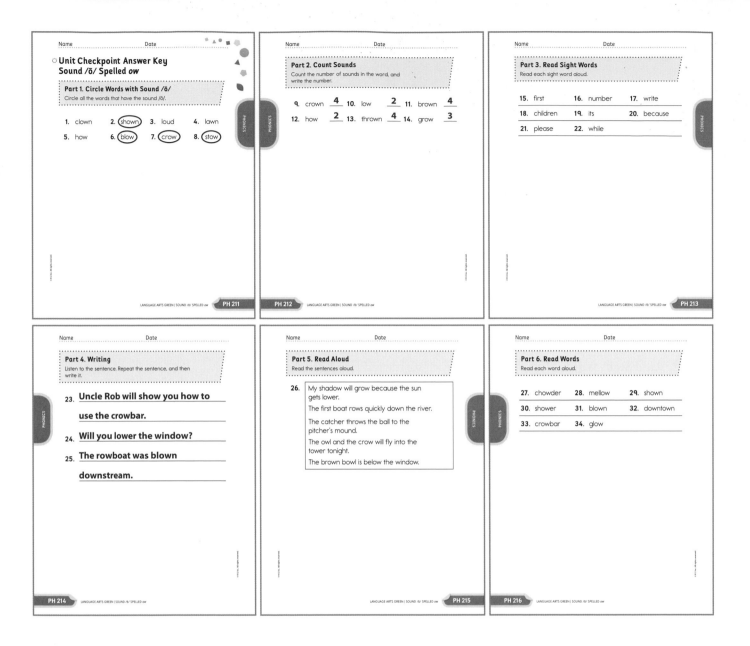

Unit Checkpoint Answer Key
Sound /ō/ Spelled ow

Part 1. Circle Words with Sound /ō/
Circle all the words that have the sound /ō/.

1. clown   2. (shown)   3. loud   4. lawn
5. how   6. (blow)   7. (crow)   8. (stow)

Part 2. Count Sounds
Count the number of sounds in the word, and write the number.

9. crown __4__   10. low __2__   11. brown __4__
12. how __2__   13. thrown __4__   14. grow __3__

Part 3. Read Sight Words
Read each sight word aloud.

15. first   16. number   17. write
18. children   19. its   20. because
21. please   22. while

Part 4. Writing
Listen to the sentence. Repeat the sentence, and then write it.

23. **Uncle Rob will show you how to use the crowbar.**

24. **Will you lower the window?**

25. **The rowboat was blown downstream.**

Part 5. Read Aloud
Read the sentences aloud.

26.
My shadow will grow because the sun gets lower.

The first boat rows quickly down the river.

The catcher throws the ball to the pitcher's mound.

The owl and the crow will fly into the tower tonight.

The brown bowl is below the window.

Part 6. Read Words
Read each word aloud.

27. chowder   28. mellow   29. shown
30. shower   31. blown   32. downtown
33. crowbar   34. glow